W9-ABQ-734

PRAIRIE GHOST

PRAIRIE GHOST
Pronghorn and Human Interaction
—— *in Early America* ——

Richard E. McCabe, Bart W. O'Gara and Henry M. Reeves
Illustrated by Daniel P. Metz

UNIVERSITY PRESS of COLORADO
A WILDLIFE MANAGEMENT INSTITUTE BOOK

DISCARDED

BOWLING GREEN STATE
UNIVERSITY LIBRARIES

The Wildlife Management Institute (WMI) is a private, non-profit, scientific and educational organization, based in Washington, DC. WMI's sole objective, since its founding in 1911, has been to advance restoration and sound management of North America's wildlife resources. As part of WMI's program, scientific information generated through research and management experiences is consolidated, published and used to strengthen resource decision making, management opportunities and methodologies, and general understanding of and appreciation for wildlife and their habitats. *Prairie Ghost: Pronghorn and Human Interaction in Early America* is one of 30 books produced by WMI since 1942, including the award-winning *Ducks, Geese and Swans of North America, Big Game of North America, Mule and Black-tailed Deer of North America, Elk of North America, White-tailed Deer: Ecology and Management, Ecology and Management of the Mourning Dove, Ecology and Management of the Wood Duck, Ecology and Management of the North American Moose,* and *North American Elk: Ecology and Management.* For additional information about WMI, its publications, programs and membership, write to Wildlife Management Institute, 1146 19th Street, Suite 700, NW, Washington, DC 20036. Or, see the website *www.wildlifemanagementinstitute.org.*

All rights reserved, including the right to reproduce this book or portions thereof in any form or by any means, electronic or mechanical, including photocopying, recording, or by any information storage and retrieval system, without permission from the Wildlife Management Institute. All inquiries should be directed to Wildlife Management Institute Publications, 1146 19th Street, Suite 700, NW, Washington, DC 20036.

© 2004 by the Wildlife Management Institute

Published by the University Press of Colorado
5589 Arapahoe Avenue, Suite 206C
Boulder, Colorado 80303

All rights reserved
Printed in the United States of America

 The University Press of Colorado is a proud member of the Association of American University Presses.

The University Press of Colorado is a cooperative publishing enterprise supported, in part, by Adams State College, Colorado State University, Fort Lewis College, Mesa State College, Metropolitan State College of Denver, University of Colorado, University of Northern Colorado, and Western State College of Colorado.

The paper used in this publication meets the minimum requirements of the American National Standard for Information Sciences—Permanence of Paper for Printed Library Materials. ANSI Z39.48-1992

Library of Congress Cataloging-in-Publication Data

McCabe, Richard E.
  Prairie ghost : pronghorn and human interaction in early America / Richard E. McCabe, Bart W. O'Gara, and Henry M. Reeves ; illustrated by Daniel P. Metz.
    p. cm.
  "A Wildlife Management Institute book."
  Includes bibliographical references (p.).
  ISBN 0-87081-758-2 (hardcover : alk. paper)
  1. Pronghorn antelope—North America—History. 2. Human animal relationships—North America—History. I. O'Gara, Bart W. II. Reeves, Henry M. III. Title.
  QL737.U52M38 2004
  599.63'9'097—dc22
                                    2004001011

Design and layout by Daniel Pratt

13 12 11 10 09 08 07 06 05 04   10 9 8 7 6 5 4 3 2 1

Credit information for endsheet artwork can be found following the index.

Dedication

Prairie Ghost: Pronghorn and Human Interaction in Early America is dedicated to Bart W. O'Gara and Jim D. Yoakum, the preeminent pronghorn scientists of the twentieth century. Few other individuals or partners have had such a profound and impressive impact on the conservation and management of a North American big game species as have these two wildlife biologists.

The co-dedication of this book to Bart, one of its co-authors, may seem a bit unorthodox. However, Bart died just weeks before *Prairie Ghost* and its companion volume, *Pronghorn: Ecology and Management*, which he co-edited with Jim, went to press. His co-authors of *Prairie Ghost,* and his other many associates, friends all, are consoled that, although he did not see these books to publication, Bart characteristically, and in his unwavering gentlemanly manner, made sure they were completed. We miss his savvy and friendship. And, whether they know it or not, so do pronghorn.

Bart W. O'Gara   Jim D. Yoakum

Contents

Figures

Tables

Foreword

What a strange, timid and elusive creature the pronghorn was to the Euro-Americans who first broached North America's western grasslands. It reminded them of a "cabri," or goat, sort of—a very speedy goat. It was difficult to approach, difficult to kill and, when brought down, its hide proved generally meager and its meat palatable but not much more. To modern civilization's vanguards in the West, the pronghorn was among the more curious features of a vast, un-chartered and infinitely perplexing landscape.

Also strange and curious to the newcomers were the aboriginals—"savages" they were called—perceived as neither timid nor elusive enough.

In time, goats became antelope. The savages became Indians. Both names still were wrong. Also in time, the antelope and Indians were abused to near extirpation. Unregulated market gunning, wanton shooting, fencing, disease, bad weather and public apathy reduced the former. Disease, bigotry, avarice, technology, Manifest Destiny, public apathy, and a tenacious and inflexible military overwhelmed the latter. Entirely lost, in a span of not more than 250 years, was the relationship of the two curiosities—a complicated nexus that had evolved since pronghorn and Native Americans, the first people, shared grassland, shrubland and desert habitats during a span of not less than 10,000 years.

This book is a sketch of that ethnozoological relationship. It begins with suspected, separate arrivals of humans and antilocaprids on the continent. It ends with the approach of the 20th century, when wild America essentially vanished.

It did not begin as a book, but as a chapter for a monograph on pronghorn ecology and management. We found that there was much to learn and tell—too much, in fact. Clearly, the emerging sketch would unreasonably affect the important monograph's size and cost. Also, as a chapter, the work would have to be reduced drastically, which, we felt, would compromise understanding of the relationship of pronghorn and people past. This volume, therefore, is a companion to *Pronghorn: Ecology and Management*, edited by Bart W. O'Gara and Jim D. Yoakum, also a Wildlife Management Institute book, published by The University Press of Colorado.

If ever a book was a team effort, it was this one. To the investment, Milt Reeves brought mounds of data, ideas and leads. Bart O'Gara brought vital organization to our stores of information. We all shared the challenge of discovery of clues to bygone natural and cultural histories. In every sense, this was and is a co-authorship.

Our only struggle in the making of this book was with what *not* to include—interesting, if not fascinating collateral information, but of limited additional insight or, worse, misleading perspective. We ex-

cluded considerable anecdotal information extracted from the historical literature because it could not be separately validated.

Special efforts were made to include only information that was fairly specific to time and place. To generalize about incredibly diverse and temporally dynamic Native American cultures would be to misrepresent them and history itself. And, that would counterfeit the relationship of those peoples with pronghorn.

History, of course, is what was. Hopefully, we learn from our past—from what was—presumably to prevent mistakes in the present and establish safeguards for the future. That really is what this book is about. Hopefully, too, it shows the values of a wildlife species to people, aboriginals, more and better connected to the environment than anyone today. We also hope that it may serve to affirm, or reaffirm for decision makers, that there is wisdom and enduring economy in the conservation and management of natural heritage. And, by acknowledging that this book is not a complete history, merely a sketch, we hope not least of all that other investigators of whatever discipline will add to and improve on the truths of it.

—RICHARD E. MCCABE

Preface

The least known, least understood and perhaps most fascinating big game animal in the Western Hemisphere is the pronghorn. Ironically, it is the most "American" of the continent's terrestrial wildlife. The pronghorn is found only in North America and is the sole living member of an ancient family, *Antilocapridae,* to survive since the early Pliocene. Although referred to as an antelope, the pronghorn is distinct from the true antelopes of Africa.

Even some people who live in the West in close proximity to pronghorn and who occasionally see the animal on open grasslands or shrublands are unfamiliar with this extraordinary species. Few know, for example, that the pronghorn is the second fastest land animal. It lopes easily at 30 miles per hour, cruises at 45 mph, and can maintain a sprint of somewhat more than 60 mph for three or four minutes, in bounds exceeding 20 feet. Such speed in an adult animal about 3 feet high at the shoulder, 4 feet long from chest to rump, and weighing 90 to 140 pounds is enabled by heavily built legs whose bones are said to have 10 times the torque of same-sized bones of cows. Also contributing are a large windpipe and lungs and a heart that is twice as big as that of other animals of similar size.

Few people know that, in addition to its speed, the pronghorn's eyesight is a major defense against predation. Protuberant eyes allow for a nearly 360-degree field of vision, and pronghorn eyesight is akin to that of a person looking through 8x binoculars. This might account for the fact that people usually only spot pronghorn at some distance, if at all. What viewers tend to see are remote splotches of white rapidly heading for the horizon. Those splotches are white rump patches, featuring 3- to 4-inch white hairs that become erect when the animals are alarmed. On open rangeland in favorable conditions, those rump patches can be seen for a number of miles, although the rest of the animal blends into the background.

The animal derives its name from the male's horns, which support a forward-point prong several inches below the tip. Females have smaller horns, usually—but not always—absent the prong. Horn sheaths fit over bony horn cores, much like swords fit into scabbards. The cores are permanent parts of the skeletal structure, whereas the sheaths—composed of compressed, cornified, epithelial cellular matter and hair—are shed each year. The pronghorn is the only hoofed animal that sheds its horn sheaths annually.

Adult males, or bucks, form harems of as many as 16 does during the autumn mating season. Occasionally one, usually two, and rarely three fawns are born to pregnant does in late May and June, after a gestation of about 240 days. Weighing only 5 or 6 pounds at birth, pronghorn fawns are able to outrun humans within a few days and elude most other predators within a few months. They reach full maturity by age three.

Pronghorn are primarily browsers, feeding on such vegetation as sagebrush, clover, alfalfa, cheatgrass, wheatgrass and sedges. In some desert areas, they receive water only from moisture in and on vegetation.

Some historical researchers have suggested that, before the West was broached by European explorers, adventurers, and settlers, the pronghorn may have been almost as numerous as the bison—which numbered more than 20 million and perhaps as many as 40 million—west of the Mississippi. In less than 80 years, 1830 to 1910, pronghorn declined from unknown millions to fewer than 15,000. The causes included unregulated gunning for market, subsistence and sport, introduction of cattle ranching on western grasslands, and disease. Other factors included the decline of Native American populations and cultures (and attendant reduction of fires that kept grasses low and produced nutritious forbs), the slaughter of bison (whose winter movements provided travel lanes through and access to plant food beneath deep snows), and some unusually harsh winters.

From near extirpation, the pronghorn rebounded to more than 1 million animals about 75 years later, thanks in part to America's unique and successful wildlife management system. That recovery also was due, in part, to the unique adaptability of the species. This book is about pronghorn and why and how, unlike today, it was widely known, understood, and appreciated by people of yesteryear, especially those who, like pronghorn, also were Native Americans.

Acknowledgments

The authors are grateful for the help, cooperation and enthusiasm extended us by a great many people during the course of preparing this book. In particular, we recognize Glenna J. Dean and staffs of the Valley Library, Oregon State University, Corvallis, the Bancroft Library, University of California, Berkeley, and the Smithsonian Institution's Anthropological Archives and Anthropology Library—both of Washington, DC. Deserving special thanks for their contributions are Lyla Baumann, Bette McKown, Kelly Stockwell, Virginia Johnston and Wilma O'Gara. And without the assistance, patience and skill of Jennifer Rahm, the Wildlife Management Institution's Assistant Director of Publications, completion of *Prairie Ghost: Pronghorn and Human Interaction in Early America* would not have been possible.

PRAIRIE GHOST

Introduction

The age-old battle between the wilderness and civilization was waged anew on the western plains, with the age-old results: the disappearance of the wilderness, the depletion and degradation of its aboriginal population, and the virtual extinction of its characteristic fauna.
—Hoopes (1975:12)

Early in *wecukanheyaye* of a sweltering day of *Wípazuk wašté wi* in the year remembered as *Pehin Hanksa ktepi*, fewer than 500 *akixita œuktayka*, led by vainglorious *Hi-es-tze*, fell upside down into a huge village of *Tsististas* and *Lakota* temporarily encamped along a 3-mile (4.8 km) serpentine stretch of the *Hetanka* watercourse of the *Cukanweta* region. The aggression was ill-conceived, poorly timed and badly executed. Unable and perhaps unwilling to retreat, as many as 1,200 *mdetahunka* swarmed from the encampment to defend against the improvidently divided force of *wasichus*.

When the dust of the season When the Ponies Grow Fat finally settled a day and a half later, still during the moon of the chokecherries, the Allies and the People retired south from Greasy Grass Creek to safer havens and better pasturage, 263 longknives were dead, including the man they called Creeping Panther, Long Hair and Yellow Hair.

The defeat by Northern Cheyenne and Sioux Indians of the U.S. Army's Seventh Cavalry under command of Colonel George Armstrong Custer along the Little Bighorn River in Montana Territory occurred nine days before the centennial celebration of the founding of the United States. The battle was a decisive victory for the Indians. But, it also signaled the last truly successful military resistance by North American Indians to social subjugation and cultural dispossession. Custer's Last Stand was duplicitously the highwater mark of American Indian defense of homeland, but, in fact, a pyrrhic victory, it was their own last stand.

The fateful scenario that played out on the rolling and gullied steppelands of southcentral Montana actually was a tragedy long in the making. In many respects, such a violent clash of humanity was made inevitable by grossly disparate societies, forced by misunderstanding, arrogance, racism and mutual antipathy to compete for independence on common landscape. In broad, historical context, the Little Bighorn battle site represents the convergence of myriad, backlogged, anthropological indignities. In an empirical, geophysical context, the site, 14 miles (22.5 km) upstream from confluence with the Bighorn River, was mostly a matter of happenstance.

The conjoining of approximately 12,000 "renegade" and AWOL "agency" Hunkpapa, Oglala, Minneconjou, Sans Arc and Blackfeet Sioux and Northern Cheyenne was an alliance borne of desperation and wishful thinking. Brought together to strengthen against offensive actions by the U.S. Army, to escape the drudgery and meager charity of reservation life, and to embrace again the relatively carefree, drifting, hunter/gatherer mode of living, the temporary confederation undoubtedly was the largest assembly of Indians ever on the Great Plains and perhaps anywhere in North America.

Twelve thousand people and their "gigantic" horse herd represented an unprecedented logistical problem (Ambrose 1986:415). They needed an abundance of fresh food, water and forage. A week before the battle, the Indians moved from the valley of Rosebud Creek to adjacent Little Bighorn Valley in search of bison. Despite initial plans to travel elsewhere, they eventually camped (June 22) at the location where Custer was to find them because it was a favorable place from which "hunters went across to the west side of the Bighorn River and killed antelope from vast herds" (Marquis 1967:3, see also Stewart 1955). Interestingly, at the time of the Reno column's attack on the south end of the sprawling encampment, the Indians were planning to relocate because the horse herd had depleted grasses on benchlands above the camp and because the pronghorn—*vó-ka-e* to the Cheyenne and *tatokadan* to the Sioux—had been scattered, and the quest for bison needed to continue.

Hundreds of pieces of literature have been written about the Little Bighorn battle—its causes, players, mysteries and far-reaching consequences—from which emerged a certain loser and, ultimately, no winner. Because no one of the divided command with Custer survived, the perspective of the vanquished was lost, except to the speculation and imagination of chroniclers who invariably are drawn to historic events so momentous as to defy objective reporting. No matter the viewpoint and discovery of new information, the battle's outcomes remain the same. The investigators and reporters seem unanimous only about that and the fact that, had the Indian encampment been anywhere else along the Little Bighorn River at that particular time, the conflict and history itself, for better or worse, would have been significantly different. Ironically, "little bighorn" is a Lakota idiom for pronghorn (Hill 1979).

By no means was that propitious occasion in *Ipehin Hanksa Ktipi* the first time that pronghorn had been an important aspect and variable in the culture, economy and general welfare of Native Americans.

Prehistory

A cool April wind blows across the sagebrush-covered ridge while the imposing south flank of the Wind River Range stands large against the northern horizon. A herd of pronghorn antelope is bunched up, and the animals appear nervous as they peer across the narrow ridgetop that lies across their traditional route to summer range. The Indians hidden behind parallel rows of ripped-up sagebrush await their compatriots as they drive the antelope past the sagebrush rows. The antelope trot over a small knoll and into the suddenly-visible corral. The Indian[s] behind the rows of sagebrush show themselves and fill in behind the antelope as the herd passes, forcing the antelope into the corral where other hunters are waiting with their stone-tipped weapons. The antelope circle the interior of the corral as the hunters hurl spears into their flanks. Soon, the bodies of the dying antelope lie in the soft dune sand. The Indians rejoice—long days of planning, preparation, and anticipation have gone into this hunt. Prayers are said in thanks to the spirits for the success of their efforts. Many antelope have been killed, but now it is the time to remove the hides and strip the meat. The bones of the victims are left behind, telling the story of a people that were intimately familiar with animal behavior and habitats, a skill that meant survival, and they tell a story about the antelope as well.

—Sanders (2000:30–31)

Successors of the Sublette pronghorn herd still migrate annually between Grand Teton National Park and their winter ranges south of Pinedale, Wyoming, as they have for 8,000 years or more. During particularly severe winters, they continue southward to rangelands near the town of Green River, Wyoming, nearly 200 miles (322 km) from their summer range (Sawyer and McWhirter 2000).

To comprehend the ancient interactions between humans and pronghorn, it is necessary to regress through geologic time to an arbitrarily chosen point of beginning. We have selected a time when North America was unpopulated by humans, but many strange animals—herds of camels and horses, huge cave bears, giant ground sloths and armadillos, plus another antilocaprid besides our pronghorn—were ranging over much of western North America. Wooly mammoths grazed on the grasslands and elephant-like mastodons browsed in the forests and shrubsteppes. These creatures were preyed on by wolves, lions, and saber-toothed tigers (Byers 1997). The evolution of the unique pronghorn is addressed in O'Gara and Janis (2004), but humankind's intrusion into the New World is yet to be told. Anthropologists generally agree that the momentous event occurred near the end of the recently concluded 1.8 million-year Pleistocene Epoch, or Ice Age (Parfit 2000).

During the Pleistocene, successive ice sheets—perhaps as many as 50 (Ruddiman and Wright 1987, Dansgaard et al. 1993)—separated by intervening warming periods, formed and pushed southward.

3

Each retreated northward and to higher mountain elevations as mysteriously as it had formed and breeched the continent. The Wisconsin glacier, last of the great North American ice sheets, persisted until about 10,000 to 12,000 years ago.

Sometime during the Pleistocene, a monumental event having incalculable consequences was to occur in a remote quarter of today's world. As Bordes (1968:255) declared, "There can be no repetition of this [event] until man lands on a [habitable] planet belonging to another star." The Americas, the largest landmass yet undiscovered by hominids, was about to be found and inhabited.

Long before the vanguards of European civilization penetrated the vast open spaces of the American West, the pronghorn was a resource for the region's native people—mistakenly and forever called "Indians." By the time humans reached the prairies, shrub-steppes and deserts of western North America, only two genera of antilocaprids persisted—*Antilocapra*, the pronghorn, and *Tetrameryx*. The latter were four-horned animals that were slightly smaller, heavier built and probably not as swift as pronghorn (Colbert and Chaffee 1939). These four-horned animals apparently were hunted and carried into caves by southwestern Indians. Roosevelt and Burden (1934) uncovered two skulls, a mandible, pelvis, some vertebrae, numerous limb bones and a fire-cracked bone in a southern Arizona cave. Colbert and Chaffee (1939) also found *Tetrameryx* fossils in Papago Spring Cave near Sonoita, Arizona.

Why the tetra-horned antilocaprids became extinct and pronghorn prospered remains speculative. Bromley (1977) suggested that pronghorn were pre-adapted to withstand overheating and dessication when subjected to climatic changes. Other genera may not have been as well adapted. The *Antilocapra* first encountered by Stone Age hunters were nearly identical to those we know today. The encounters almost certainly occurred within the known historic range of the species, as have the only known fossilized remains of pronghorn associated with aboriginal dwellings.

THE FIRST PEOPLE

> . . . there is no reason to deny that antelopes . . . were not important from earliest times.
> —Sherratt (1980:357)

Using new technologies, a growing contingent of specialists—archaeologists, physical anthropologists, DNA experts and linguists—are busily trying to solve the long-perplexing problem, "Who were the first Americans?" At least four theories find some support (see Parfit 2000). Recent findings cause some scientists to place the arrival of humans in the Americas at 15,000, 20,000 or 30,000 or more years ago (Figure 1). And, the search for evidence of America's oldest people continues (Parfit 2000).

Those early North American pioneers did not come alone or empty-handed. Dogs surely accompanied them and were used as beasts of burden. The first Americans also made use of fire and had a few rudimentary stone and wooden weapons, such as the knife, club, spear and atlatl (dart-thrower), but not the bow and arrow. These resourceful people learned how to exist in their new, often harsh and hostile environment, gathering plant food but mainly exercising the relative nutritional efficiency of hunting large terrestrial game (see Kelly and Todd 1988).

OCCUPYING NORTH AMERICA

> Whilst beholding these savages, one asks, whence have they come? What could have tempted, or what change compelled a tribe of men, to leave the fine regions of the north, to travel down the Cordillera or backbone of America?
> —Darwin (1906:206)

Upon reaching North America, the discoverers from Siberia probably pressed southeastward through passages formed between the retreating Laurentian and Cordilleran ice sheets or along the West Coast (Parfit 2000). Some lingered in the North, whereas others continued southward. Martin (1967), using megafaunal biomass and human reproduction rate information, advanced the notion that people swept southward in a relatively dense wave, obliterating many mammalian species—the now-murky "aboriginal overkill" hypothesis (Martin 1978, Kay 1994, cf. Krech 1981, 1999). Because of the rapidity of the human advance and the unwariness of the animals, Martin theorized that there was no need for game drives and traps, which he believed could have eliminated local if not regional populations of some species. He argued that this may account for herding

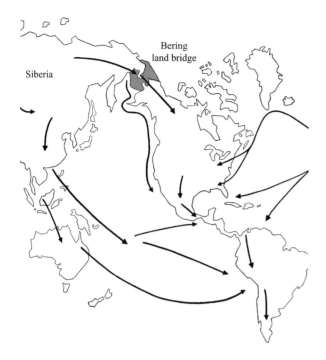

FIGURE 1. *The most prevalent theory concerning the peopling of the Americas is that nomadic Asians crossed the Bering land bridge, possibly in several waves, to reach North America. With the lowering of seas, a land bridge—Beringia—connecting the present Chukchi Peninsula of easternmost Siberia with western Alaska was exposed (Parfit 2000). Today, with the retreat of the last polar ice sheet and the rise of seas, Beringia lies beneath the Bering Strait between East Cape, Russia, and Cape Prince of Wales, Alaska, a distance of only 56 miles (90 km). A second postulation is that other Asians reached North America by watercraft, following the exposed Beringian shoreline. Third, a few anthropologists, who see similarities between eastern North American tools and those of the Solutrean culture that disappeared from southwestern Europe about 19,000 years ago, believe that the populating of North America by European stock using a water route warrants consideration. Also, stone tools dated between 14000 and 11000 B.C. were found near Meadowcroft, Pennsylvania (Schobinger 1994). Last, the possibility of an epic crossing of the Pacific by Polynesians to a South American landfall has a few adherents. A major cause for revision of the long-held view that North America was first populated about 11,200 years ago was verification that the Monte Verde site in southern Chile was inhabited more than 12,000 years ago (Dillehay 2000). Furthermore, stone points dating from about 11,000 to 10,000 years ago were found in five caves of southern Argentina (Schobinger 1994). Archaeologists also found evidence of many differing cultures that flourished almost simultaneously in South America roughly 12,000 to 13,000 years ago.*

species, such as bison and pronghorn, escaping extinction.

Other authorities maintain that a changing environment caused the precipitous extinction of many indigenous North American animals (Weaver 1991). In any event, of some 14 pronghorn-like genera, only the pronghorn and *Tetrameryx* survived the great extinction, according to Kurtén and Anderson (1980). Archaeologists found a broken flint flake and the leg bone of a horse, which appeared to have been scratched by a flint knife, in the layer of a Texas cave estimated to be from about 8000 B.C. "With these," wrote Baldwin (1962:93), "were bones of mammoth, camel, bison, and antelope."

Human skeletal remains, believed to be those of a 30-year-old woman, were found during 1953 near Midland, Texas, in a deposit of sand that also included chipped-stone tools and the remains of extinct horses, bison and antilocaprids. The human bones originally were estimated to be 800 to 10,000 years old, but subsequent tests of the sand using the "Rosholt method"—a refinement of a uranium clock process for dating rocks—have hinted at a much older age (Josephy 1981). In caves and rock shelters about Tehuacán in the arid highlands of the central Mexican state of Puebla, a team of experts in many sciences laid bare a sequence of cultural development of the inhabitants in the area, from approximately 12,000 years ago until historic times (1500 A.D.). The work revealed, among many other things, the development of agriculture in that region. Until about 9,000 years ago, the studies showed the sparse population in the neighborhood lived predominately by gathering wild plant foods, trapping and hunting small animals, birds and turtles, and occasionally killing the remaining species of Pleistocene pronghorn and horses (Josephy 1981).

Before the introduction of the horse, relatively few nomadic Indians lived on the plains proper (Wedel 1961, Holder 1970). During the moist millennia immediately following retreat of the Wisconsin glacier, a thin veneer of Paleo-Indians spread out across the plains from the eastern slope of the Rocky Mountains. About 11,000 years ago, one group devised a long spear point for killing mammoths. Now known as Clovis-fluted, from the site on the high plains where the first one was found with bison bones, the point was chipped from both edges and then from the base. This fluting enabled tying the point to a long wooden handle (Tanner 1995). From 10,000 B.C. to 1000 A.D., a series of transitory cultures of nomadic, prepottery, preagricultural societies vacillated as wet periods and alternating dust bowl climates made habitation of the plains intermittently possible and then nearly untenable. Beginning about 500 A.D. immigrants from the woodlands of the Mississippi Valley and the East brought farming to the river bottoms of the Missouri and its tributaries. These people established villages of earth lodges or grass-domed houses, and grew maize (corn), squash and tobacco. They lacked domesticated animals other than dogs. Necessarily, they traveled afoot to hunt bison and pronghorn, but always near home, apparently driving them into funnel-shaped pens opening onto bluffs over which the stampeding animals tumbled to their deaths. They also fought, but warfare was stylized and not a central interest according to Jennings and Edwards (1948). The coming of the horse from the Southwest and the westward displacement of tribes by eastern Indians armed with guns, beginning in the 17th century, changed all this (Wallace and Hoebel 1952).

Water, to a large extent, determined where prehistoric Indians settled. It limited or impacted their environment, their food and their physical prosperity. These factors, in turn, influenced their social structure, material culture, religions and trade patterns. Archaeologists variously divide the span of time between the appearance of the first Indians and the arrival of Europeans into sometimes overlapping and geographically distinct periods that reflect major cultural advances among these vanished people. They roughly include the hunters of the Paleo-Indian period—with their fluted Clovis spear points designed for killing very large mammals—the hunter–foragers of the Dalton period, the forager of the Archaic periods, the prairie/forest potters of the Woodland periods, and the village farmers of the Mississippian periods (Weaver 1991).

One ancient civilization that foreshadowed and merged into Archaic times (8000–1000 B.C.) was the Desert Culture of about 8500 B.C. (Maxwell 1978). Essentially, it persisted with little change in Nevada, Utah, eastern Oregon and southern Idaho until the middle of the 19th century. The Paiute and Shoshone

Indians are descendants of the Desert people (see D'Azevedo 1986). Their projectile points were broader, shorter and generally smaller than those of the big game hunters of the plains and in northwestern North America from the Rocky Mountain divide to the Pacific Ocean. The Desert Indian's projectile points were mounted on darts or spears hurled by the atlatl or spear thrower (Jennings 1986). Animals of various sizes were hunted, the larger ones often being bighorn, pronghorn and deer, although some bison bones have been found at Desert sites (Driver 1972).

The best known archaeological site for the Desert Culture is Danger Cave on the edge of the Great Salt Lake in western Utah, where carbon-14 tests have shown human occupation as early as 11,500 years ago (Maxwell 1978). During the 1950s, this cave yielded the remains of bighorn, deer and pronghorn. In the oldest levels of the cave, excavators found small points, apparently used as the tips of throwing-stick darts in the hunting of relatively small animals, such as deer and pronghorn. Some objects in the newer layers range from 9,000 to 3,000 years in age—proof that Danger Cave had been occupied, although perhaps not continually, over many thousands of years.

Desert foragers of 5,000 years ago in the southwestern desert hunted pronghorn and used their skins for clothing and blankets. Pronghorn meat surely provided a welcome relief from their meager diet of wild vegetables, nuts and berries (Maxwell 1978).

For the western Anasazi, who occupied the Four Corners area of Utah, Colorado, Arizona and New Mexico from about 100 B.C. to 1300 A.D., hunting and gathering were the most important food procurement strategies (Plog 1979). Major prey included bighorn, deer, elk, pronghorn, rabbits and turkey. Bighorn, deer and elk were hunted at higher elevations and pronghorn at lower elevations. "Animal resources also vary seasonally. For example, it is easiest to harvest deer, elk, and antelope during periods when these animals are in large herds, which occurs only when they are moving from higher to lower elevations or back, and during the breeding period; thus the spring and especially the fall would have been the seasons when these animals were most easily taken" (Plog 1979:111).

Before the arrival of whites, Indians of the upper Missouri River valley relied primarily on animal food, apart from their own horticultural produce. "Though

(Top left) *Danger Cave, 2 miles (3.2 km) northeast of Wendover, Utah, was inhabited as early as 8000 B.C. by nomadic Paleo-Indians and later by Northern Paiutes. At an elevation of 4,250 feet (1,295 m), it overlooks the Great Salt Lake Desert to the east. Pronghorn bones and fragments are the most common ungulate remains. Pronghorn hair was found in 32 of 46 human caprolites examined. A one-piece stitched moccasin of pronghorn skin, with hair on, was found. Its origin was radiocarbon-dated at about 6000 B.C. (Scarre 1988). (Top right) The location of Dirty Shame Rockshelter (lower left) at the base of a cliff in southeastern Oregon on the northwest side of Antelope Creek, which is at bottom right. The scale of the site can be approximated by noting the excavators at work in the site. Evidence of human occupancy dating back to 7520 B.C. has been found. Small numbers of pronghorn food bones, plus human feces containing pronghorn hair and bone fragments, were excavated there. (Bottom left) Excavation of abandoned pueblos in the Southwest, such as Arroyo Hondo Pueblo in northern New Mexico, provides clues to food habits of the Anasazi and the tribes who replaced them after their mysterious prehistoric disappearance. Examination of whole and fragmented bones indicated that at least 7 bison, 6 elk, 157 mule deer, and 56 pronghorn had been consumed there. Total numbers undoubtedly were larger, as many causes may explain the absence or paucity of faunal remains at early habitations. (Bottom right) Coxcatlan Cave in the Tehuacan Valley of south-central Mexico during the dry season. The deciduous nature of the vegetation is clearly seen. The man standing on the talus demonstrates the scale of the shelter that extends across the face. The cave was inhabited by Paleo-Indians. At deep levels, dated to about 5000 B.C., 44 cobs of maize were discovered, making them the oldest found (Byers 1967). Perhaps they represent the beginning of New World agriculture. The remains of antilocaprids were unearthed from the four deepest levels of the cave. Flannery (1966:801) concluded: "The pronghorn antelope . . . is almost certainly the species represented in the Early Ajuereado levels in Coxcatlan Cave. . . ." Flannery (1967:152) wrote: "These antelope had apparently disappeared from the Tehuacan Valley by 7000 B.C." Thus, some 2000 years before the dawn of agriculture, Coxcatlan humans were subsisting on pronghorn at their southernmost known range. Top left photo from Jennings (1957). Top right photo from Aikens et al. (1986). Bottom left photo from Lang and Harris (1984). Bottom right photo from Byers (1967).*

they made some use of deer, elk, and antelope, the game of greatest importance to them, as to other Plains tribes, was the bison, which they hunted on the Plains during the summer and often along the river when winter's cold drove the animal down into the well-timbered valley floor" (Meyer 1977:2).

MEANS OF SUBSISTENCE

A review of the available archaeological, ethnographic, and historical data reveals that there is compelling evidence for communal pronghorn hunting across western North America in the protohistoric and early historic periods. The evidence is particularly compelling for the Great Basin, where corrals were in common use, as well as for the Great Plains, where drives into corrals or pits were common. Evidence for such activities in the remote past, including projectile point concentrations, hunting facilities, and bonebed sites, is considerably sparcer and more ambiguous. Nonetheless, it appears that communal pronghorn hunting did not decrease through, but rather was maintained or has increased within the last 1,500 years.

—Lubinski (1999:158)

Paleo-Indians relied on hunting for their primary food supply. Along the coasts and waterways, marine and aquatic mammals, fish and mollusks; and in particularly game-impoverished inland areas, even insects and their larvae provided protein. A bewildering variety of seeds, fruits, nuts, berries and tubers, when available, provided other nutrients and contributed to a diversified diet (Ebeling 1986).

By 8000 B.C., most of the large animals that had provided the Paleo-Indian culture with its primary source of food were becoming extinct. The reason so many large mammals disappeared at the end of the Ice Age is a mystery, but a changing environment probably was one—if not the main—contributing factor (Weaver 1991). "Some 70 percent of large (100 pounds [45 kg] or more) North American mammals died out" (Schaefer 1975:21). Pronghorn survived, but their range may have been shrinking. They disappeared from the Tehuacan Valley by perhaps 7000 B.C., but appear to have lasted in the higher Valley of Mexico until the Formative period. Pronghorn bones were found in caves in the state of Hidalgo dating 350–1100 A.D. (Flannery 1966).

During the Archaic period (8000–1000 B.C.), most Indians increasingly relied on plant foods (Figure 2). They began exploiting aquatic resources by using nets and traps. Horticulture and agriculture became established. The introduction of pottery distinguished the Woodland period, which began about 1000 B.C. Artifact assemblages suggest that the Wood-

land Indians were organized into bands with permanent villages. The Mississippian period (900–1700 A.D.) is commonly thought of as a time when larger permanent villages were established and agriculture became the predominant subsistence practice (Weaver 1991).

Agriculture—focused on maize, beans and squash—had its origin in Mesoamerica. By about 6000 B.C., a shift from a hunter/gatherer economy to an agricultural society had begun (Stuart 1983). By 2000 to 1000 B.C., the transition was complete there, and maize production was carried northward as far as the upper Missouri River in today's mid-North Dakota.

The importance of the pronghorn in Late Prehistoric Indian economies jointly depended on its abundance and the availability of other food resources. "That long-term dependency on bison [by plains Indians] notwithstanding plains herbivores such as the pronghorn were essential to support human life, especially during unexpected food shortages" (Davis 1986:15–16). "Pronghorn have been hunted for over 10,000 years. They were an important food resource, worthy of large cooperative hunting efforts yielding up to hundreds of animals at a time" (Lubinski and Herren 2000:8).

Cressman (1977) supposed that effective hunting of pronghorn in the Great Basin developed quite late prehistorically. Driver and Massey (1957) synthesized hundreds of studies to compile maps showing the dominant features of pre-Columbian Indian life in North America, including major subsistence patterns. Maize culture in the watered valleys of the eastern plains and prairies and in the Southwest, where irrigation was employed locally, somewhat alleviated dependence on wild animals for food. Nonetheless, game was still the dominant food supply over most of the pronghorn's range, particularly on the prairies of the United States and southern Canada. Over wide areas, the abundant bison was overwhelmingly the major food source. However, bighorn, deer, elk and pronghorn contributed to basic food supplies and dietary diversity as well as providing hides, antlers, etc., for clothing, shelter and tools (see Wedel and Frison 2001).

Referring to the Great Plains Middle Missouri tradition, 500 A.D. to 1500 A.D., which gave rise to village dwelling tribes in the Dakotas, Wedel (1961) reported

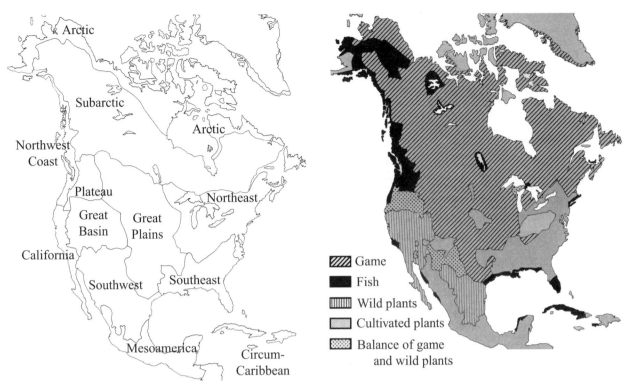

FIGURE 2. (Left) *Indian culture areas, some within pronghorn habitat.* (Right) *Dominant types of subsistence, some within pronghorn habitat, according to Waldman (1985). Unable to sustain themselves entirely by hunting big game, Indians shifted to other sources of food, including increased gathering of seeds, berries, fruits, nuts and roots. This eventually brought about the domestication of various plants and led to farming, which in turn permitted a more sedentary lifestyle for some tribes. The hunter-foragers of the Dalton period (7000–8000 B.C.) were people of a transitional time (Weaver 1991).*

that hunting and gardening were the basic sustenance activities of these people, and their principal meat sources were bison, deer, elk, pronghorn, small mammals and birds.

Figure 3 shows the estimated ranges of bighorn, bison, deer (white-tailed and mule) and elk—the most important big game food species for Indians within the macro-range (presumed maximum) of the pronghorn at the time of European contact.

Pronghorn abundance during prehistoric times seems to be estimated best by pronghorn numbers thought to be present during early historic times. However, all attempts to ascertain the abundance at a given time before use of modern censussing equipment and technology are decidedly speculative. Even today, when biologists are aware of seasonal differences in pronghorn distribution and group characteristics and have helicopters at their disposal, censuses remain crude estimates. Calculations from the early 20th century and before must be considered guesses and of limited utility.

Probably the most frequently used indices of early wildlife abundance and distribution were analyses of journals, letters and other literature from early explorations and travels through uncharted areas (Appendix A). Another significant source has been trapping and trade records. Although such information is valuable for indicating abundance at a specific time and locality, it is not applicable for lengthier periods of time or over the presumed range of the species in question.

With respect to pronghorn, certain eyewitness accounts of large populations in pristine habitat or of extensive kills by Indians or settlers tend to infer a much greater species abundance than was actually the case. The historic literature includes many presumably reliable local references to herds and kills of pronghorn much in excess of those observed or even conceivable today. For every such account, as many and often more local records reflect few or no pronghorn extant in the known historic range, including in the same areas of observed abundance during other years or at other times of year.

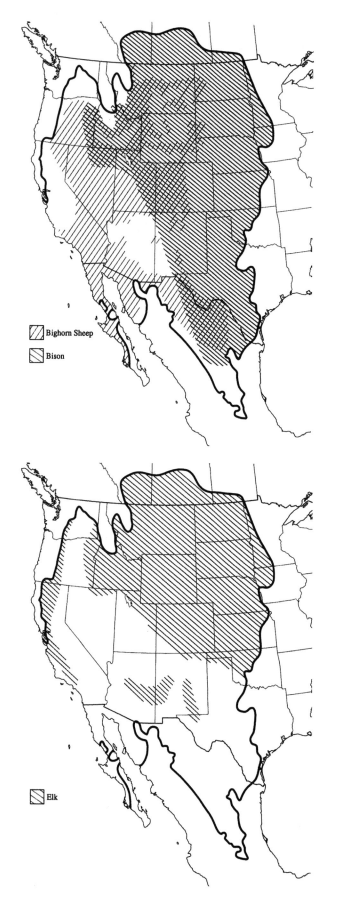

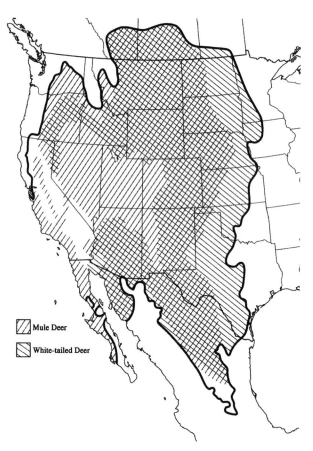

FIGURE 3. *Imposed on the presumed macro-range of pronghorn are the presumed macro-ranges of* (top left) *bighorn (Wishart 1978) and bison (Meager 1978),* (top right) *mule deer (Wallmo 1978) and white-tailed deer (Halls 1978), and* (bottom left) *elk (O'Gara and Dundas 2002).*

Seton (1909) estimated for the early 19th century: bison (on the prairies), 50 to 60 million; pronghorn, 40 million; white-tailed deer (north of Mexico), 20 million; mule deer, 10 million; and elk, 10 million. His pronghorn numbers were based on reports of huge winter congregations, of which he (1909:221) wrote: "It is extremely unlikely that they came from a greater distance than 200 miles." However, Roosevelt et al. (1902) noted longer movements from eastern North and South Dakota to the Black Hills before human-made barriers stopped them.

A more recent evaluation of pristine populations residing only in the 11 western states was offered by Wagner (1978), who adjusted Seton's (1929) basic information not only for his restricted geographical area but also for range capabilities. For the 11 western states, he estimated the following populations in prehistoric times: bison, 5 to 10 million; pronghorn, 10 to 15 million; mule and black-tailed deer (the latter outside the pronghorn's range), 5 million; elk, 2 million; and bighorn, 1 to 2 million.

Wagner's (1978) most interesting conclusion is the preponderance of pronghorn, by a ratio of two to three per bison, depending on the estimates chosen. Wagner considered pronghorn and bison symbionts, with bison grazing on climax grasses and pronghorn browsing on shrubby, herbaceous plants that tend to become the climax vegetation of the more arid West. Thus, bison densities were higher than the pronghorn's on the grassland plains and prairies east of the Rocky Mountains, whereas the reverse pattern prevailed westward. McHugh (1972) also calculated bison number based on habitat-carrying capacity and other variables and settled on a maximum count of 30 million (see also Haines 1970).

However, venturing a guess at prehistoric numbers of pronghorn is challenging. The 40 million suggested by Seton (1909) has been repeated so often that it is accepted as gospel—which it is not—by many present-day authors. On the other hand, nothing found in the earliest reports and firsthand accounts supports Wagner's (1978) supposition of a greater abundance of pronghorn than of bison. That is not to say, however, that Wagner's figure of 10 million pronghorn is wrong. One has no way of knowing, but 10 million at some time in pristine America is not implausible. If, however, bison numbers are benchmark, inasmuch as bison were the most noteworthy and, accordingly, best documented animals of the plains, and one subscribes to McHugh's (1972) estimations, there would be fair reason to conclude that the Seton and Wagner estimates are significantly liberal and conservative, respectively.

DISTRIBUTION OF PRONGHORN

... this interesting animal, like the buffalo, is now [1843] very rarely seen within less than 200 miles of the frontier: though early voyagers tell us that it once frequented as far east as the Mississippi.
—Gregg (1954:378)

The extent of the pronghorn's range during past times has been debated for nearly a century. In part, arguments have centered around the perceptions of "origi-nal" and "pristine" habitat. Those terms are without reference to geological or environmental time and have proven confusing in efforts to detail the area formerly occupied by pronghorn. In dispute has been the historic range—that area used at least periodically by pronghorn at some time or other since the discovery of North America by Europeans. Even so, historic range can be a misleading expression, for not all parts of the continent were "found" and their features documented simultaneously. Different areas of North America had historic origins as much as four centuries apart, i.e., 1600 to 1900.

Interest in the pronghorn's historic and contemporary ranges appears to have evolved about the close of the 19th century and beginning of the 20th century with public realization that the bison had been nearly exterminated (see Grinnell 1897, Roosevelt et al. 1902, Hornaday 1904). The concurrent decimation of pronghorn—at first, equated less with numerical reduction than with reduced distribution—served as supporting evidence of continental wildlife loss, validating that North America's natural resource bounty was not limitless after all.

Before historic time, pronghorn thrived on the temperate grassland prairies and shrub steppes of North America west of the Mississippi River. The only barriers to the species' distribution and prevalence were vegetational complexes, water and climate. By no means was the species' former range spatially or temporally continuous. The animals were not in heavily forested regions or mountain ranges.

Based primarily on review of historical documents, and such reviews by others (Seton 1909, Nelson 1925, Buechner 1950, Hall and Kelson 1959, Leopold 1959, Yoakum 1978, Kitchen and O'Gara 1982), the historic, extreme south-to-north pronghorn range was from central Mexico at about 20 degrees latitude to about 53 degrees latitude in Alberta and Saskatchewan, Canada. From east to west, the range limit was from about 93 degrees latitude in portions of Minnesota and Iowa to about 122 degrees latitude in California.

More than 850 documents—including journals, diaries, correspondence, reports, maps and anthologies—of early travelers and explorers in Mexico, western Canada and the United States (in which pronghorn were specifically identified) were reviewed to

Before the White Man Came (top) *is how Charles M. Russell illustrated in pen and ink, his vision of the western landscape before 1800. The scene, featuring elk, pronghorn, prairie wolves, geese and bison, probably is less romantic and more realistic that most people today would realize. On the other hand, such congregations and interactions of wildlife, were limited to certain times (mainly autumn, as shown) and places in the West, more so than implied by Russell's artwork, but as shown by Albert Bierstadt's spectacular painting,* Western Landscape with Antelope (bottom). Top photo courtesy of the Amon Carter Museum, Fort Worth, Texas. Bottom photo courtesy of the George F. McMurray Collection, Trinity College, Hartford, Connecticut.

The pristine habitats of pronghorn were predominantly short and tall grass prairies and the shrub steppes west of the Mississippi. It was in these settings that the species was first seen and recorded by Euro-American adventurers. Independence Rock—Groups of Antelope and Buffalo *was sketched and painted by Alfred Jacob Miller. Miller accompanied the Wilham Drummond Stewart expedition along the Platte River Valley and beyond in 1837. Perhaps most famed for his in-person renderings of mountain men and the fur rendezvous that year (along the Green River in Wyoming), Miller was the first to reproduce images of such places as Chimney Rock, ·Scott's Bluff, and Independence Rock, all of which were to become famous landmarks on the Oregon Trail. Also, Miller, like contemporaries George Catlin, Karl Bodmer, Rudolph Kürz and John J. Audubon, provided accurate and indelible views of the early West—its flora, fauna and people, as well as its landscapes. Like most of the early artists of the West, Miller sketched scenes "in the held," and painted them when back from the frontier. And, like most of such artists, he made several paintings of the same scene—as he did for* Independence Rock—*each slightly different.* Photo courtesy of the Northern Natural Gas Company Collection, Joslyn Art Museum, Omaha, Nebraska.

learn where and when the animals existed. Particular emphasis was placed on those areas bordering reported limits to historic pronghorn range. Nearly all the accounts of pronghorn distribution that were considered reliable fell within the range suggested by the reviewers previously cited. (We came across reference to skeletal remains of two pronghorn in an unlikely tall grass portion of what became northern Illinois, in the mid-1800s. This puzzle was solved months later when we chanced on a local history about the same Illinois county, which reported on a family that had two pet pronghorn fawns brought from the western plains several years before the skeleton finding. It was noted that the animals simply disappeared, so quite possibly accounted for the remains. Isolated and wholly inconsistent zoogeographic anomalies of late prehistoric and early historic time are not unusual and invariably have that sort of explanation or conjecture. We mention only this one.)

After firsthand sightings of pronghorn from the historic literature were pinpointed as closely as possible, the documented range was compared with various biogeographic delineations (Figure 4). There is a distinctive, although not precise, correlation of the historic pronghorn distribution and certain ecoregion divisions—prairie, steppe, mediterranean and desert.

The eastern limit of the pronghorn's historic range was at the terminus of grassland prairie and the adjoining vegetative biomes of oak and bluestem parkland in Texas, Oklahoma and southeastern Kansas, of oak/hickory/bluestem parkland in eastern Kansas and Iowa, of maple/basswood and oak savanna in northeastern Iowa and Minnesota, and of spruce and fir forest in northern Minnesota and Manitoba. It also appears that, within the grasslands of the Great Plains, mixed-grass prairies were zones of transition, where pronghorn were not regular or common inhabitants, except perhaps following extensive fires.

The northern boundary of pronghorn range historically matched fairly closely the termination of prairie and beginning of subarctic forest and parkland. To the west, the extent of yesteryear pronghorn range occurred almost exactly where steppe and prairie end or are interrupted by northern hardwood/fir forest in Montana, Idaho and Washington, by silver fir/Douglas-fir forest in Washington, Oregon and northern California, and by the Pacific Ocean in southern California and Baja California. To the south, pronghorn within historic times were unknown beyond where Mexican highland shrubsteppe meets the humid tropical savanna.

The pronghorn was, as Grinnell (1911) wrote, a creature of the yellow prairie.

VULNERABILITY TO HUNTING

The pronghorn has many physical characteristics and behavioral traits that facilitated or hindered its exploitation by people. Some populations do not migrate and are relatively available much of the year. Those that migrate usually do so along established routes. Pronghorn are remarkably fleet afoot over short distances, but their endurance is limited. The species avoids perceived obstacles and will seek a way around them; unlike deer, they seldom jump over even low barriers. The pronghorn's eyesight at long distances is legendary, but perhaps because of a pervasive curiosity, it may not identify an Indian in pronghorn skin or head at a few yards as an enemy.

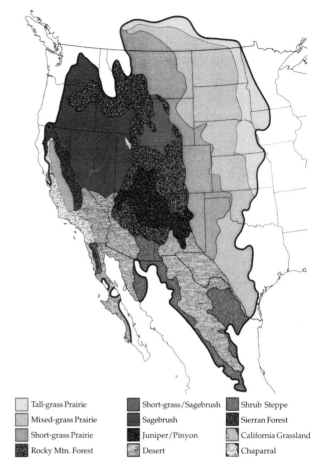

Tall-grass Prairie	Short-grass/Sagebrush	Shrub Steppe
Mixed-grass Prairie	Sagebrush	Sierran Forest
Short-grass Prairie	Juniper/Pinyon	California Grassland
Rocky Mtn. Forest	Desert	Chaparral

FIGURE 4. *Biogeographical zones within the macro-range of pronghorn (adapted from Leopold 1959, Küchler 1964, Allen 1967, Hunt 1974, Bailey 1978, 1995) show that the distribution of pronghorn was not continuous, just as the designated biotic zones exhibit more variety than evident. Records indicate that, historically, pronghorn were least abundant in the desert and Sierra Rocky Mountain forest regions. Conversely, the most heavily used habitats were the short-grass plains (dominated by gramma, needlegrass, wheatgrass and buffalograss) and the short-grass/sagebrush zone (dominated by wheatgrass, needlegrass and sagebrush).*

Pronghorn frequent open plains and prairies, and they seem unapproachable. When contained within physical barriers, such as a valley or by encircling hunters, they typically run a circular course without trying to break free. They are habitual in their daily activities, such as visits to the watering holes or salt licks, even after being shot at (Curtis 1926). There is a weakness of innate curiosity, and an inclination to approach strange objects and sounds. Also, a pronghorn band or herd tends to follow a lead animal.

Once the pronghorn's weaknesses are understood, it becomes an exploitable resource. In the autumn and winter it gathers into herds of a hundred or more individuals. Such assemblages justified elaborate hunting strategies and construction of large capture structures.

CAPTURING PRONGHORN

It is well understood that most hoofed game— buffalo, antelope, deer, elk, and sheep—usually traveled by certain established trails. In the days of their abundance, they always followed such trails and were not turned from them except by some alarming object. The Indians, who were consistently studying the habits of the animals on which they subsisted, were well informed as to their ways, and commonly built their pens, pitfalls, and other traps, lay in wait for, and laid their snares on or near these trails. The Indians expected the game would come to them, instead of their being obliged to search for the animals and bring them to the traps. This was not only a labor-saving practice, but also added greatly to the probability of success in securing food.

—Grinnell (1972 (1):277)

The prehistoric hunters at Trappers Point, in Sublette County, Wyoming, characterized earlier by Sanders (2000), took advantage of a natural migration corridor, a low ridge bordered on one side by the Green River and on the other by the New Fork River (Sawyer and McWhirter 2000). Predictable movements drew the attention of the Stone Age hunters to the possibility of harvesting numbers of animals. A bottleneck, such as at Trappers Point, was an ideal location for a trap.

Archaeologists began excavations in 1992 at Trappers Point—a large prehistoric site that occupies a narrow ridge that is on Bureau of Land Management land. The excavations revealed three layers of prehistoric tools, stone flakes from the manufacture of the tools and butchered animal bones; 258 whole and fragmentary projectile points were found (Sanders 2000). The upper layer was radiocarbon-dated at 4,690 years ago. Radiocarbon dates from the lowest stratum indicate that the charcoal there was created 6,180 to 7,880 years ago, so possibly the Sublette herd might have been migrating past Trappers Point for almost 8,000 years.

The middle layer held the fragmentary bones of nearly 30 pronghorn along with the fatal stone points and the stone tools that were used to dismember them. Radiocarbon dates from the plentiful sagebrush and juniper charcoal indicated that this stratum was about 5,800 years old, nearly 4,000 years older than any other known pronghorn kill/processing site. This level yielded the most complete record of a pronghorn kill. All three layers contained the same types of broken stone points, butchering tools, butchered pronghorn bones, burned rock and charcoal, suggesting that this pronghorn kill site had been used on several occasions. Fewer bones were found in the upper and lower levels, perhaps because smaller portions of those layers were excavated.

As at other prehistoric kill/processing sites in this region, pronghorn bones were systematically smashed, seemingly for boiling to extract all of the marrow grease and nutrients possible. Discarded bone fragments, burned rocks and charcoal-darkened soil from the final processing of the skeletons are scattered over the site along with a cluster of basin-shaped pits that apparently were used to heat rocks for cooking purposes (Sanders 2000).

Pronghorn fetal remains were found at the site. Comparing their bones and the mandibles of fawns with those of modern pronghorn, biologists concluded that the kill occurred during March or April, when modern pronghorn pass through the area toward their summer range.

One is inclined to believe that prehistoric communal hunts for pronghorn took place mainly in autumn, when the animals were concentrated and their skins (hides), muscle (meat) and marrow fat were in prime condition. Communal hunts for pronghorn at other times of the year would have required greater effort for relatively poor-quality animals. From contemporary standpoints of ecology, biology and subsistence, communal hunts in spring make little sense except in places and times of unusual privation. However, as evidenced by historic hunting by Indians, pronghorn fawns and fetal pronghorn were favored food. More so, Indian hunting—communally and otherwise—tended to be predicated on spiritual dictates. Also, spring migrations of pronghorn were opportunistic occasions for Indians to hunt them with reasonable chance of success because of the animals'

Pronghorn bones uncovered during excavations at Trappers Point, near Pinedale, Wyoming, proved to be approximately 6,000 years old. From such remains, archaeologists can determine not only what species of animals were killed, but the age at death, the season of death, the method of butchering and, to some extent, what parts of the kill were used. Charcoal from the ancient cooking fires allows carbon dating of some levels of a bone bed. Photo courtesy of the Wyoming State Archaeologist Office, Cheyenne.

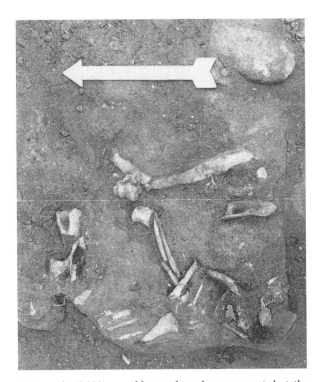

Among the 6,000-year-old pronghorn bones excavated at the Trappers Point archaeological site in Wyoming, were 258 whole and fragmented atlatl points, indicating the type of hunting weaponry used at the time and suggesting a great deal of hunting skill by those who used them to procure such wary and elusive prey as pronghorn. Photo courtesy of the Wyoming State Archaeologist Office, Cheyenne.

Artifacts found at the Trappers Point pronghorn kill site included a hafted, biface knife (left), two biface atlatl tips (center) and a drill (right). Photo courtesy of the Wyoming State Archaeologist Office, Cheyenne.

predictable routes and behavior. And, assuming that the religious belief system of prehistoric Indians was not too dissimilar from that of historic Indians, there would have been little reason for the hunters to equate seasonal hunting with conservation, at least in the modern context of the term. Many historic Indians subscribed to the general belief that game abundance was a function of a spiritually or metaphysically based punishment and reward system (i.e., if an ani-

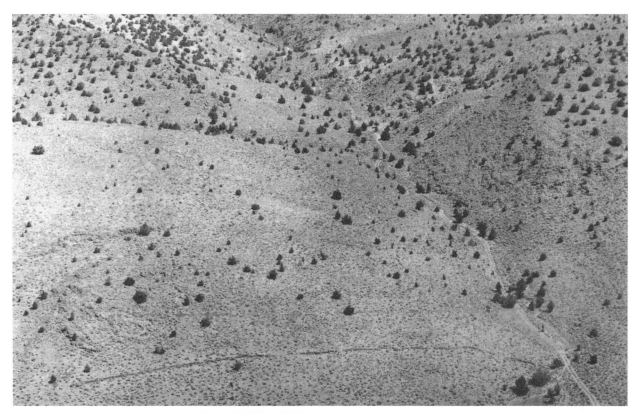

Paleo-Indians constructed fence-like structures to direct pronghorn to hunters. The Fort Sage Drift Fence (top), located about 31 miles (50 km) north of Reno, Nevada, is nearly 1.1 miles (1,800 m) long and, in places, almost 33 inches (1 m) high. It extends across three low hills and intercepts three drainages. The fence has five major segments, and arrowheads seem to document its use as an ambuscade. No evidence indicates whether target animals simply passed through breaks or openings in the drift fence (left) during natural foraging movements or were herded from below by Indians. Another possibility is that pronghorn were lured to or through the fence by concealed hunters. Regardless, the strategy must have been quite successful, because construction of the wall was very labor intensive. The Fort Sage Drift Fence was constructed well before 1300 A.D., and the accumulation of artifacts suggests that it was used over a long period of time. A similar drift fence, dated from about 1000 to 1300 A.D., is near Austin, Nevada (Thomas and McKee 1974).

mal was available to be killed, it was killed because it made itself available), not as a matter of personal restraint or herd conservation (see Martin 1978, Krech 1981, Brown 1992, Harrod 2000).

A drift fence, dated from about 1000 to 1300 A.D., exists near Austin, in central Nevada (Thomas and McKee 1974). Two walls are located on opposite sides of a ridge. The 330-foot (100 m) eastern section contains about 3,000 rocks, some weighing more than 50 pounds (22.7 kg), suggesting that its construction was a cooperative effort involving many Indians.

Many stone blinds are located in the upper Warm Springs area of Saline Valley, in Inyo County, California, and evidently were used since about 1200 B.C. to ambush bighorn and pronghorn (Brook 1980). Shooting from such blinds took place during spring and autumn when animals migrated along well-known adjacent trails.

The Fort Bridger pronghorn trapsite in Uinta County of southwestern Wyoming, encompassing approximately 27 acres (10.9 ha), was constructed of juniper (since vandalized for firewood). Archaeologists believe it was too unsubstantial to contain bison and that deer would have jumped over it. Pronghorn evidently were attracted in late summer and autumn to nearby rain-filled basins. Hunters herded the pronghorn into the oval-shaped corral where they were exhausted, or shot. Such traps were used repeatedly. Its form is marked on the photograph. Photo from Frison (1991).

Frison (1978) speculated that the corral trap for pronghorn evolved from its successful use for bison. Pronghorn pens familiar to him date from Late Prehistoric (ca. 200 to 1500 A.D.) to Protohistoric (1500 A.D. to present) times, but he believes that the hunting strategy may be much older. As Frison observed, such structures for pronghorn can be far less substantial than those necessary to direct or contain bison. Most of these geologically fragile structures have disappeared with time. For example, the remains of more than 200 pronghorn were found at the Eden-Farson site (a protohistoric Shoshonean campsite of 12 lodges) in the Green River basin of southwestern Wyoming (Frison 1971). Their demise had been catastrophic, suggesting that they had perished in a communal trapping operation. However, no apparent trapping structure was found.

A type of drive employed by the Hopi involved building a masonry wall across the narrow neck of a mesa. "Antelope were driven up the mesa and through a gap in the wall which was subsequently closed with brush. Trapped on the mesa-top, the antelope were killed by waiting hunters or by leaping from the edge of the mesa to the rocks below. Such a wall was found on a small mesa in northwestern New Mexico, and it may be that prehistoric inhabitants of the area trapped antelope in the same manner" (Peckham 1965:20).

QUANTIFYING FOODS USED

Determining the food habits of long-deceased cultures or communities is a vital but difficult challenge confronting an archaeologist, especially if it involves aborigines who lacked a written language—the case north of Mesoamerica. An attempt to assess prehistoric Indian use of pronghorn throughout the species' presumed range by a systematic review of archaeological site investigations met with mixed success. Few conclusions could be drawn, primarily because most reports of animal remains in Indian middens and other sites are insufficient with respect to species composition. Also, pronghorn bones and artifacts, except in some locations during the Late Prehistoric period, were too few or fragmentary to be useful (see Cressman 1977).

Bones, usually as fragments, often are among artifacts and debris excavated from human-occupied sites. If in fairly good condition and having certain diagnostic characters, they may be identifiable by experts to species. However, the animal may have strayed onto the site and died, or been brought there by predators (McGuire 1980). Their evidence as food becomes stronger if the bone bears butchering marks, has been disarticulated or broken in a consistent pattern, is charred (suggesting it had been heated by fire) or is associated with a hearth (Deaver and Greene 1978). A single bone may mean little. However, if a number of such bones are found in stratifications or in association, or with bones of other recognized food items, there may be reason to believe that they represent a food item.

Most early archaeologists merely listed the species whose remains had been identified at a site—if, in fact, they had the ability to identify them or even took pains to examine them. Eventually, zoological identification techniques and expertise developed to the point that systematic methodology of interpreting bone deposits came into being.

The first of two such designations is number of identified specimens (NISP), which refers to the number of bones or bone fragments that can be identified to a species, such as a pronghorn. By arranging and comparing bones, the number of animals necessary to have produced a given collection of bones can be determined. Thus, the minimum number of individuals (MNI) present, by species, is calculated. These are two of the major standards by which faunal remains at archaeological sites often are expressed.

Some crude estimation of the relative minimal amounts of food provided by each species can be made by multiplying the averaged dressed weight for each species by MNI. Such estimates are imprecise and biased because they ignore the size and condition of the animal and the noncarcass parts (e.g., internal organs, brain, marrow and blood) that usually were eaten.

Unfortunately, these approaches also usually ignore many biases resulting from Indian hunting and processing practicalities. The larger an animal and the farther from the point of consumption it was killed, the fewer of its bones likely were transported to a camp or village (Daly 1969). For example, large pieces of meat were deboned to lessen weight and facilitate their transportation.

Other problems abound. For example, some pronghorn and deer bones are similar and often indistinguishable, so sometimes are simply combined (Deaver and Greene 1978). Also, most food bones are fragmented, so are difficult to identify. Dogs, common to nearly all tribes, and wild carnivores would forage on or carry away discarded bones. Bones and skeletal fragments of larger animals (particularly bison) persist longer than those of small animals (Hurt 1953). Other bones were used in tool, implement and weapon manufacture, thus are overlooked or absent as food bones. Even if the meat source is fairly well understood, its relationship to other available food might be unknown. Clearly, bone remains are a biased sample of food habits.

Another way of quantifying aboriginal food sources is to examine their nutritional qualities. Roll and Deaver (1980) compiled data showing the calories provided by individuals of various wildlife species, based on the total of muscle tissue, internal organs and bone marrow. An adult bison provided 562,500 calories, compared with 45,000 yielded by a pronghorn. Therefore, 12.5 pronghorn would have to be taken to equal the caloric contribution of a single bison. The elk (277,200 calories) ranked second in value among the commonly taken artiodactyls. A jackrabbit produced 2,800 calories, and a cottontail, 700 calories. Both lagomorphs were important Indian foods in the Great Basin and Southwest. A single pronghorn was calorically equivalent to about 16 jackrabbits or 64 cottontails. Although Indians lacked such information to guide their decision making while hunting, they surely had a pragmatic sense of an animal's worth for food and made their decisions accordingly. Table 1 gives a perspective regarding numbers of animals probably used.

Evaluation

Recognizing various limitations, particularly with respect to archaeological findings, we nonetheless

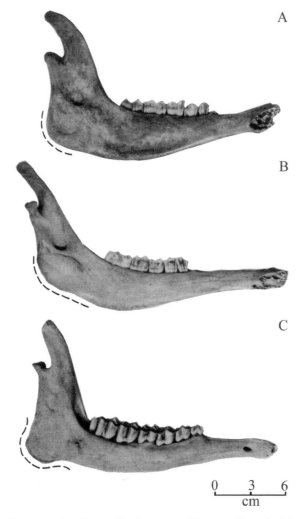

A

B

C

0   3   6
cm

By comparing diagnostic characters of bones, paleontologists sometimes can identify them according to species. Shown above are mandibles from the Awatovi site in northeastern Arizona: A = domestic sheep, B = pronghorn and C = mule deer. Photo from Olsen (1978).

undertook an extensive review of the archeological literature for information about Indian-occupied sites where unworked pronghorn bones had been reported. The study produced 146 sites containing pronghorn remains. Of these, the bones at 124 sites represented food items (Figure 5, Table 2). The sites were widely scattered, except for clustered pueblos of the Southwest.

With few exceptions, pronghorn food bones rarely were abundant at a site. Throughout pronghorn range, food bones of deer were common, being found at 100 (81%) of the 124 sites having pronghorn food bones. In its eastern range, pronghorn bones, usually far less abundant than those of bison, were found at 62 sites. In the southwestern part of the range, food bones of bighorn were found at 37 sites. Elk food bones were found at 30 sites. Because the analysis was based solely on sites where pronghorn bones were found, it is biased to the extent that other sites within the pronghorn's range produced no bones of that species but had other big game bones.

Where substantial samples of pronghorn were found (NSIP = 50+, MNI = 5+), pronghorn outnumbered other ruminants only at: Caldwell Village, Utah; Danger Cave on the Utah/Nevada border; Hosterman and Angostura Reservoir, South Dakota; Lost Terrace, Montana, and Eden-Farson, Wyoming. The latter two apparently were pronghorn kill/processing sites (Frison 1971).

Danger Cave, situated on the western shoreline of Lake Bonneville, was occupied nearly continuously from about 9500 B.C. until Late Prehistoric time. Wrote

TABLE 1. Approximate maximum number of mature big game animals of various species hypothetically necessary to support a band of 100 Indians

Species	Approximate live weight[a]		Approximate food yield[b]		Number of animals needed per unit of time			
	Pounds	Kilograms	Pounds	Kilograms	Day	Week	Month	Year
Bison	1,382	627.4	937	425.4	0.32	2.2	9.7	116.9
Moose	1,105	501.7	759	344.6	0.39	2.7	11.9	142.4
Elk	600	272.4	407	184.8	0.73	5.1	22.2	266.5
Caribou	295	133.8	212	96.2	1.41	9.9	42.4	516.5
Deer	165	74.9	115	52.2	2.60	18.2	79.0	949.0
Bighorn[c]	161	73.2	106	48.1	2.83	19.8	86.1	1,033.0
Pronghorn	104	47.2	43	19.5	6.97	48.8	211.9	2,544.1

This information is based on an arbitrary year-round animal food consumption rate of 3 pounds (1.4 kg) per person per day (modified from McCabe 1982, Reeves and McCabe 1998).

[a] Averaged for both sexes of adults (3 years old and older).

[b] Calculated on the basis of 90% of dressed carcass weight (minus most bones), plus 60% of viscera. These percentages are based roughly on what is known of food utilization of carcasses by plains Indians.

[c] Bighorn weight is for both sexes of adults, averaged for the Desert, California and Rocky Mountain bighorn, from Wishart (1978).

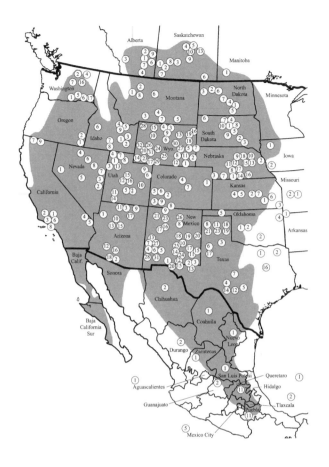

FIGURE 5. *Human-occupied or used archaeological sites containing pronghorn remains. Depicted sites might represent kill sites, butchering or cooking locations, caves used as living quarters, middens, etc. Pronghorn remains at a few locations may bear no relationships to humans. For instance, a wolf could have carried a bone into a cave sometimes used by humans. A site is defined as a human-occupied location at which pronghorn remains were dated to a specific geologic time period. Remains occasionally were found in two strata (e.g., Saskatchewan, Heron Eden, where remains dated to both the Late Glacial and Early Holocene periods). Human use of such sites probably was discontinuous. Thus, Heron Eden is regarded as two sites and is so numbered. Sites are numbered consecutively and chronologically within each province or state. Mexican sites are not identified to specific locations. The number of sites associated with specific states is shown within one circle. Because of obvious spatial limitations, site locations are approximate. Where several sites overlap, the following type of notation was used—28 to 31 enclosed in circles. This example is from New Mexico, where sites 28, 29, 30 and 31 are in close proximity. Table 2 provides basic information for each site as well as the source of that information. The shaded area represents pronghorn macro-range. Naturally, pronghorn did not inhabit unsuitable habitat, such as steep mountains and dense forests within the delineated area.*

TABLE 2. Archaeological sites containing pronghorn remains, corresponding to Figure 5

Country	Province/state	Geological period[a]	Number on map	Designation	Site number
Canada[b]	Alberta	Late Wisconsin	1	Galt Island Bluff	EaOq-VP
		Middle Holocene	2	Cactus Flower	EbOp-16
			3	Metke	EdPl-01
		Late Holocene	4	Unnamed	DgOv-93
			5	Unnamed[c]	DjOu-5
			6	Larson	DlOn-3
			7	Laidlaw	DlOu-9
			8	Kenney[c]	DjPk-1
			9	Cactus Flower	EbOp-16
	Manitoba	Late Holocene	1	Stendall	DkMh-1
	Saskatchewan	Late Glacial	1	Heron Eden	EeOi-11
		Early Holocene	2	Heron Eden	EeOi-11
		Middle Holocene	3	Gray	EcNx-1a
			4	Gowen 1	FaNq-25
			5	Thundercloud	FbNp-25
		Late Holocene	6	Oxbow Dam	DhMn-1
			7	Bracken Cairn	DhOb-3
			8	Gray	EcNx-1a
			9	Sjovold	EiNs-4
			10	Tipperary Creek	FbNp-1
			11	Newo Asiniak	FbNp-16
			12	Newo Asiniak Kill	FbNp-16
			13	Amisk	FbNp-17
United States[d]	Arizona	Late Glacial	1	Vulture Cave	1058
		Middle Holocene	2	Ventana Cave	1145
		Late Holocene	3	Black Mesa D:7:0023	1272
			4	Black Mesa D:7:0216	1274

continued on next page

21

TABLE 2—*continued*

Country	Province/state	Geological period[a]	Number on map	Designation	Site number
United States (*contd.*)	Arizona (*contd.*)	Late Holocene (*contd.*)	5	Black Mesa D:7:0236	1254
			6	Black Mesa D:7:3013	1259
			7	Black Mesa D:11:0320	1285
			8	Black Mesa D:11:2025	1283
			9	Black Mesa D:11:2030	1278
			10	Grand Canyon Airport Site 5145	1519
			11	Heltagito Rockshelter	1491
			12	Point of Pines	1158
			13	Red Lake Wash Site 5137	1513
			14	Red Lake Wash Site 5150	1514
			15	Red Lake Wash Site 1515	1515
			16	Snaketown	1251
			17	Tallahogan	1213
			18	Ventana Cave	1145
	Arkansas	Early Holocene	1	Albertson	950
	California	Late Wisconsin	1	Maricopa	1373
			2	McKittrick	1374
			3	Rancho La Brea	1335
		Glacial	4	Antelope Cave	1355
			5	Kokoweef Cave	1356
		Middle Holocene	6	Glen Annie Canyon	2916
			7	Nightfire Island	953
		Late Holocene	8	CA-Ven-294	1350
			9	Nightfire Island	953
	Colorado	Late Glacial	1	Dutton	14
			2	Haystack Cave	736
		Late Holocene	3	5MT3	584
			4	Dutch Creek	583
			5	Grass Mesa Village	609
			6	Mesa Verde Site 499	675
			7	Recon John Shelter	557
			8	Serrano	763
			9	Windy Wheat Hamlet	612
	Idaho	Late Wisconsin	1	Dam Local Fauna	1496
			2	Rainbow Beach	1495
		Late Glacial	3	Owl Cave	1497
		Middle Holocene	4	Bison Rockshelter	1522
			5	Veratic Rockshelter	1523
		Late Holocene	6	Dry Creek Rockshelter	20
			7	Meacham	1532
			8	Spaulding	1551
			9	Veratic Rockshelter	1523
	Iowa	Late Holocene	1	Arthur	544
			2	Hanging Valley	2242
	Kansas	Middle Holocene	1	Milbourn	2396
		Late Holocene	2	Elliott (14GE303)	353
			3	Roth	2280
			4	Solomon River 14ML5	352
			5	Solomon River 14ML15	351
			6	Williamson	2245
			7	Witt	732
	Missouri	Middle Holocene	1	Rodgers Shelter	2576
		Late Holocene	2	Rodgers Shelter	2576
	Montana	Middle Holocene	1	Sun River	568
		Late Holocene	2	Bootlegger Trail	575
			3	Cremer	348
			4	Drake	590
			5	Ellison's Rock	574
			6	Hoffer	374
			7	Pictograph Cave	592
			8	Sun River	568

continued on next page

TABLE 2—*continued*

Country	Province/state	Geological period[a]	Number on map	Designation	Site number
United States (contd.)	Nebraska	Early Holocene	1	Lime Creek	429
		Middle Holocene	2	Logan Creek	445
			3	Spring Creek	797
		Late Holocene	4	25FT17	441
			5	25FT39	439
			6	25FT70	444
			7	25RW22	794
			8	Aiken	442
			9	Bill Packer	428
			10	Brown	436
			11	Clarence Allen	440
			12	Compton	443
			13	Cunningham	437
			14	Doyle	792
			15	Hulme	558
			16	Mowry Bluff	425
			17	Owens	438
			18	Schmidt	426
	Nevada	Late Wisconsin	1	Hidden Cave	117
			2	Owl Cave 2	1191
			3	Smith Creek Cave	114
		Late Holocene	4	Ezra's Retreat	1174
			5	Gatecliff Shelter	1001
			6	James Creek Shelter	1250
			7	Kachina Cave	1060
			8	Newark Cave	1353
	New Mexico	Late Wisconsin	1	Conkling Cave	1337
		Late Glacial	2	Burnet Cave	1163
			3	Dry Cave	1164
		Late Holocene	4	Apache Creek Site 8887	1241
			5	Apache Creek Site 8888	1242
			6	Apache Creek Site 8891	1243
			7	Armijo Springs Site 5939	1240
			8	Arroyo Hondo Pueblo	1235
			9	Bancos Village	1478
			10	Block Lookout	1229
			11	Bloom Mound	1224
			12	Bonnell	1226
			13	Castle Rock	1244
			14	Fresnal Shelter	1738
			15	Garnsey Spring Campsite	1501
			16	Guadalupe Ruin	1165
			17	Henderson	1918
			18	Hiner	1227
			19	Middle Pecos Valley Site P4	1499
			20	Middle Pecos Valley Site P24	1500
			21	Navajo Reservoir LA 3427	1472
			22	Navajo Reservoir Site LA 4065	1471
			23	Navajo Reservoir Site LA 4385	1481
			24	Penasco	1225
			25	Phillips	1228
			26	Tesuque By-Pass	1919
			27	Tularosa Cave	1249
			28	Whiskey Creek Site 4986	1245
			29	Whiskey Creek Site 4987	1246
			30	Whiskey Creek Site 4988	1247
			31	Whiskey Creek Site 4989	1248
	North Dakota	Late Holocene	1	Bendish	486
			2	Mahaha	492
			3	Mondrian Tree	452
			4	Pretty Point	489

continued on next page

TABLE 2—*continued*

Country	Province/state	Geological period[a]	Number on map	Designation	Site number
United States (contd.)	North Dakota (contd.)	Late Holocene (contd.)	5	South Cannonball	481
			6	Upper Sanger	449
			7	White Buffalo Robe	448
	Oklahoma	Late Holocene	1	Delaware Canyon 34CD157A	319
			2	Lee	280
			3	McLemore	279
			4	Pohly	282
			5	Roy Smith	287
	Oregon	Early Holocene	1	Dirty Shame Rockshelter	1034
		Middle Holocene	2	Dirty Shame Rockshelter	1034
	South Dakota	Early Holocene	1	Walth Bay	423
		Late Holocene	2	Crow Creek	410
			3	Dinehart	408
			4	Jake White Bull	398
			5	Jiggs Thompson	422
			6	Lightning Spring	573
			7	Lower Grand	395
			8	McKensey Village	388
			9	Sommers	414
			10	Travis I	396
	Texas	Late Wisconsin	1	Clear Creek Local Fauna	135
		Late Glacial	2	Ben Franklin	136
			3	Lake Theo	2225
		Middle Holocene	4	Baker Cave	162
			5	Hall's Cave	2240
			6	Lubbock Lake	13
		Late Holocene	7	41TG91	740
			8	Alibates	9
			9	Antelope Creek 22	639
			10	Antelope Creek 22A	638
			11	Antelope Creek 24	637
			12	Baker Creek	162
			13	Caldwell Ranch No. 1	752
			14	Hinds Cave	164
			15	Hueco Tanks State Historical Park	167
			16	Kyle	151
			17	Lubbock Lake	13
			18	Medford Ranch	636
			19	Pickett Ruin	634
			20	Pickup Pueblo	2222
			21	Roper	8
			22	Sanford Ruin	633
			23	Spring Canyon	7
	Utah	Early Holocene	1	Hogup Cave	1048
			2	Sudden Shelter	1153
		Middle Holocene	3	Danger Cave	1047
			4	Hogup Cave	1048
			5	Sudden Shelter	1153
			6	Thorne Cave	1159
		Late Holocene	7	Bear River No. 3	1450
			8	Bear River No. 2	1459
			9	Caldwell Village	1462
			10	Clyde's Cavern	1529
			11	Evans Mound	1552
			12	Hinckley Mound 2	1546
			13	Hogup Cave	1048
			14	Median Village	1454
			15	Seamons Mound	1549
			16	Spotten Cave	1545
	Washington	Late Glacial	1	Umatilla Mammoth	1035
		Middle Holocene	2	Chief Joseph Dam 45DO243	1435

continued on next page

Table 2—*continued*

Country	Province/state	Geological period[a]	Number on map	Designation	Site number
United States (contd.)	Washington (contd.)	Middle Holocene (contd.)	3	Chief Joseph Dam 45OK11	1425
			4	Chief Joseph Dam 45OK287/2881418	
			5	Marmes Rockshelter	1040
			6	Tucannon	1181
		Late Holocene	7	Avey's Orchard	2891
			8	Chief Joseph Dam 45DO214	1433
			9	Chief Joseph Dam 45DO242	1434
			10	Chief Joseph Dam 45DO326	1422
			11	Chief Joseph Dam 45OK2	1426
			12	Chief Joseph Dam 45OK2A	1427
			13	Chief Joseph Dam 45OK4	1416
			14	Chief Joseph Dam 45OK11	1425
			15	Chief Joseph Dam 45OK258	1424
			16	Chief Joseph Dam 45OK287/288	1418
			17	Timothy's Village	1146
	Wyoming	Late Wisconsin	1	Horned Owl Cave	186
			2	Little Box Elder Cave	22
			3	Prospects Shelter	180
		Full Glacial	4	Natural Trap Cave	24
		Late Glacial	5	Agate Basin	175
			6	Colby	181
			7	Sheaman	169
		Early Holocene	8	Casper	176
			9	Eagle Shelter	179
			10	Horner	227
			11	Little Box Elder Cave	22
			12	Rattlesnake Pass	2241
			13	Sister's Hill	237
		Middle Holocene	14	48UT199	233
			15	Dead Indian Creek	202
			16	Hawken	190
			17	Maxon Ranch	140
		Late Holocene	18	48CA403	261
			19	48CA1391	218
			20	48UT199	233
			21	48UT779	234
			22	Austin Wash	232
			23	Bessie Bottom	221
			24	Birdshead Cave	262
			25	Buffalo Hump	229
			26	Butler-Rissler	170
			27	Castle Gardens Access Road	268
			28	Lamar	837
			29	Maxon Ranch	240
			30	Spring Creek Cave	372
			31	Taliaferro	247
			32	Wardell Buffalo Trap	193
Mexico[e]	Aguascalientes			Cedazo	1
	Coahuila			Cuatro Ciénegas	1
	Chihuahua			Cueva de Jiménez	2
				Los Moctezumas	
	Durango			Bolsón de mapimi	2
	Guanajuato			Cerro de la Mesa	2
	Hidalgo			Cueva La Nopalera	2
				Tepetitlán	
	Mexico			Cuanalan	11
				Frente 2	
	Teotihuacán				
				Oztoyahualco	
				Santa Maria Coatlán	
				Temamatla	

continued on next page

25

TABLE 2—*continued*

Country	Province/state	Geological period[a]	Number on map	Designation	Site number
Mexico	Teotihuacán			Teotihuacán	
(*contd.*)	(*contd.*)			Tlatilco	
				Tlailotlacan	
				Ventanilla frentre 3	
				Teotihuacán	
				Xocotitla	
				Zohapilco	
	Mexico City			Teremote-Tlaltenco	5
	Nuevo Leon			Mina	1
	Puebla			Cholula	11
				Cueva Coxcatlán (Tehuacan Valley)	
				Cueva Coxcatlán (Coxcatlan Cave)	
				Cueva del Tepeyolo	
				Cueva del Texcal	
				Hueyatlaco	
				Puente de Atepetzingo	
				San Antonio Arenillas	
				Sta. Catarina, Cholula	
				Tehuacán	
				Tlapacoya	
	Queretaro			Zona Arqueológica de Ranas	1
	San Luis Potosi			Laguna de la Media Luna	1
	Zacatecas			Osario de la Quemada	1

[a] Geological time periods: Late Wisconsin, 40,000–10,000 years ago (ya); Glacial 20,000–10,000 ya; Full Glacial, 20,000–15,000 ya; Late Glacial, 15,000–10,000 ya; Early Holocene, 10,000–8,000 ya; Middle Holocene, 8,000–4,000 ya; Late Holocene 4,000–500 ya (from Graham and Lundelius 1994).
[b] Morlan (1999).
[c] Not mapped because of insufficient information.
[d] Not mapped because of insufficient information.
[e] Graham and Lundelius (1994).
[f] Arroyo-Cabrales et al. (2001).

Jennings (1957:22), "The chief game resource appears to have been ungulates. Of these the most frequently encountered is the antelope." Bighorn were next in frequency, and bison were scarce. The Danger Cave bones were not subdivided by genera, so the relative abundance of genera by occupation level was not given, but 78% were in the top two layers—dating from about 2250 B.C. to 20 A.D. Consequently, there is no reliable way to determine relative food values. Peoples in the Angostura Reservoir basin exhibited a preference for pronghorn, according to White (1952).

Using ethnological information in his analysis of elk as an Indian food, McCabe (1982, 2002) ranked various nonvegetable foods according to the amount eaten, seasonal significance and preference, for regions of North America (Table 3). In the eight regions where pronghorn occurred, it failed to rank first in any. Pronghorn and deer ranked second (tied) only in the Southwest, third in the southern plains and Great Basin and fourth in the central plains and central California. Even in the Southwest, pronghorn ranked below jackrabbits; in the Great Basin, it placed third, behind jackrabbits first, and reptiles and insects combined.

The ranks were weighted by assigning a value of 4 to Rank 1, 3 to Rank 2 and so forth. Within a possible ranking total of 80 points, bison was first with 18.0, followed by deer with 14.5, elk with 8.1, fish with 8.5 and pronghorn with 7.0. A variety of other mammals, plus birds, reptiles and insects comprised the remainder.

In another ranking study of 19 prehistoric sites in Utah, comparative meat importance values were mule deer at 2.0, bighorn at 1.2, pronghorn at 1.1, bison at 0.8 and elk at 0.5 (Harper 1986).

Although one may question these crude, subjective values, they uniformly suggest that pronghorn were not the major sustaining source of meat for Indians. In a few places, notably communal kill sites, pronghorn were dominant, but this importance was local and temporal. On the other hand, pronghorn provided a moderately important food supply to quite

TABLE 3. Approximate rank of importance of pronghorn and other animal foods in diets of historic North American Indians

| Region | Rank[a] | | | |
	First	Second	Third	Fourth
Plains				
Northern	Bison	Beaver	Deer	Elk
Central	Bison	Deer	Elk	Pronghorn
Southern	Bison	Deer	Pronghorn	Elk
California				
Northern	Fish	Birds Deer	Bear Elk	Small mammals
Central	Rodents Birds	Fish	Deer	Pronghorn Elk
Great Basin	Jackrabbit	Reptiles Insects	Pronghorn	Bighorn sheep Deer Elk
Southwest	Jackrabbit	Pronghorn Deer	Bison	Elk

[a] Based on amount eaten, seasonal significance and preference, in that order.
Source: McCabe 1982, 2002.

a number of tribes. To tribes within its range, pronghorn probably offered some welcomed dietary diversification. Geographically, bison far outranked pronghorn on the prairies; in the Southwest and on the western plains and foothills, bighorn probably was more important. Throughout most of the Great Basin, where impoverished environments made human existence tenuous, the acquisition of a single pronghorn must have been a memorable occasion.

Wedel (1961:42) reasonably summed up the situation when he wrote: "Normally an inhabitant of the open plains, gifted with keen vision, and possessing great powers of endurance, the antelope was less easily taken by hunters than was the bison. Moreover, its weight seldom exceeded 120 pounds, as against 700 to 1,200 pounds for the female and 1,500 to 2,000 pounds for the male bison, and so its taking netted much less sustenance per animal. Its bones and horns occurred in small quantities in the refuse deposits of Indian camp and village sites."

PREHISTORIC WEAPONS

Like other aborigines, North American Indians had an arsenal of hand weapons at their disposal. These included knives, clubs, spears and even rocks. These often were used to dispatch animals that were being restrained by other means. A design engineer who examined Indian weaponry from his professional perspective, observed that primitive hunters used re-

liable and maintainable weapons systems optimal to their situations (Bleed 1986).

By far, the simplest Indian weapon was a rock cast by the hand itself. George Bird Grinnell (1923), noted chronicler of the Cheyenne and Blackfeet, told of the unerring skill of Strong Left Hand in killing animals, including on one occasion a pronghorn, with nothing more than a stone. The old Cheyenne told Grinnell that a pronghorn once approached him while he was lying on a hill. When the animal stopped nearby to nibble at some grass, Strong Left Hand threw a rock just as the pronghorn raised its head. The stone killed the animal or wounded it such that its hunter completed the kill. That incident, of course, was during historic time, but throwing stones in self-defense or to procure food most likely was practiced from earliest time.

Sling

The sling consists of a small strap, pouch or socket of leather or fabric to which two cords are attached. The slinger holds the two ends in one hand, whirls the pouch and its missile rapidly around the head and, by releasing one end sharply, dispatches the missile with considerable centrifugal force. The sling was a marked improvement over casting stones by hand, and it was widely used by Indian youths for taking small mammals and birds.

Use of the sling has been documented for dozens of tribal groups inhabiting at least nine western states (Heizer and Johnson 1952) and Mexico. But not until 1952 was the first intact prehistoric example found in North America, at Lovelock Cave, Nevada.

Atlatl

The atlatl is perhaps the least known and understood of all weapons used by North American aborigines. Names given it over the years—dart-thrower, spear-thrower, spear sling, throwing stick and throwing board (Grant 1979)—have caused confusion. It was known as atlatl in ancient Mexico (Taylor 2001), where it reached its highest level of development, by progressing from a very effective weapon to the supreme symbol of Aztec authority and power (Hamilton 1982).

Countless glyphs depict the atlatl grasped in the hands of Aztec emperors and officials. Although a Nahuatl text, dated 1576, credits the Aztecs with inventing the atlatl (see Nuttall 1891), the weapon was widely used in the Old World for thousands of years prior (Krause 1905). The earliest dated atlatl artifact was found near the Dalles, on the Columbia River in Oregon (Cressman et al. 1940). It was dated to about 8,500 years ago.

The atlatl is a device for hurling a spear or dart; it consists of a rod or board, often with a groove on the upper surface, and a hook, thong or projection at the rear end to hold the missile in place until its release. The missile of the atlatl is a spear, a long shaft with a sharp head or blade, often barbed, or a shorter dart, both usually feathered at the rear end. The penetration of a projectile thrown by an atlatl is greater than that of a comparable one thrown by hand and is about equal to that of an arrow shot from a bow (Butler 1975). Bernal Diaz related how, when the Spaniards first battled the Tlaxcallans, they were the recipients of cast barbed spears, which "could traverse any sort of armor and against them there was no means of protection" (Nuttall 1891:9).

Early Aztec codices show the atlatl being used in warfare and for taking waterfowl and spearing fish. Some depict large quadrupeds being stalked by atlatl-armed hunters, but it is unclear whether the quarry are deer or pronghorn. In the Casas Grandes area of Mexico, seminomadic aborigines of the Viejo period are known to have hunted bison and pronghorn as had their ancestors, the Chichimecs, whose killing tools included traps, curved or flat wooden clubs and the atlatl (Di Peso 1979). The broad distribution and abundance of atlatl points documented that the device was in wide use, virtually throughout the range of pronghorn, and for some period of time, it probably was the major weapon (Heizer 1938, Ekholm 1962, Newman 1967, Riddell and McGeein 1969).

Bow and Arrow

Replacement of the atlatl by the bow and arrow was gradual and temporally varied among Indian groups and locales (see Kellar 1955, Cressman 1977). Stuart (1983) noted that the shift from the atlatl to the

The atlatl, also called dart-thrower, spear-thrower or spear sling, supposedly was brought to North America by Asian pioneers. It was the major weapon used by prehistoric people for taking big game in the West, and was far superior in power and accuracy to the hand-thrown spear. Eventually the atlatl was largely replaced by the more advanced bow and arrow. However, it still was used by the Aztecs at the time of the Spanish conquest. Photo from Amsden (1931).

bow and arrow had begun by the end of the first century, but the replacement rate varied widely.

The bow and arrow was more powerful, accurate and efficient than the atlatl. It could be slung over the shoulder and discharged from a concealed position, or later from horseback. Arrows were more portable than spears. Thus, the bow and arrow seems the weapon most used by Indians for hunting pronghorn.

The atlatl was not abruptly discarded but still used for generations, perhaps centuries, after the advent of the new weapon. Cressman (1977) saw the period of

Before Indian acquisition of firearms, and even thereafter for most Indians, the bow and arrow was the most popular means of the communal killing of big game, including pronghorn. Pronghorn driven to traps or pits were killed as well by clubs and lances, but the bow and arrow was most effective. Illustration of an Indian at a waterhole in the Colorado Desert is from Brander (1971).

synchronous use as about 750 years, indicating reluctant divestment of atlatl technology, skill and hunting methods in favor of those of the bow and arrow (see also Kroeber 1948). According to Driver and Massey (1957), the bow and arrow was the chief hunting weapon in western North America at the time of European contact.

A study of missile points at Dry Creek Rockshelter, in southwestern Idaho, supports the notion that the bow and arrow was in use in the Great Basin by 1370 B.C. (Webster 1978). Webster (1980) later reported that five dart (atlatl) points—but no arrow points—were found in the stratum of the same rock shelter dated at 1600 B.C.; in strata dated since 270 A.D., the proportion of arrowheads increased, whereas dart points declined and vanished altogether (Webster 1980).

ARTIFACTS

Prehistoric artifacts identifiable as pronghorn are scarce; most are bone tools found in caves (Table 4).

Pottery

Probably the most outstanding decorative effigies of pronghorn are those on pottery from the Swarts Ruin, a Mimbres site in southwestern New Mexico (Cosgrove and Cosgrove 1932, Figure 6). This enormously rich site was largely ignored by early archaeologists. Its inconspicuous mounds seemingly paled in comparison to the cliff-houses and open ruins of nearby areas.

Table 4. Prehistoric pronghorn artifacts, generally found in caves during archaeological excavations

Site	Artifact	Reference
Broken Cave, Arizona	Four bags made of deer or pronghorn whole hides; a dog-skin bag contained two small pronghorn-skin bags	Guernsey (1931)
Danger Cave, Utah	Highly polished pendant of horn sheath with serrated edges; five horn cores used as flakers to shape projectile points	Smith (1952)
Danger Cave, Utah	Knives and scrapers of scapulae	Jennings (1957)
Deadman Cave, Utah	Knapping tool for flaking obsidian made from a scapula	Clark (1884)
Catlow Cave, No. 1, Oregon	Knife handle made from a pronghorn sheath	Cressman et al. (1942)
Grand Gulch, Utah	A rattle of deer or pronghorn hooves	Goddard (1975)
Grave in Nevada	Necklace of unborn pronghorn hooves and abalone shell, found on the skeleton of an 8- to 10-year-old girl	Ulrich (1995)
Green River Basin, Wyoming	Many edged tools from long bones, possibly used for fleshing skins of the many pronghorn processed at the site; beads from diastema of mandibles	Frison (1971)
Hogup Cave, Utah	Horn core considered to be a knapping tool	Aikens (1970)
Southwestern New Mexico	Awl made from an excavated metatarsal bone	

FIGURE 6. *The prehistoric Mimbres peoples lived in several hundred small villages in the isolated valleys and scorching deserts of present-day southwestern New Mexico (Brody 1977). They decorated their pottery with remarkably attractive and mystical motifs drawn from their environment. The art form reached its zenith between about 1000 A.D. and 1250 A.D., after which the Mimbres civilization mysteriously collapsed. Shallow bowls, about 3 inches (7.6 cm) deep and the size of our dinner plate, bearing on the inner surface stylized images are particularly numerous. The pronghorn was one of the animals most commonly depicted. More than 4,000 Mimbres bowls are now in private collections, but countless others were irreparably damaged or destroyed by looters. Frequently the bowls were "killed" (pierced or broken) before being placed as offerings or tokens in Indian burials (Cosgrove and Cosgrove 1932).*

Paintings

Prehistoric pronghorn paintings appear on the walls of kivas at Jemez and Kawaika-a (Smith and Ewing 1952). Oddly, some animals are depicted with tassel-edged blankets thrown over their backs. Although the animals were sometimes painted blue, there is no uncertainty about their identity. Pronghorn also are evident in kiva wall paintings at Pottery Mound in the Puerco Valley of northcentral New Mexico, an Anasazi site that dates from about 1300 to 1475 A.D. (Hibben 1975, Figure 7).

Figurines

More than 375 ancient animal effigies, each intricately bent and fashioned from a single split, long willow twig, have been found in at least 15 locations in Arizona, California, Nevada and Utah (Tuohy 1986). Their ages range from about 1020 to 2145 B.C. (Schroedl 1977). Although these stick figures surely represent ungulates, we do not know whether they are bighorn, deer or pronghorn (all resident in the general area) or perhaps all three species. The utility of split-twig figures is unknown, but Schroedl (1977)

Dating from 1400 to 1625 A.D., the ceramic bowl above is of the Sikyatki style, named after a prehistoric Hopi site in Arizona. Its type is considered superior to nearly all other prehistoric bowls. The pointed image of a pronghorn, shot in the flank by a bowman, is not regarded as superior period artwork. Photo courtesy of The Brooklyn Museum, Brooklyn, New York.

FIGURE 7. *A pronghorn effigy from a wall painting at Pottery Mound, an Anasazi site in the Puerco Valley of northwestern New Mexico. Approximately 800 frescoes, dating to about 1300 A.D., have been unearthed there. Hibben (1975:xiii) wrote: "The paintings discovered at Pottery Mound constitute the most extensive body of kiva art ever brought to light, an art form which is probably the earliest found within the boundaries of the United States, except for petroglyphs and pictographs." Pronghorn were dually depicted as a live animal and as a disguise for a hunter-dancer (from Hibben 1975).*

A split-twig figure (top) from a cave above Marble Canyon, in Coconino County, Arizona, was made by the prehistoric Hakataya, and may have been served totemically or ceremonially to improve hunting of the ungulate the figure represents, perhaps a pronghorn. The bottom photo is a Zuni earthenware figure, the date and source location of which are unknown, but the Zunis, from northern New Mexico, descended from the prehistoric Anasazi. Photos courtesy of the Smithsonian Institution, Department of Anthropology, Washington, DC.

supposed that they evolved as magico-religious objects.

BURIAL OFFERINGS

At Gran Quivira, in central New Mexico, the ancient Anasazis buried their dead or cremated them in shallow pits beneath the floors of their living quarters

31

A rattle, partially made of pronghorn horn sheaths, was recovered from Lovelock Cave, Churchill County, Nevada, in 1911 by miners excavating bat guano. The rattle was buried with the body of a child. Photo from Loud and Harrington (1929).

(Hayes et al. 1981). Of 154 cremations examined, 87% were accompanied by funerary offerings, including pottery and food remains. The 614 identifiable food bones from eight species of birds and mammals included 328 pronghorn bones or fragments. The preponderance of pronghorn remains, 53%, suggests that the species had special, probably religious significance to the Ancient Ones.

History

North America on the eve of the European invasion was a mosaic of distinctive peoples. Some were nomadic hunter–gatherers, others farmed intensively and lived in populous towns. . . . The first European settlements in North America were no more than footholds, but their effect was catastrophic. The newcomers carried diseases, and Native Americans, who had no immunity to them, died in their millions.

—TANNER (1995:30, 42)

An aspect of pronghorn history of minor practical importance is identification of which humans first saw or recorded the species. By the time Old World explorers visited pronghorn range and observed this species unknown to the rest of the world, the animal had been well known to indigenous people for many millennia. Inasmuch as those Native Americans probably knew as much about pronghorn as is known by wildlife scientists today, by virtue of greater pronghorn numbers then, but primarily because of the Indians' pragmatic use of and reliance on them to varying degrees over countless generations, it is absurd in the extreme to suggest that pronghorn were undiscovered before European contact. That long-standing awareness and familiarization notwithstanding, there is, among contemporary society, a fascination with as-

signing credit for the "discovery" of natural phenomena, including life forms.

Beginning in 1519 and continuing through 1879, about 40 documented expeditions ventured into uncharted landscapes within the range of pronghorn. Seven Spanish explorations and one each English and Portugese explorations took place in the 16th century, but only two Spanish explorations during the 17th century. The 18th century brought renewed excursions into pronghorn habitat—seven Spanish, three French, and one each from England and Scotland. The 19th century saw 16 investigations, all United States enterprises (Fernandez-Armesto 1991, Goetzmann and Williams 1992). For most areas, expeditions, especially the earlier ones, marked the end of prehistory and the beginning of history. The following highlights a selected few.

SPANISH

There has been considerable speculation that Francisco Vasquez de Coronado was the first "white man" to see pronghorn when he arrived in Mexico (named "Nuevo España" by Cortés) about 1535 or, subsequently, between 1540 and 1542, when he and his conquistadors probed our Southwest to as far north as modern Kansas (Seton 1929). However, by the time Coronado headed northward from Compostela in February 1540, hundreds—perhaps thousands—of Spaniards had traveled over or settled in portions of central and northern Mexico known to be within historic pronghorn range. Furthermore, Spanish explorers had reached and traversed the Gulf Coast of Texas by 1519, and Franciscans were proselytizing among Indians north of New Spain by 1537 (Castañeda 1936). Pronghorn surely were seen and hunted, even if the newcomers were uncertain of the genus and seldom bothered to write of them. The first Europeans in the Spanish West were conquistadors and missionaries, not journalists or naturalists.

Still, the first modern record of pronghorn may have been from the pen of the most celebrated conquistador of all, Hernán Cortés. In a letter to the King of Spain, written on July 10, 1519, from his seaport fortress at Vera Cruz, Cortés observed: "There is every kind of game in this country, and animals, and birds such as are familiar to us—deer, fallow deer . . ." (McNutt 1908:22). That, at least, was the translation into English. In the Castillian Spanish that Cortés wrote, the passage reads: "Hay en esta tierra todo género de caza y animales y aves conforme á los de nuestra naturaleza, ansi como ciervos, corzos, gamos. . . ." (Gayangos 1866:161). Translated literally in the vernacular of the era, "ciervos" (stags), "corzos" (roe deer) and "gamos" (fallow deer) may have referred to elk, white-tailed deer, mule deer, brocket deer and pronghorn, or some age or gender cohort of any or all. The qualifier "ansi [sic:asi] como," or "such as," adds to speculation that the artiodactyls in reference may have represented even more than the three types named. In other historic literature, untrained observers of wildlife who used those classifications tended to characterize mule deer and whitetails as fallow deer, and pronghorn as roe deer. Still, there is no consistency of association of North American wild ungulates to Old World forms in the historic literature, with the exception of pronghorn usually associated with the wild or domestic goats, or "cabrie," of Europe. In any case, pronghorn historically were present west of Vera Cruz and into the Valley of Mexico, so may have been among the animals Cortés identified (Figure 8).

The Cortés reference points to a not uncommon conundrum—namely, liberal, anglicized translations of historical literature from foreign languages (J. C. Porter personal communication:1989). First, zoological precision of original or early observations in the New World was rare, in part because the flora and fauna were unfamiliar, in part because the trailblazers' interests, missions and priorities were oriented to other values—such as minerals, spiritual or national dominion and survival—and, in part, because

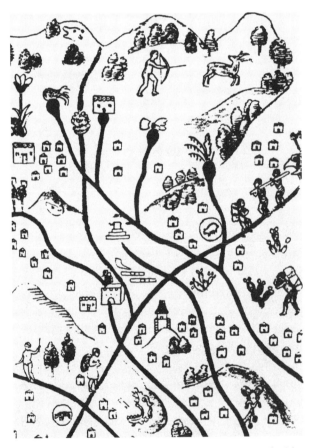

FIGURE 8. *A pronghorn being pursued by a native armed with a bow and arrow* (upper right*). The scene is an enlarged detail of panel 3 of the 11-panel map preserved in the University of Uppsala Library, Uppsala, Sweden (Linné 1948). The map, sometimes known as the* Mapa de Santa Cruz, *dates to 1555–1556 (Thomas 1993).*

the observations were made or recorded by persons not trained in natural sciences. Second, many of the early records were first edited and redescribed. Third, some of the early records edited and translated abroad or in North America decades and even centuries later tended to confuse or misinterpret terms that had undergone a denotative change. Misspellings and somewhat arbitrary replacement of archaic words or period vernacular also have altered or obscured original meaning. Initial descriptions sometimes identified several species, not realizing they were identifying different age and sex classes of the same species. Subsequent references to translations of those first records often perpetuate and compound historic error. These are not uncommon phenomena in the zoological literature, and verification or correction usually is possible only by reexamining the first records in their original language.

The earliest modern records of pronghorn are in Spanish, then French, with the former predating the known, firsthand English accounts by approximately 150 years. Townsend (2000) and Linné (1948) presented interesting maps, beginning in 1519, of New Spain (Figure 9).

There is a strong likelihood that another Spaniard, Alvar Núñez Cabeza de Vaca, was the first—with several companions, notably Andrés Dorantes, Lope de Oviedo, Alonzo del Castillo and Estévanico (or Black Stephen)—to encounter pronghorn, at least within what is now the United States. Lost and afoot in the Gulf States and Southwest from 1527 to 1536, Cabeza de Vaca (1542) wandered from east to west along much of the Gulf coast, often as a captive of various Indian tribes. Within a few years after staggering out of the wilderness and regaining civiliza-

tion, he wrote of his epical experience. He reported on the now-extinct Yguaces, a Coahuiltecan tribe closely related to the Karankawas, that inhabited the coastal plain inland from San Antonio Bay, Texas. Covey's (1984:79–81) translation and annotation of the narrative identified pronghorn as the animals Cabeza de Vaca saw being hunted "occasionally" by the Yguaces and by Mariames Indians in the vicinity of present-day Austin, Texas. Covey clearly distinguished between pronghorn and deer, although certain other translators of the original account did not (cf. Bandelier and Bandelier 1904, Hodge 1984).

The next reasonably certain record of pronghorn concerned a hunt in 1540 on the Llano del Cazadero in the extreme southwestern portion of the State of Hidalgo, Mexico, and "adjoining parts" (Nelson 1925:1). Indians made a great drive of game in honor of Viceroy Antonio de Mendoza, and 600 deer were killed, including "those which they call verrendos . . . [that] not only ran but flew" (Torquemada 1723 [1–5]:611–612). The name verrendos (pronghorn still are known in Mexico as berrendos), is a distinction between other game (i.e., "stags"), and the noteworthy description of the verrendos' speed almost certainly indicate pronghorn. (Interestingly, Nelson [1925:1] noted that this "first record of the pronghorned antelope having been seen by Europeans was published in 1723. . . ." In fact, it was not the first-recorded sighting—long postdating both Cortés and Cabeza de Vaca—and the Torquemada description was originally printed in 1618.)

With some degree of certainty, and despite assurance to the contrary by the usually reliable Seton (1909), sightings of pronghorn by Coronado and his company did not represent Europeans' initial con-

FIGURE 9. *Two pronghorn, each impaled by an arrow, are shown in this page from the* Mapa de Quinatzin, *a colonial pictoral map that documents the journey of the Chichimecs to the Valley of Mexico in the 13th century (from Townsend 2000:55). The map dates between 1542 and 1546. The upper pronghorn is running from the site where a native with a bow and arrow is about to shoot another wounded pronghorn a second time. The Chichimecs were a nomadic hunter-gatherer tribe that lived in north-central Mexico. They and three other tribes that settled the Valley of Mexico were the progenitors of the Aztecs.*

tact with the species. Nevertheless, Coronado surely did encounter pronghorn during his conquistadorial travels and, although natural history observations obviously were not among his priorities, both Coronado and his chronicler, Pedro de Castañeda (1936), made reference (in 1554) to animals that probably were pronghorn (Winship 1896).

Preceding the departure of Coronado's northward expedition, two advance parties had been sent to Cíbola by Viceroy Mendoza. Fray Marcos de Niza supposedly traveled from 1538 to 1539 in search of rumored cities of gold. Based on the Franciscan's glowing, but faulty report, Melchior Díaz was dispatched in 1539 to reconnoiter further. He and his men returned after Coronado's march was underway. From Fray Marcos, Díaz or perhaps via courier from Coronado, Mendoza was able to report to King Charles V, in a letter dated April 17, 1540, that, in Cíbola or thereabouts, "There is a great abundance of wild goats, the colour of bay horses" (Winship 1896:550).

Just when and where Coronado's army first saw pronghorn are not recorded. However, the expedition's first report of pronghorn was in late May 1540, in the vicinity of Casa Grande, Arizona. "Between Suya and Chichilticalli," wrote Castañeda (Winship 1896:516), "there are many sheep and mountain goats ['carneros y cabras montesas' (Winship 1896:449)] with very large bodies and horns. Some Spaniards declare that they have flocks of more than a hundred together which ran so fast that they disappeared very quickly."

It can be argued that Castañeda was referring only to bighorn. However, earlier in the narrative, he provided a definitive description of bighorn and referred to them then exclusively as "sheep" (Hodge 1907:305). The large flocks and the animals' speed suggest that the "goats" were pronghorn.

Several months later, in July, when the expedition was on the plains in central New Mexico, Castañeda wrote of "siervos, remendados de blanco," or "stags pied with white" (Hodge 1907:363). This, too, is an apt characterization of pronghorn, but why Castañeda termed the animals stags instead of sheep or goats, as he may have two months previously, is uncertain.

After Coronado's return to Mexico and for the next two centuries, numerous other expeditions were launched from Mexico. For God, glory and gold, the Spaniards trekked through a significant portion of

the pronghorn's range in the Southwest and southern California. In the many chronicles of these excursions, very little attention was given to the region's flora and fauna. With few exceptions, only bison ("cows") were noted with any regularity.

Among the exceptions was the anonymous record of the second Marquis of San Miguel de Aguayo's expedition to defend Texas against a supposed invasion by the French in 1721. He reported seeing wild goats on flat prairie in what now is northern Frio County, Texas (Buckley 1911). Another exception was that of Pedro Fages, who, in 1769, said that the pronghorn he observed in the San Joaquin Valley of California were "a kind of mountain goat" (Priestley 1937:77). In June 1776, Lieutenant Commander Don Jose Joaquin Morago and a small contingent of soldiers and colonists departed the Presidio of Monterey to establish a mission to be named for Our Father San Francisco de Asis, on a large bay to the north. The chronicler of this founding of San Francisco described an animal the party observed and hunted while en route: "In the said plains of San Bernardino [Santa Clara Valley] . . . there is another species of deer about the size of three-year-old sheep. They are similar in appearance to the deer, except that they have short horns and also short legs like the sheep. They live in the plains where they go in herds of 100, 200, or more. They run all together over the plains so fast that they seem to fly. . . . These animals are called berrendos and there are many of them also in the southern Missions wherever the country is level" (Dane 1935:104). Also, in 1776, Franciscans Silvestre Velez de Escalante and Francisco Atanasio Dominguez, on an ambitious crusade through what is now Utah, Colorado, Arizona and New Mexico, found some wild sheep (pronghorn) larger and "much swifter" than domestic sheep, and evidence of large herds of them in south-central Utah (Briggs 1976:149).

Although the Spanish never found the mythical seven cities of gold in Cíbola, they did, among other things, introduce the pronghorn, however obliquely, to the rest of the world. More importantly, their *entrada* into the Southwest and central Great Plains inadvertently helped to seed the frontier with horses, which were to have extraordinary impact on Indian life in the West, including the native people's relationship with each other as well as to pronghorn and other wildlife.

FRENCH AND ENGLISH

Presumably, the next people to take note of prong-horn were French explorers, although it may be argued that Englishman Sir Francis Drake probably saw or learned of pronghorn when he sailed along the California coast in 1579 (Vaux 1854). Also, nearly a decade earlier, while on an ill-fated slaving expedition in the Caribbean, Drake put ashore a number of his crew at San Juan de Ulúa (near Vera Cruz) in Mexico. Three of the men made their way northward and one, David Ingram, when back in England, wrote of their journey (Hakluyt 1589). Although their claim to have walked the length of the North Atlantic coast to Cape Breton Island, Nova Scotia, is suspect, they did, in fact, travel a good distance in Mexico and made some reliable observances of the flora, fauna and Indian life. Of northern Mexico or coastal Texas, Ingram reported a "great plenty of . . . goats" among the region's wildlife (Wright 1965:59).

Henri Joutel—a Frenchman on Robert de La Salle's 1684 to 1687 voyage to the New World—made shipboard observations of "goats [pronghorn] and bullocks [bison] . . . running along the coast" between Galveston Bay and Lavaca Bay in Texas (Stiles 1906:72). Joutel and others subsequently went ashore before reaching Matagora Bay and reported seeing herds of "goats."

In 1685, La Salle established Fort St. Louis on Garcitas Creek above Lavaca Bay. When, in recent years, the fort site was excavated by the Texas Memorial Museum, pronghorn remains were unearthed (Newcomb 1961). The fort had been occupied until 1689, when the inhabitants were annihilated by Karankawa Indians. The fort was burned by Spaniards the next year. It can be assumed, therefore, that the pronghorn remains found there were from a brief period (1685–1689) when pronghorn would have been procured locally.

During the 1700s, while the Spanish pressed into the Southwest in search of souls and silver, the French broached the western wilderness of the United States from the north and southeast in pursuit of furs. As early as 1719, the French were seeking fur trade outposts in Texas and New Mexico, and gradually moving up the Mississippi and westward (Ghent 1936). Free trappers and *engagés* encountered pronghorn,

but like the conquistadors before them, were little interested in documenting natural history.

From Canada, more adventuresome voyageurs had made their way, by 1740, at least to the Black Hills in South Dakota, to Mandan villages along the Missouri in North Dakota, perhaps to Montana, and to the forks of the Platte River in western Nebraska and from there southward to distant Santa Fe (Ghent 1936, Wood and Thiessen 1985). Each of these reaches—achieved before famed American explorers Meriwether Lewis and William Clark were born—was through areas of pronghorn abundance.

In 1738, Pierre Gaultier de Varennes, the Sieur de La Vérendrye, was the first European to broach the northern Great Plains. With a party of 51, including his two sons, La Vérendrye headed southwest on October 18, 1738, from Fort La Reine, south of Lake Manitoba. Less than 2 months later, on December 3, the party arrived at a Mandan Indian village along the Missouri River, just north of modern Bismarck, North Dakota, where La Vérendrye noted, "there are many antelope ['chevreuille'] here, a very small animal" (Smith 1980:59).

On December 24, La Vérendrye met with Assiniboine Indians who told him that he was heading in the direction of an area where other white men had been encountered. Seeking clarification, the trader/explorer was told that the whites were men "covered with iron" in a region where "The water is salty. It is a country of mountains with great valleys. . . . There are many buffalo . . . deer and antelope . . ." (Smith 1980:64). The Assiniboine were speaking of conquistadors in the Southwest or Great Basin.

Ascending the Mississippi River Valley from 1751 to 1762, as far north as modern Illinois, Jean-Bernard Bossu (1771:356) wrote: "On going toward the head of the river Missouri, you find all sorts of wild beasts. The wild goats and their young ['Les boucs, les chevres fauvages and les cabrits'] are very common at certain seasons. These animals are lively and pretty. . . ." Bossu did not claim to ascend the Missouri, nor did he clarify the source of his information, other than "the French." However, he did visit Fort de Chartre and Fort Cahokia along the Mississippi River (Feiler 1962), then fur trade establishments where traders knew of pronghorn. The "head of the river Missouri" was as far upstream as was then known.

From 1783 to 1788, Edward Umfreville (1790:165–166) explored the frontier regions of the Red and Saskatchewan rivers in Canada, and subsequently provided a reasonably detailed description of pronghorn: "I am not sufficiently conversant in the science of Zoology to give this beautiful animal its proper name in the English language; perhaps it has never yet been described in natural history. The French people resident in these parts call it Cul Blanc, from a white mark on its rump. A more beautiful creature is not to be found in this or perhaps any other country. Extreme delicacy of make, and similarity of proportion, are observable in all parts. No animal here is so swift of foot. They herd together in large droves, but sometimes three or four are found in a place. Its horns are not ossified like [those of] the other species, nor are they branched. Both male and female have them, but they never fall off: they resemble more the horns of the Goat than those of the Deer species. They feed upon most kinds of grass, and the tender twigs of trees. The whole length may be about four feet and a half; the legs are white and slender; the rest of the body a light red, with a white space on the rump."

An Irish merchant named O'Crouley, who lived in Cadiz, Spain, made several trips to New Spain (present-day Mexico) during the late 1700s. While there, O'Crouley produced extensive notes about the day's flora and fauna, including pronghorn: "There are some mountain goats and mountain sheep, the latter being often the hunter's quarry. Though these animals are goatlike and sheeplike in form, there pelts are like that of a deer. Their hides are thin but workable like deer hides; yet, pliant as the goatskin may be, they are not soft like buckskin" (Galvan 1972:87).

INTRODUCTION OF THE PRONGHORN TO SCIENCE

While at Fort Mandan in present-day North Dakota, William Clark wrote a letter, dated April 2, 1805, to William Henry Harrison, in which Clark stated the region was abundant "in a great variety of wild animals . . . many [of which] are uncommon in the U. States . . . such as antelope or goat" (Thwaites 1969 [VII]:316). Neither Clark nor his expedition coleader are known to have made any further allusion or claim to their discovery of pronghorn. On February 11, 1806,

however, President Thomas Jefferson, in possession of Lewis' faunal specimens, wrote to Constantin François de Chasse-Boeuf Compte de Volney that the collection included "an antelope" and other animals "not before known to the northern continent of America" (Thwaites 1969 [VII]:327). George Ord (1815) provided the first taxonomic binominal name for the pronghorn, based on the specimen to which President Jefferson referred and erroneously credited Lewis and Clark for the species' first description. Also, Richardson (1829:262) wrote that "it is to Lewis and Clark that naturalists owe the present knowledge of the animal."

Jean Louis Berlandier traveled through Texas and northeastern Mexico during 1826 to 1834. He reported on herds of pronghorn (berrendo), which he falsely assumed were unknown to science (Ohlendorf 1969). Caton (1877:24) accurately wrote that the pronghorn had long been known to frontiersmen, but parroted the misconception that "the scientific world is indebted to Lewis and Clark for the first accurate information concerning it; not from the description they give . . . but rather from the specimen they brought with them." Coues (1893), who edited and republished the expedition journals, unequivocally asserted that *Antilocapra americana* was new to science when discovered by Lewis and Clark. Skinner (1922:88) was equally direct in his statement that "the pronghorn was first made known to science on the return of Lewis and Clark." Seton (1929:416) opined that Lewis and Clark were the first "to give the world detailed information about the Pronghorn of the Plains." And other writers in more recent times have parroted or paraphrased those assertions.

The criteria by which Jefferson, Caton, Coues, Skinner, Seton and others came to their respective aforementioned conclusions are not known. Whatever the basis, they were incorrect because the pronghorn was clearly identified in text and by illustration in an extensive work on the natural history of Mexico, compiled by Francisco Hernández, edited by Nardo Antonio Reccho and published in Latin in 1651 (Figure 10). In the Hernández (1651:324–326) account of New Spain's deer, or *Mazame*, pronghorn are identified as *Teuthlalmazame* and *Temamazame* (buck and doe). The illustration, presumably by Italian artist Federigo Cesio, is one of the earliest known renderings of a pronghorn.

FIGURE 10. *Apparent doe and buck pronghorn are depicted in Francisco Hernández's* Natural History of New Spain *(in Hernández 1651). His description, developed during 1570 to 1577, was translated by Diana Doan-Crider in 2001. The left animal, named* Teuhtlalmazame *by the Aztecs, was described first as approximately the size of a goat, covered with grayish or brownish hair and having a white belly. Also, pelage was easily plucked out. The horns were thick at the base and forked into small, cylindrical branches. Eyes were beneath the horns. Criollos, colony-born Spaniards, usually called them berrendos. The* Temamazame *(right) was smaller with shorter horns, tawney brown in color and white undersides. Both of those names end with deer (Mazame), but Cancino and Reygadas (1999:81) translate various Mexican names for pronghorn as meaning "deer with blunted horns," "deer with lengthened face" and "deer of the sacred land." The people who drew the animals probably did so from descriptions. Body shape, tails, length of legs and dewclaws all resemble goats. The suggestion of neckbands and mane on the buck also indicate that the illustrator never saw the animal.*

Even earlier (1569), Fray Bernardino Sahagún (1963), however poorly, described and illustrated an animal of the Valley of Mexico (Figure 11) now thought to have been a pronghorn (Dibble and Anderson 1963).

CORPS OF DISCOVERY

Clearly, Lewis and Clark were not the first to identify pronghorn as a distinct species, nor were they the first to describe the species. Nevertheless, their remarkable transcontinental journey from 1804 to 1806, principally along the Missouri and Columbia rivers, provided extensive documentation of the pronghorn, including its description, habitats, behavior, food habits, distribution, abundance and value to Indians. In total, the expedition leaders made nearly 200 references in their journals to the species which, when first sighted northwest of modern Niobrara—Nebraska—on September 5, 1804, were called by Lewis "wild goats or antelopes" (Moulton 1986 [3]:50).

After this initial observation, and as the expeditioners pressed up the Missouri River through what is now southern and central South Dakota, pronghorn were seen and recorded almost daily (Figure 12, Table 5).

FIGURE 11. *Sahagún's* Florentine Codex *(1963) was completed about 1569. In Book 11, Earthly Things, Sahagún assigns the Nahuatl name, Tlamcazcamacatl, to the species. He briefly described it as, "very big, very tall. Its face is painted, darkened in the hollows of its eyes. It is also ashen" (Sahagún 1963[11]:15). The forest deer, white deer, pronghorn and a dog were depicted. The brevity of the passage and its lack of detail suggest that he did not know the pronghorn well. In an accompanying section, Nahuatl artists sequentially depicted the various animals. There is little doubt that the center drawing is the "white deer," and that the one at the lower right is the dog. The lower left illustration evidently was intended as a pronghorn buck. Its horns are somewhat realistic but the body and face are caninelike. Animals in many early works appear doglike or horselike, just as native North Americans often were given European features. Illustrators of early books probably never saw the animals, but drew them from descriptions by others.*

FIGURE 12. *Locations of select observations and commentary (corresponding to Table 5) about pronghorn by Meriwether Lewis and William Clark, during the Voyage of Discovery, 1804 to 1806.*

TABLE 5. Observations of pronghorn by Meriwether Lewis and William Clark on the Voyage of Discovery, 1804 to 1806

Location[a]	Date	Expedition proximity	Author	Remarks (quoted material)	Volume and page[b]
1	Sept. 5, 1804	Northwest of Niobrara, NE	Clark	Goats . . . Seen today . . . First sighting	I:140
2	Sept. 6, 1804	Near Choteau Creek, NE	Clark	saw several	I:141
3	Sept. 14, 1804	South of Chamberlain, SD	Clark	First kill	I:147
4	Sept. 16, 1804	South of Fort Thompson, SD	Lewis	Antilopes seen feeding in every direction as far as the eye of the observer can reach	I:151
5	Sept. 17, 1804	South of Fort Thompson, SD	Lewis	immence herds	I:153
6	Oct. 14, 1804	Near Fort Yates, ND	Lewis	Antilopes are passing to the Black Mountains [Hills] to winter as is their custom	I:177
7	Dec. 12, 1804	Fort Mandan, ND	Clark	Great numbers . . . near our fort	I:237
8	Feb. 6, 1805	Fort Mandan, ND	Clark	Killed 3	I:255
9	Apr. 10, 1805	Near Garrison Dam, ND	Clark	saw several	I:294

continued on next page

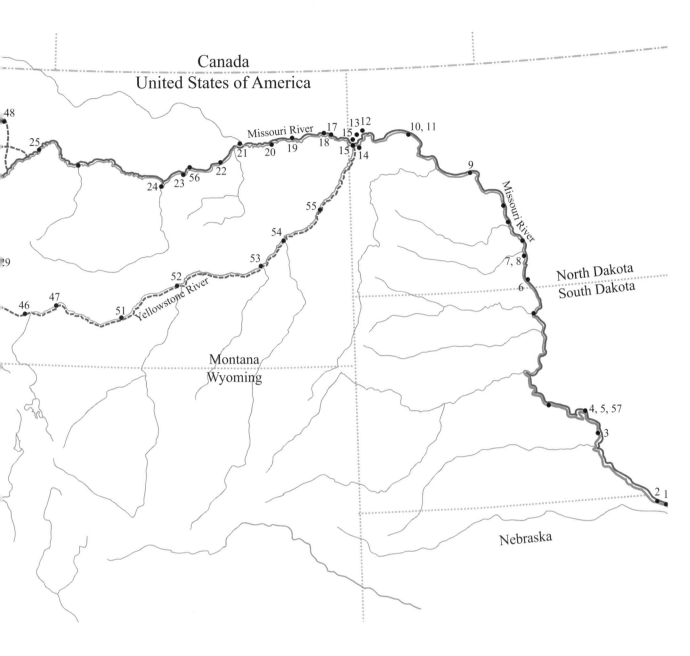

continued on next page

TABLE 5—*continued*

Location[a]	Date	Expedition proximity	Author	Remarks (quoted material)	Volume and page[b]
10	Apr. 17, 1805	Between Tobacco Garden and Beaver Creeks, ND	Lewis	immence quantities of game [including] herds of . . . Antelopes	I:317
11	Apr. 18, 1805	Between Tobacco Garden and Beaver Creeks, ND	Clark	verry plenty	I:322
12	Apr. 21, 1805	Near Williston, ND	Clark	emence number	I:327
13	Apr. 22, 1805	West of Williston, ND	Clark	extinsive vallee . . . covered with Buffalow, Elk & antelopes	I:331
14	Apr. 25, 1805	Near Fort Buford State Historic Site, ND	Lewis	whol face of country was covered with herds of Buffaloe, Elk & Antelopes	I:335
15	Apr. 26, 1805	Confluence of Missouri and Yellowstone rivers, ND	Clark	emence numbers	I:343
16	Apr. 27, 1805	Near Fort Union National Historic Site, MT	Clark	great numbers of Goats or antelopes	I:346
17	Apr. 28, 1805	West of Culbertson, MT	Lewis	great quantities	I:348

TABLE 5—*continued*

Location[a]	Date	Expedition proximity	Author	Remarks (quoted material)	Volume and page[b]
18	Apr. 29, 1805	Near confluence of Missouri and Big Muddy rivers, MT	Lewis	we can scarcely cast our eyes in any direction without perceiving . . . Antilopes	I:351
19	May 3, 1805	Near Poplar, MT	Lewis	vast quantities	I:362
20	May 5, 1805	Southwest of Wolf Point, MT	Lewis	goats or Antilopes feeding in every direction	I:370
21	May 8, 1805	Confluence of Missouri and Milk rivers, MT	Clark	enumerable herds . . . in every direction."	II:19
22	May 11, 1805	South of The Pines Recreation Area, MT	Clark	inumerable and so jintle	II:27
23	May 14, 1805	East of Devil's Creek Recreation Area, MT	Lewis	immence herds	II:33
24	May 18, 1805	UL Bend National Wildlife Refuge, MT	Lewis	number of	II:45
25	June 3, 1805	Confluence of Missouri and Marias rivers, MT	Lewis	solitary antelope . . . with young were distributed over it's [vast plain] face	II:113
26	June 26, 1805	Great Falls, MT	Lewis	still continued [to be] scattered and separate in the plains . . . females with . . . young . . . and males alone	II:189
27	July 19, 1805	Near Gates of the Mountain Wilderness, MT	Lewis	a few	II:248
28	July 24, 1805	Near Townsend, MT	Lewis	great number	II:266
29	July 25, 1805	Near Townsend, MT	Lewis	again is [*sic*: in] small groups	II:268
30	July 27, 1805	Near confluence with the Madison River, MT	Lewis	great numbers	II:278
31	July 31, 1805	Near Jefferson Island, MT	Lewis	few	II:291
32	Aug. 2, 1805	Near Whitehall, MT	Lewis	an abundance	II:299
33	Aug. 9, 1805	Northeast of Beaverhead Rock, MT	Clark	Could kill only two . . . game . . . scerce."	II:324
34	Aug. 11, 1805	Between Beaverhead Rock and Dillon, MT	Lewis	some	II:332
35	Aug. 20, 1805	West of Clark Canyon Dam, MT	Lewis	Soshone reported few in region immediately over the Continental Divide	II:383
36	Aug. 21, 1805	West of Clark Canyon Dam, MT	Lewis	Soshone reported pronghorn "abounding . . . beyond the barren plain towards the Ocean in a S. Westerly direction"	III:5
37	Oct. 11, 1805	West of Clarkson, WA	Clark	Indians reportedly hunting pronghorn nearby on both sides of the Snake River, WA	III:109
38	Feb. 15, 1806	Fort Clatsop, OR	Lewis	Pronghorn among a list of quadrupeds of the country "from the Rocky Mountains to the pacific Ocean"	IV:73, 76
39	Feb. 22, 1806	Fort Clatsop, OR	Lewis	Antelope is found in the plains of the Columbia . . . [but] by no means as plenty on this side of the Rocky Mountains as on the other	IV:95
40	Apr. 1, 1806	Near Washougal, WA	Clark	Indians reported, above the falls (Celilo Falls at The Dalles, Or) on through the Plains from thence to the Chopunnish (Nez Perce villages in the vicinity of Weippe, ID) there are no Deer Antelopes or Elk (at that time of year) on which we could depend for subsistence	IV:231
41	Apr. 16, 1806	Near The Dalles, OR	Lewis	some	IV:287
42	Apr. 27, 1806	Near Waitsburg, WA	Clark	Walla Walla Indians reported a plenty . . . Antilopes in the area between Walla Walla and confluence of Snake and Clearwater rivers; no pronghorn reported by expeditioners who took the shortcut route from April 30 to May 4, 1806	IV:330
43	July 5, 1806	East of confluence of Blackfoot and Clearwater rivers, MT	Lewis	saw a gang . . . said to be many about the head of the Yellowstone river	V:190
44	July 8, 1806	Between Lower Dearborn River and south fork of the Sun River, MT	Lewis	great number	V:197
45	July 10, 1806	South of Twin Bridges, MT	Clark	scattered	V:256
46	July 15, 1806	Between Bozeman and Livingston, MT	Clark	great numbers	V:265
47	July 16, 1806	Near Big Timber, MT	Clark	Nearly 200 seen	V:266

continued on next page

TABLE 5—*continued*

Location[a]	Date	Expedition proximity	Author	Remarks (quoted material)	Volume and page[b]
48	July 16, 1806	Near Lake Ewell Recreation Area, MT	Lewis	a number . . . always in passing through the plains of the Missouri above the Mandans. . . . [A]t this season they are thinly scattered over the plains, but universally distributed in every part	V:205
49	July 19, 1806	Southwest of Shelby, MT	Lewis	a number	V:208
50	July 22, 1806	Along Cutbank northeast of Browning, MT	Lewis	very few	V:215
51	July 24, 1806	Plains around Pompeys Pillar, MT	Clark	to . . . give estimate . . . would be increditable	V:290
52	July 26, 1806	Mouth of the Bighorn River, MT	Clark	plenty	V:297
53	July 27, 1806	Near Miles City, MT	Clark	scarce	V:302
54	July 28, 1806	Near Powder River confluence, MT	Clark	not abundant	V:306
55	July 31, 1806	Near Glendive, MT	Clark	more . . . than usial	V:312
56	Aug. 5, 1806	Near Frazer, MT	Lewis	many	V:235
57	Aug. 28–29, 1806	South of Fort Thompson, SD	Clark	Hunters unable to collect any pronghorn in two days of search; *cf.* September 17, 1804	V:363–365
	Post-expedition		Clark	The Antilope of Cabra are found in great abundance as low as the Chyenne River [confluence with Missouri River in central South Dakota], and are seen scattering as low down as the neighborhood of the Mahar [Omaha] village (or 800 Ms. [up])	VI:122

These observations reflect the species' numbers and distribution along the expedition route (extrapolated from Bakeless 1964, Thwaites 1969, Satterfield 1978, Appleman 1975, Moulton 1986, Salisbury and Salisbury 1993).
[a] Corresponds to numbers on figure 12.
[b] From the Thwaites (1969) volumes.

On September 14, Clark shot "a (Buck) Goat which is peculiar to this Countrey," which he described as "about the hight of the Grown Deer, its body Shorter, the Horns which is not very hard and forks 2/3 up one prong Short the other round & Sharp arched, and is imediately above its eyes the Coulor is a light gray with black behind its ears, and its Jaw white round its neck, its Sides and its rump round its tail which is Short & white verry actively made, has only a pair of hoofs to each foot. his brains on the back of its head, his Norstral large, his eyes like a Sheep—he is more like the Antilope or Gazella of Africa than any other Species of Goat" (Moulton 1986 [3]:70–71).

Three days later, in pursuit of a pronghorn doe for the expedition's collection, "having already procurred a male," Lewis made cogent observations about pronghorn behavior: "we found the Antelope extreemly shye and watchful . . . when at rest they generally seelect the most elivated point in the neighbourhood, and as they are watchful and extreemely quick of sight and their sense of smell very accute it is almost impossible to approach them within gunshot; in short they will frequently discover and flee from you at a distance of three miles [4.8 km]. I

had this day an opportunity of witnessing the agility and superior fleetness of this animal which was to me really astonishing . . . when I beheld the rapidity of their flight . . . it appeared reather the flight of birds than the motion of quadrupeds" (Moulton 1986 [3]:81–82).

Except when they were in the most rugged parts of the Rocky Mountains and again while overwintering along the Pacific Coast, the Corps regularly found pronghorn to be a source of scientific curiosity, food and leather products (Table 6).

Not all discoveries beyond the Mississippi River were made by expeditions; trappers and traders swarmed through unexplored country seeking furs and fortune and were the first to see many of the West's secrets. South Pass in Wyoming, for example, was widely regarded as the "gateway to the West" because its gentle summit over the Continental Divide provided the avenue for mass overland travel to the Oregon Territory. Initially, it was discovered in late October 1812 by Robert Stuart and six other members of John Jacob Astor's Pacific Fur Company on a misadventurous journey from the Pacific Coast eastward (Spaulding 1953). However, the discovery re-

TABLE 6. Ecological characteristics of pronghorn in the journals of Lewis and Clark, 1804 to 1806

Subjects	Date	Author	Observation (quoted material)	Volume and pages
Morphology	Sept. 5, 1804	Lewis	their track is as large as a deer reather broader & more blont at the point	VI:128
Anatomy	Sept. 14, 1804	Lewis	this day Capt. Clark killed a male wild goat so called it's weight 65 lbs F I lenght from point of nose to point of tail 4 9 hight to the top of the wethers 3 Do behind 3 girth of the brest 3 girth of the neck close to the sholders 2 2 do near the head 1 7	VI:129
Behavior	Sept. 20, 1804	Lewis	Antilope is now rutting	VI:175
Seasonal movement	Oct. 17, 1804	Lewis	Antelopes are passing to the Black mountains to winter as is their custom	VI:177
Name and morphology	Mar. 31, 1805	Lewis	the cabie, as they are generally called by the French engages . . . is a creature about the size of a small deer	VII:311
Seasonal movement	Apr. 9, 1805	Lewis	the Antelope repasses the Missouri from N. to South in the latter end of Autumn, and winter in the black hills	I:290
Food and behavior	Apr. 14, 1805	Lewis	the other ['herb'] about the same size ['2 or 3 feet'], has a long, narrow, smo[o]th, soft leaf of an agreeable Smel and flavor; of this last the A[n]telope is very fond; they feed on it, and perfume the hair of their foreheads and necks with it by rubing against it	I:307
Behavior	Apr. 25, 1805	Lewis	The . . . Antelope are so gentle that we pass near them while [they are] feeding, without apearing to excite any alarm among them; and when we attract tehir attention, they frequently approach us more nearly to discover what we are, and in some instances pursue us a considerable distance apparently with that view	I:335
Food	Apr. 26, 1805	Lewis	the Antelope feed on this herb ['wild hyssop']	I:338
Pelage	Apr. 28, 1805	Clark	The antilopes are nearly red, on that part which is subject to change i.e. the sides & 2/3 of the back from the head, the other part as white as snow	I:349
Predation, behavior, and physiology	Apr. 29, 1805	Lewis	they [wolves] kill a great number of Antelopes at this season; the Antelopes are yet meagre and the females are big with young; the wolves take them most generally in attempting to swim the river; in this manner my dog caught one drowned it and brought it on shore; they are but clumsey swimmers, tho' on land when in good order, they are extreemly fleet and dureable. We have frequently seen the wolves in pursuit of the Antelope in the plains; they appear to decoy a single one from a flock, and then pursue it, alturnately relieving each other untill they take it	I:351
Reproduction	May 17, 1805	Lewis	the Elk begin to produce their young, the Antelope and deer as yet have not	VI:190
Reproduction	May 31, 1805	Lewis	The Antelope now bring forth their young	VI:191
Behavior and reproduction	June 26, 1805	Lewis	The antelopes still continue scattered and separate in the plains, the females with their young only of which they generally have two, and the males alone	II:189
Behavior and habitat	July 25, 1805	Lewis	these anamals appear now to have collected again [in] small herds several females with their young and one or two males compose the herd usually. Some males are yet scattered over the plains which they seem invariably to prefer to the woodlands. If they happen accedentaly in the woodlands and are allarmed they run immediately to the plains, seeming to plaise a just confidence in their superior fleetness	II:268
Pelage	Mar. 11, 1806	Clark	in winter they [mule deer] also have a considerable quantity of very fine wool intermixed with the hair and lying next to the skin as the Antelope has	IV: 157
Distribution and behavior	July 16, 1806	Lewis	at this season they are thinly scattered over the plains but seem universally distributed in every part; they appear very inquisitive usually to learn what we are as we pass, and frequently accompany us at no great distance for miles, frequently halting and giving a loud whistle through their nostrils, they are a very pretty animal and astonishingly fleet and active	V:205

Source: Thwaites 1969.

mained a virtual secret until late March 1824, when it was located serendipitously by Jedediah Smith, Thomas Fitzpatrick, James Clyman, William Sublette and several others of the Rocky Mountain Fur Company. The party was following Crow Indian directions to a beaver-rich portion of the Sage Hen (Green) River: "On the sixth day, Clyman and Sublette brought down an antelope, and when the rest of the party came up, 'we butchered our meat in short order many of the men eating large slices raw.' The next morning 'we found we had crossed the main ridge of the Rocky mountain.' Unknowingly, Smith and his companions had celebrated a historic moment by gorging on raw antelope" (Utley 1997:60–61, see also Clyman 1984).

The first of the U.S. topographic expeditions of the West, following the Lewis and Clark Voyage of Discovery, occurred between 1819 and 1820, under the leadership of Major Stephen H. Long. Prevented from going far up the Missouri River, the expedition followed the Platte River westward, eventually reaching the Rocky Mountains (James 1823). Engraver and landscape artist Samuel Seymour, an Englishman residing in Cincinnati, Ohio, was enlisted as the expedition's official artist (Monaghan 1863). He would produce more than 150 drawings and paintings of the unchartered wilderness and its inhabitants. Also among the expedition members was 19-year-old Titian Ramsey Peale, assigned as assistant naturalist. Titian, youngest son of Charles Willson Peale, perhaps the most famous American painter of their day (Poesch 1961), made 122 artistic studies of wildlife and more of Indian life on the plains. Among Peale's wildlife studies is what was incorrectly claimed to be the "white artist's . . . first representation" of a pronghorn (Ewers 1965:29). It (right) is titled "American Antelope." Interestingly, the pronghorn in the foreground of Seymour's "Sketch of the Rockies" (below) are identical to Peale's pronghorn family, including the erroneous dewclaws. Such composite art was the right and prerogative of the official illustrator. Peale artwork photo courtesy of the American Philosophical Society, Philadelphia, Pennsylvania. Seymour artwork photo courtesy of the Joselyn Art Museum, Omaha, Nebraska.

INDIANS OF THE WEST

'To understand fully the culture of a region,' proposed Henderson and Harrington (1914:5), 'it is necessary to know something of the native animals. . . .' We believe the reciprocal to be equally valid.
—McCabe and McCabe (1984:19)

In any discussion of the attributes, characteristics or proclivities of North American Indians, particularly in those relating to ethnozoology, there is a grave danger that historic information may be mistakenly applied more universally than is warranted. Within the span of recorded time, American Indians represented a diversity of languages, cultural traditions, economies and general lifestyles. Even for single tribal entities within that time period, most experienced dramatic

cultural adaptations and geographic shifts that altered their lifestyles and, accordingly, their relationships with wildlife (Martin 1978). The arrival of Europeans and the attendant introductions of horses, diseases, metal trade-goods, alcohol, firearms, livestock and other byproducts of western civilization caused great upheaval of virtually all North American Indian groups—some more so or faster than others. That said, figure 13 presents the approximate location of various tribes within pronghorn habitat during the 19th century.

By the time the new Americans pressed into the West and the range of the pronghorn, the multitude of Indian groups there already had been disrupted by antecedent goods, goals and guise of the invaders, by way of explorers, traders, trappers and missionaries. European diseases drastically lessened some populations and altered balances of power and territory. In particular, the horse and gun altered many Indians' mobility, subsistence quests and social structures. Also, many woodland and prairie Indians of the East were forced west of the Mississippi River and further complicated the already volatile spacial and societal chemistry of the Indian groups indigenous to the region. For the most part, the Indians that were encountered and chronicled by the white-skinned newcomers were in a relatively abrupt period of transition. By the early 1800s, and unknown to anyone at the time, the momentum of cultural dispossession of the American Indian, all American Indians, was closer to its finish than to its start.

Therefore, any historic aspect of Indian life, including ethnozoology, must be represented and understood only in the contexts of specific time, place and cultural composition. It is no more accurate to characterize Indians otherwise than to imply that residents of the 19th century boomtown of Deadwood, South Dakota, truly and fully represented all the people who pioneered and settled the West.

According to Denig (1961), two groups of writers, equally wrong, each declared Indians as a noble, generous and chivalrous race far above the standards of Europeans or represented them as inferior. Correct knowledge of any nation, particularly a wild-living one, can only be attained by being—as it were—raised in their camps, entering into their most intimate feelings, practicing their occupations, speaking and un-

FIGURE 13. *The approximate locations of various Indian tribes about 1850. Even before the exertions of European influence, most Indians survived somewhat precariously, by virtue of internecine warfare and the eternal vagaries of weather. A single event of war or bad weather could be and often was catastrophic, since each affected the ability of the native people to provide for themselves by hunting, gathering, fishing or farming, and to defend themselves. Tribal rivalries for space, subsistence commodities and other advantages often were intense enough to preclude constant or simple changes of locality when and where resources became scarce. Such rivalries frequently amounted to genocidal conflict. Nevertheless, the dynamic ebb and flow of tribal dominance was considerably more stable before Europeans arrived—armed with their own territorial ambitions, advanced technologies, artifice and social/cultural/racial prejudices—than afterward (Hyde 1959, Wedel 1961, Ewers 1975).*

derstanding their language, studying their minds and motives, and being thoroughly familiar with their government, religion, customs and capabilities. Most extant information has been published by transient visitors among the tribes, travelers through part of their

In August 1805, a shipment of botanical and zoological speci-mens from Lewis and Clark to President Jefferson was received at the White House. Advised of the shipment and its contents, Jefferson, at his home at Monticello near Charlottesville, Vir-ginia, directed that certain items be sent to Charles Willson Peale, famed artist and owner of the Philadelphia Museum. Among those items, sent that April from Fort Mandan, in present-day North Dakota, where the Lewis and Clark expedi-tion had overwintered, were the skins, horns and skeletons of a male and a female pronghorn. At his museum, housed in Inde-pendence Hall in Philadelphia, and working with the "badly damaged skins and bones," Peale produced a mount of the ani-mal, which was "long the only known example in the East" (Sellers 1980:177). He also illustrated the mount in 1806 (see Miller et al. 1988), which subsequently was engraved sepa-rately for at least three publications. The first of these engrav-ings, Antelope furcifer *(top), was for Richardson's (1829) book that documented Sir John Franklin's early explorations in Canada, in search of the fabled Northwest passage. The engrav-ing, by Thomas Landseer, featured a coniferous landscape, a second, deerlike pronghorn standing in the background and a third animal bounding away. "The Prong-horned Antilope" (center) appeared in Doughty's (1833) three-volume* Cabinet of Natural History and American Rural Sports. *Its en-graver, A. Stone, presented the same pronghorn, but with slightly different markings, in reversed direction and a rocky, montane setting. In 1852, Peale's pronghorn resurfaced in the annual report of the U.S. Patent Bureau.* "Antilocapra americana *Ord." (bottom) is the modified Richardson treat-ment, minus the two background animals and much of the scen-ery. The engraver is not known. It is likely that Peale's prong-horn artwork was reproduced in other publications and docu-ments, especially before the early 1820s, when other renditions were prepared by artists who visited the West and witnessed the species firsthand, including Charles Peale's son, Titian (see Godman 1826, Griffith 1827, Poesch 1961). Of particular inter-est is the fact that none of the above works credited Charles Peale as the original artist or noted that his subject was the sole Lewis and Clarke pronghorn specimen. Top and center pho-tos courtesy of the Smithsonian Institution, Washington, DC. Bottom photo courtesy of the Library of Congress, Washington, DC.*

country, or collected from half-civilized interpreters who impressed their credulous hearers with fiction mingled with ceremonies. Such hastily collected and poorly digested masses of information formed the basis of many works by which the public was so deceived concerning the true nature of Indians. For-eigners—who passed a winter at some trading post and saw an Indian dance or a bison chase—returned home to enlighten Europe, if not America, regarding the Indian's character, "which is only the product of their own brains and takes its color from the peculiar nature of that organ" (Denig 1961:xxx).

Into early historic times, hunting continued to play an important part in the subsistence patterns of the village tribes along the upper Missouri as long as

The Journal of Charles LeRaye *(LeRaye 1926) was a narrative of the 1801 capture of French-Canadian trapper LeRaye and his six voyagers by Sioux, and of the captives' adventures among the Indians along the upper Missouri River as far west as Montana. The work—anonymously authored and published in 1812 by a Charles Williams, in Boston, as a supplement to* A Topographic Description of the State of Ohio, Indiana Territory, and Louisiana—*contained various topographical descriptions of the wilderness regions purportedly traveled. Accompanying one such description was an illustration of a pronghorn (above), drafted by Jervis Cutler. The total volume is detailed and entertaining. That the descriptions predated those of Lewis and Clark gave the volume stature in the historic literature until the work was deemed fraudulent. No other record of LeRaye could be found and the anonymity of the author raised doubt. Careful analysis by Dollar (1982) and others discredited the journal, which apparently was fabricated by Cutler, and perhaps his brothers, using references from a variety of sources available by 1812. The journal's imaginative drawing of a pronghorn, entitled "Cabree or Missouri Antelope," features an animal with horns indicative of a waterbuck, sable antelope, blackbuck or impala, but not a pronghorn, further evidence that the journal was bogus.* Photo courtesy of the Library of Congress, Washington, DC.

game was obtainable. Although they hunted deer, elk, pronghorn and, indeed, any edible game, their mainstay was the bison (Meyer 1977).

THE COMING OF HORSES

The horse also represented a unique and valuable item of capital that had the unprecedented value of not having to be carried, but of moving itself. In the past, differences in wealth would depend on a much more direct kind of personal skill. The man who was the swiftest on his feet and most skilled with the bow and arrow got the best buffalo, and his wife could produce the finest packaged meat and the best skins. These in turn could be traded for other valuable things—valued ornaments or participation in the sacred ceremonies. Now skill in horsemanship, which became an indispensable factor in hunting the buffalo, implied also major successes on the warpath and the capturing of horses as well as their subsequent care and protection. The horse thus provided a material basis for a greater degree of social differentiation.

—Weltfish (1977:143)

The arrival of horses in North America at the dawn of historic time was of nearly unimaginable importance and consequence. Several scholars have addressed the dispersal of horses from early Spanish intrusions into Mesoamerica and the Southwest (Haines 1938a, 1938b, Jacobsen and Eighmy 1980, Hanson 1986). Tribes of the southern plains are thought to have first obtained horses about 1640 and, by about 1780, horses had been adopted by the northern plains tribes. Among some western Indians, the horse preceded the first white man by only a few years or decades. Some tribes in the Great Basin and mountainous areas apparently never acquired horses, at least other than for food.

Possession of horses led to drastic changes in the lifestyles of most tribes. Apaches of the plains were not regarded as "bad Indians" by Spaniards until the 1660s, when horses and metal weapons became available (Hyde 1959). Horses increased intertribal warfare, modified hunting cultures to raiding cultures and prompted increased trade in the Southwest. After about 1692, Apaches no longer came to trading fairs at Pecos, Taos and Picuris to exchange dried meat or tanned bison and pronghorn skins for maize,

The horse greatly altered Indian culture and economy by providing a swift, reliable mode of human travel, scouting, hunting, warfare, transport of heavy items (including game carcasses) and, as a last resort, a source of food. Horses virtually eliminated the need to hunt afoot. Soon-to-be-acquired firearms, when coupled with the horse, gave the Indian enormous flexibility and efficiency when hunting pronghorn. The aborigine's improved hunting capabilities, eventually augmented by the reckless exploitive activities of the white man, guaranteed the near-total destruction of pronghorn and most other North American big game. In this painting by Albert Bierstadt (1830–1902), pronghorn are seen escaping at far left. The scene probably accurately depicts the drama of the horseback hunt, but the center Indian's headdress and feathered lance are entirely imaginary. Despite that and other minor discrepancies, the art clearly shows that the horse enabled Native Americans to prey effectively on bison and, consequently, develop an anthropologically brief, intense culture predicated on those two animals. Photo courtesy of the Joslyn Art Museum, Omaha, Nebraska.

but instead brought slaves to barter for metal weapons. The transition from one form of trade to another was the result of the Apaches becoming horsemen.

Some tribes made long, annual treks to hunt bison and pronghorn. Such hunts generally were to procure meat for the following winter. Even with dried meat, the amount that could be carried (sometimes hundreds of miles) back to a camp or village must have been quite limited before the introduction of horses. Tribes that made such annual horseback expeditions included the Nez Perce and Kalispel (Walker 1978), Lemhi Soshone (Steward 1938), and Santa Clara (Arnon and Hill 1979) and Taos Pueblos (Bodine 1979). Although horses ordinarily provided improved mobility for Indians during autumn and winter, the opposite may have been true in many cases.

At least some Plateau and northern and central plains tribes were restricted to areas where cottonwoods were abundant because the bark was an important source of food for their horses at that time of year (Boller 1972). Also, during open or mild winters, Indians could readily move camp, but under heavy snow conditions, their horses were a handicap. Periods of famine could follow, with meals reduced to one a day (Ewers 1980).

Walker (1978) observed that horses decreased Shoshone/Bannock dependence on small game and plants, allowing them to penetrate the haunts of bear, bighorn, deer and pronghorn.

On the Great Plains, horses were exchanged for guns and other objects of European manufacture—an irresistible stimulus for acquiring horses at any cost (Jablow 1951). Horses were wealth; stealing horses—the nominal aim of plains warfare—increased personal and tribal wealth, and personal status and esteem. Reciprocally, it reduced the wealth of enemy tribes. It was an exciting, dangerous and honorable vocation, a rite of passage for young men of many tribes and validation of bravery for all participants, which was the actual motive for warfare (see McMurtry 1999). Boller (1972:54) noted: "Horse flesh is uncertain property in any part of the world, and nowhere more so than in the Indian country."

As many luxuries do, horses soon became a necessity to some tribes. Boller (1972:54) observed: "An Indian without horses is reduced to a pitiful strait indeed, crippled in hunting and unable often to carry home the meat he may kill, or to move his family when the camp travels." Denig (1961) maintained that horses were an absolute necessity to Sioux existence during the mid-1800s.

BOWS AND ARROWS

The superiority of bow and arrow over the old type musket was recognized by the Comanches. When muskets first became known to them, they were all eager to obtain them. But when the novelty of the weapon had worn off, they realized that it was inferior to the bow and arrow both in hunting and in war. The muskets had a greater range, but a much slower rate of fire, they were difficult to load on horseback, and ammunition could be obtained only infrequently. As a result the Comanches were reverting to the bow and arrow when introduction of repeating firearms turned the tide again.

—Linton (1940:474)

Western Americana artists and illustrators appear to have been more taken with the hand-thrusted lance than were the Indians. Although the lance, or spear, was used sometimes to kill large game driven to deep snow, soft sand, and mud, deep water and impoundments, it was rarely the primary weapon of choice for hunting pronghorn and other large terrestrial mammals during historic time.

Bows and arrows from three major collections were field tested at the University of California (Pope 1923). Results showed that even the rather inferior Mohave bow with a 40-pound (18.1 kg) draw would cast an arrow 110 yards (100.5 m). Distances shot by

other aboriginal bows included 120 yards (109.7 m) by a Luiseño bow and up to 210 yards (192 m) by a Yaqui bow. However, the pragmatic Indian archer probably chose ranges seldom exceeding 40 to 50 yards (36.7–45.7 m), if distances of hunting blinds from game trails are any indicator. At 10 yards (9.1 m) an obsidian-pointed arrow, cast by a 35-pound (15.9 kg) draw bow, penetrated 30 inches (76.2 cm) of animal tissue. Pope concluded that aboriginal bows and arrows varied greatly, and those of the California Indians generally were better than those of the plains Indians. In his opinion, an arrow was as effective as a bullet when shot into abdominal or chest cavities. Tests with ancient plains weapons indicated that the average arrow cast from a bow attained a speed of about 150 feet (46 m) per second (compared with a pitched baseball speed of about 60 feet [18 m] per second), and was capable of killing a large animal as quickly and cleanly as a rifle bullet (Mails 1972).

Delano (1854) made reference to severe depredations on his wagon train's livestock by raiding Paiute Indians, and he remarked at the power of their bows. He observed a horse shot in the side with a stone-pointed arrow that broke the backbone and protruded 6 inches (15 cm) beyond.

Accuracy was important in hunting the comparatively small pronghorn. According to Carter (1935) and Marcy (1938), a Comanche warrior could hit an object the size of a doorknob with four out of five arrows at up to 50 yards (46 m). Also, an expert Comanche hunter could kill twice the number of bison with a bow and arrows as a Euro-American could with a pistol. At Fort Laramie in 1866, U.S. Army Private William Murphy (1930:384) observed that young Cheyenne and Sioux boys "could hit a button, pencil or any small article at about 30 yards with bow and arrow." During 1886, Mead (1986) met an Indian (presumably a Pawnee) armed with a bow. Mead told him he should have a gun, and the Indian replied that his bow was light, easy to carry and never misfired. Mead pointed to a bison skull at 80 paces and challenged the Indian to hit it. He pulled four or five arrows from his quiver, selected one without a head and straightened it a little. Sitting on his horse, he drew and let fly. The arrow splintered in pieces as it hit the skull dead center.

The weapon and hunting device most closely associated with Native Americans, at least those within historic time, is the bow and arrow. There is suggestion in the literature that, at least during protohistoric time, lances were used mainly by hunters to dispatch wounded animals, those caught in surrounds and those chased into deep snow, prudently conserving arrows or bullets. The bottom scene to the contrary shows equestrian hunters using bow, lance and rifle, presumably during a drive and probable relay. Note the location of the wounds, indicating that Indian hunters were very acquainted with shot or strike placement for efficient, fatal results. Top drawing (detail), circa 1878, by Howling Wolf, a Southern Cheyenne; photo courtesy of the Joslyn Art Museum, Omaha, Nebraska. Bottom drawing by Making Medicine, a Cheyenne prisoner at Fort Marion, Florida, in 1875; photo courtesy of the Smithsonian Anthropological Archives, Washington, DC.

FIREARMS

In the area of the Great Plains . . . the gun never attained such imperative importance in subsistence activity. As a matter of fact, it was rarely used in hunting buffalo, and was actually prohibited by the Assiniboine on such occasions (McDonnell 1889). Though the rule on the hunt was not so stringent among the Mandan and Hidatsa, they gave a decided preference to the bow and arrow (MacKenzie 1889). [The loading of the cap-and-ball rifle of those days was a] "meticulous and time consuming task. The powder had to be measured and poured, the ball had to be rammed down the barrel with a long rod, the tube must be 'primed,' and the cap or flint had to be adjusted. All this took about a minute . . . the Indian could in that time ride 300 yards and discharge 20 arrows."

—Webb (1931:168–169)

Crow Indians seldom used guns to hunt, except when snow was too deep for horses to overtake bison (Denig 1930). Also, on hunting grounds distant from villages, Indians were hesitant to use guns, because shots could be heard at considerable distance on the prairies and "might be the means of discovering us to the enemy" (Boller 1972:146).

Indian expertise with firearms appears to have depended on how long a tribe had possessed them, favorable association with whites who could mentor the weapons' use, care and repair, and how available ammunition was. "Thirty years ago," wrote Dodge (1885:450), "the rifle was little used by mounted Indians, as it could not be reloaded on horseback, but many of them were armed with guns of the most nondescript character, old Tower muskets and smoothbores of every antique pattern. Powder and lead were obtainable from traders. The former was carried in a horn, the latter was cut into pieces, which were roughly hammered into spherical form. These bullets were purposefully made so much smaller than the bore of the gun as to run down when dropped into the muzzle. When going into a fight, the Indian filled his mouth with bullets [see also McHugh 1972]. After firing he reloaded at full gallop by turning up the powder horn, pouring an unknown quantity of powder into his gun and spitting a bullet into the muzzle. There was so little danger from weapons so loaded that troops did not hesitate, even with the saber alone, to rush on any number of Indians."

The breech-loading rifle and metallic cartridges transformed the plains Indian from worrisome threat to a terrifyingly capable adversary. Already an accomplished horseman and accustomed to the use of arms on horseback, the Indian needed only an accurate weapon that could be loaded rapidly at full gallop

Firearms appear to have been some Indians' weapon of choice for hunting pronghorn alone and in small groups. Rifles—muzzleloaders primarily—were not especially efficient for communal drives because, compared with bows and arrows, these guns were slow to reload, loud and unwieldy. Ledger art by an unknown Northern Cheyenne about 1877; photo courtesy of the Foundation for the Preservation of American Indian Art and Culture, Chicago, Illinois.

"Late in the fall, antelope collect in herds, hundreds, even thousands, running together like sheep. Of late years, that is, since he has obtained the breachloading rifle, such a herd is a true godsend to the Indian. Riding slowly and carefully as near as possible to the herd without alarming it, he suddenly dashes in, and riding almost among the terrified animals, pumps his bullets into them until his ammunition is expended, or his horse tired out. The antelope crowd together in their fright and make present a mark not easy to miss. Eight or ten antelope is not an unusual number for a good hunter to bag from a large herd, in one such case" (Dodge 1885:580). Artwork (1837) by Alfred Jacob Miller; photo courtesy of the Walters Art Gallery, Baltimore, Maryland.

(Malouf 1974). With breech-loading rifles, Indians also became much more efficient hunters of pronghorn.

The development of long-range, black-powder cartridges and heavy, extremely accurate rifles to handle those cartridges hastened the demise of the bison. The rifles then were turned on the elk and pronghorn of the plains by the hide and market hunters (Blair 1982).

Concerning the best rifle for pronghorn hunting, DuBray (1890) reported a great diversity of opinions among old prairie hunters, each proclaiming emphatically that his favorite was the best. This will sound familiar to modern hunters, but DuBray's own choice sounds more like a rifle for moose than for pronghorn. "For antelope-shooting, then, or, in fact, for any kind of big game shooting, I prefer the Winchester, my choice being the repeater of large bore, say 50 caliber, with its 100 grain powder-charge and hollow-point, 300-grain bullet" (DuBray 1890:321). DuBray was partial to Winchesters because they were safe, accurate, durable, made in all calibers, relatively

inexpensive and more reliable than other repeaters of the day. Murphy (1879) considered the Sharp's rifle of 45 caliber with 100 grains of powder an excellent weapon for stalking pronghorn. They espoused such heavy calibers, in part, because, as Dodge (1877:201) observed: "Antelope possess a great vitality and will carry off more lead in proportion to their size than any other animal."

ABORIGINAL HUNTING

On the vast grass plains he steals upon wild beasts and he snares those that provide him with sufficient food, clothing, and fuel. To accomplish that on the open prairies requires cunning: to entrap a shy creature like the antelope or bison under a disguise made up of the wolf's skin or bison's hide and the head of a stag marks a distinct advance in the intelligence of the hunter.

—Hewitt (1970:349–350)

The techniques, strategies, weaponry and timing of Indian pronghorn hunts differed regionally within the West. Differences apparently were not primarily consequences of cultural or spacial distinctions, but because of other subsistence considerations. Pronghorn were not the principal, regular (on an annual basis) diet component of any known aboriginal tribe, thus the attention the species received depended on availability of other foods. "Because it [the pronghorn] seldom exceeded 120 pounds, Plains Indians did not pursue it for food with sustained energy," wrote Carlson (1998:17). Even in parts of the northern plains where they were co-dominant with bison (Davis 1986), pronghorn generally were hunted only when bison were difficult to procure.

Hunting success often meant the difference between survival and starvation. Becoming a superb hunter also contributed to individual worth, warrior qualities, status and authority within the tribe, attractiveness to the opposite sex and respect among neighboring tribes.

Given permission to leave the Standing Rock Reservation during autumn 1880, a party of Sioux killed 200 pronghorn, 150 to 200 bison and a number of deer, otter and beaver in three days (Dodge 1885). When the bison were first sighted, the Indians were forbidden to shoot before a major hunt commenced. Some, however, shot at pronghorn and consequently had their guns taken away, and the men were soundly beaten.

Seasonality

Pronghorn were hunted seasonally in some areas and, in others, they provided subsistence throughout the year (Table 7). Possible alternative foods, as well as the availability and condition of the pronghorn itself, determined whether, when and how pronghorn would be hunted. Fichter (1987), after 20 years observing pronghorn, synthesized 31 combinations of sex and age class assemblages. These reflected seasonal and environmental changes and the species' biological cycle, plus the noncohesiveness of group membership. Aggregations ranged from single animals to bands of many dozens. Similar knowledge of behavior enabled Indians to determine when and what sort of hunting strategy could best be employed (e.g., stalking by a lone hunter, communal drives). Communal drives and surrounds were limited to autumn, winter and spring when pronghorn were gathered in herds (Newhouse 1869). Burton (1862:68) qualified the pronghorn were hunted "especially in winter, when the flesh is fattest." A solitary hunter or a small group of hunters might be more effective at other times. The ambush of migrant pronghorn was, of course, confined to autumn and spring (Hill 1979).

TABLE 7. Examples of seasonality of pronghorn hunting by North American Indians

Time of year	Tribe or area	Remarks	Reference
February	Hopi/AZ		Hill (1938)
	Navajo/AZ		Hill (1938)
Early spring	Saline Valley, CA	Hunted from blinds during migration	Brook (1980)
Spring	Sierra Blanca, NM	Hunted communally	Driver (1985)
March	Honey Lake Paiute/CA	Pronghorns tired easily when ground muddy	Riddell (1960)
March and April	Hopi/AZ	When adults have young with them	Beaglehole (1936)
July	Modoc/CA	Hunting commenced at end of camass harvest	Ray (1963)
Warmest weather	Hopi/AZ	Animals pursued to exhaustion	Curtis (1922)
Summer and "other favorable months"	Spring Creek Cave, WY		Frison (1965:94, 282–283)
August-October	Hopi	When animals were fattest	Beaglehole (1936)
Mid-August	Klamath, OR	After camass harvest	Spier (1930)
Late summer and autumn	Southwestern WY	Hunted by driving into trap	Frison (1965)
Late September and October	Wadatika/OR	Hunted communally	Aikens and Greenspan (1988)
Autumn	Saline Valley, CA	Hunted communally when grouped	Brook (1980)
Autumn	Southern Paiute	Hunted communally when grouped	Kelly (1964)
Late autumn	Northern Paiute	Hunted communally by drive traps	Smith (1974)
December	Hopi/AZ	Tracked in snow	Beaglehole (1936)
Winter	Achomawi	Hunted animals stranded in deep snow	Curtis (1924 [13])
Winter	Modoc/CA	Hunted communally	Ray (1963)
Seasonally	Paiute		Fowler (1989)
Year-round but chiefly autumn and winter	Surprise Valley Paiute/CA	Hunted communally	James (1983)

Arikara hunters prevented pronghorn from exiting the Missouri River in present-day North Dakota during migrations; on October 16, 1804, they killed 58 pronghorn with arrows and sticks (Coues 1893). Audubon and Bachman (1851) also reported that Indians along the upper Missouri River during the mid-1800s frequently shot pronghorn trying to cross the river.

Fletcher and la Flesche (1972) indicated that pronghorn were hunted by Omaha Indians only during autumn and winter. Summer hunting by individuals and small parties apparently would have interfered with tribal bison hunts. When individuals or small groups impulsively hunted during summer and disturbed nearby bison herds, those hunters were dealt with harshly.

After the summer (communal) bison hunt, Pawnees could hunt without special permission (Weltfish 1977). A man with a gun was likely to go pronghorn hunting by himself. Bow and arrow hunters generally went in small groups. These were mostly young men, hunting for sport as much as meat. They ate what they killed or carried meat back to the camp or village to share with family or friends.

Shamanism and Charming

The term shaman is a corrupted form of the Sanscrit word meaning ascetic (Mallery 1893)—one who leads a life of contemplation or rigorous self-denial. Its use was somehow carried to North America where it was applied to medicine men,

Hunting big game was the vocation, avocation and education for most North American Indians within the range of pronghorn. It was done mainly by individuals or small groups of hunters, except when it interfered with communal hunts or spiritual sanctions. Communal hunting for pronghorn occurred most often in winter or autumn, but pronghorn were otherwise hunted year around. "The Antelope Hunt" (1897), by Charles M. Russell; courtesy of the Montana State Historical Society, Helena.

some women, priests, doctors or sorcerers of Indian tribes.

Procuring food sometimes involved shamanistic practices. Certain shaman were thought to possess the power to charm pronghorn—to capture the animal's very soul by magic from revelations in dreams or trances (Steward 1941). The shaman expressed and invoked power by songs, dances, music, ritual paraphernalia, pipe smoking, taboos, acts of magic and incantations to the pronghorn and instructions to communal hunt participants. Communal drives invariably were sacramental events, replete with ceremony, song and sacrifice (Table 8).

Instances of supposed successful use of shamanism are reflected abundantly in Indian accounts. The Atsugewi, for example, reportedly encircled *charmed* pronghorn with a rope and easily killed them (Garth 1950). The shaman of the Honey Lake Paiute charmed pronghorn the evening before the hunt; the next day, they were simply herded into a corral and slaughtered (Riddell 1960). A Shoshone legend combines charming, drive hunting to a pen and mythology to explain pronghorn hunting (Smith 1993).

Sarah Winnemucca Hopkins (1883), a Paiute, told how pronghorn were charmed by two men who circled the herd on five successive nights with sagebrush bark torches. Six piles of sagebrush were made,

where in the early morning and evening, shamanism (smoking, drumming, singing and magical acts) was practiced. On the fifth night, the pronghorn were said to be so bewitched that they followed torch-bearing men to the brush piles where they were easily killed by concealed hunters.

Unlike the Paiute, Shoshone participants sometimes included women, although no one menstruating was allowed because such women might break the charm and cause the pronghorn to run away (Trenholm and Carley 1964).

In the Great Basin, "perhaps once every eight years, depending on the mysterious cycles of abundance and scarcity, there might be signs of enough pronghorn antelopes to call for a drive. This was the responsibility of an antelope shaman well versed in charms and incantations. He was the one who picked the time and place for the drive and the direction in which the herd was to be driven into the corral, or killing pen" (Maxwell 1978:258).

In the 19th century, magical pronghorn surrounds became infrequent, but occasionally a shaman staged or invoked such an event. The basic pattern described below is widespread among Indians of the plains, Great Basin and Southwest (Underhill 1948:28–34). "The antelope shaman receives his power from Maiyun in a series of dreams. When he feels ready to

TABLE 8. Examples of ritualistic beliefs and behaviors imposed on pronghorn hunters

Tribe	Time period	Belief or behavior	Reference
Hopi	Before hunt	Any man might organize a hunt, thus becoming the hunt chief; chief took prayer sticks to Badger clan chief, whose clan owns all animals, and he announces the hunt; in discussing the hunt, they used the pseudonym "rat" (ka la) for pronghorn so they would know nothing of hunt and not run away; prayer sticks were taken to the altar of Mother of All Animals and prayers were offered for success and safety of hunters; hunters abstained from sex for four days before hunt; dreams were looked upon as omens; hunt preparations were completed and hunters departed on the fifth day; hunters covered their bodies with yellow pigment and an eagle feather was tied in the hair; hunters did not joke, and had to think only of hunting; hunters ridded themselves of the odors of women and babies (which pronghorn dislike) by drawing hands over various parts of the body and blowing with breath; prayer sticks were offered to coyote so that he would chase pronghorn at night, tiring them for the hunt day; another was made for pronghorn that he might breed and increase; special songs were sung the evening before the hunt; two hunters took prayer sticks to a place away from camp and listened for omens (hearing the coyote, wolf or crow was good news); hunters returned to camp and reported on omens, and all smoked and went to sleep.	Beaglehole (1936)
	During hunt	At sunrise another prayer stick was offered to the Sun deity with prayers for success; hunters passed hands through campfire to make them strong; hunt commenced; head of pronghorn was turned toward camp and the animal was killed by smothering the nose in the sand.	
	After kill	Pronghorn head was turned toward the east before skinning commenced; each animal was divided among the hunter and the next three hunters to arrive on the scene; intestines were removed, emptied, sprinkled with meal and prayed over for the increase of animals and rain; animals were butchered	

continued on next page

TABLE 8—*continued*

Tribe	Time period	Belief or behavior	Reference
Hopi *(contd.)*	After kill *(contd.)*	and divided according to ritually prescribed patterns; upon returning to the village the hunter purified himself of the odor of pronghorn so their spirits might not haunt the village; each hunter made an offering at a shrine to signify that he had ended hunting; pronghorn meat was cooked and eaten according to ritual; food bones were marked with red ochre, sprinkled with meal and placed on a shrine with prayers for an increase in animals.	
Navajo	General	If the hunter observed all the rituals, the game would allow itself to be killed; game did not die but returned to its "home"; hunt was organized and directed by a shaman or chanter; hunters were admonished to focus minds on killing and death; joking and levity were forbidden.	Hill (1938)
	Before hunt	Preparations included making new clothing and moccasins drab in coloration; packing food supplies (meat prohibited); and taking sweat baths.	
	During hunt	Hunters kept a serious mein; accidents would befall those who talked or acted foolishly; prayers for toughness and swiftness were said after each meal; hunters were forbidden to kill crows, wolves, wildcats or coyotes because they were thought to be hunting partners; owls calling at night indicated direction of game; nighttime shelters were constructed in a set manner, and pollen scattered on ground; hunters slept in prescribed positions and directions; weapons were stashed in a certain way at night; no one could pass between the shaman and the fire; no one retired too early; hunters urinated and defecated in holes and then filled them; sneezing, coughing or laughing was forbidden as it might frighten game; during evening, hunters related stories of past hunting successes; hunters were reminded how to walk (never flatfooted) and hold weapons (pointed forward and on downhill side); in the morning, dreams were interpreted as omens of success; several hunting songs were sung; weapons were "blessed" with pollen; hunters communicated by imitating animal calls; great importance was placed on killing the first animal shot at; in the Stalking Way of hunting, a "holy" piece of turquoise was placed between the horns of the pronghorn head disguise; in the Corral Way, hunters were forbidden to spit or urinate within the enclosure; once the corral was completed, an all-night Blessing Ceremony was held during which no one was allowed to sleep; successful "listeners" for game were given responsibility for unwrapping and rewrapping the shaman's two medicine bundles, each of which was comprised of a preserved bluebird; the bluebirds and a small pronghorn fetish of white shell were used in the Blessing Ceremony; hunters were handed their weapons by others; hunters marked faces with charcoal to resemble pronghorn; prayer sticks and the bluebirds were placed near the corral entrance to entice pronghorn; some captured pronghorn were released so that "they would increase in the future for men"; in Sacred Buckskin Way, water and pollen were poured into the pronghorn's mouth, its nose tied, and it was choked to death with a rope (such skins were considered sacred); hunters avoided inhaling the breath of the dying animal.	
	After kill	If the hunt was very successful, the two finest animals were given to the shaman; if only moderately successful, he might receive only one; animals were removed from the corral for skinning; heads of killed animals were turned toward the camp; the animal was eviscerated, skinned and dismembered in a prescribed manner; sex organs were buried in the stomach content and it was then buried; meat was arranged in the order that it had been taken, and the first taken eaten; horns were removed from the skulls and placed in center of night shelter in order taken; heads were cooked and eaten first; turquoise and pollen offerings were left at the abandoned campsite; upon returning to the village hunters resumed a normal lifestyle.	
Northern Paiute	Before hunt	Hunt conducted by shaman who also was a pronghorn charmer, and he set the time for the hunt.	Fowler (1989)
	During hunt	Women (except those pregnant or menstruating) assisted men in hunt; sexual intercourse was forbidden during hunt; shaman led the dance at the site where the corral was to be constructed the next day; the next morning hunters scouted for animals; the shaman fell into a trance and was covered with sagebrush; from this point they shaped the corral; shaman revived; hunt commenced next morning; women assisted men in driving pronghorn into corral; entrance closed after capture, usually in late afternoon, and fires were lit in evening to contain animals overnight; a runner entered corral next morning and chased and tired the animals; sacred dirt placed in fire was believed to paralyze animals; runner killed a young pronghorn with bow and arrow.	
	After kill	Same pronghorn was presented to shaman and killing of remainder commenced; intestines were buried in a cool place and covered with sagebrush so that pronghorn would not see them; meat was distributed equally.	

Based on information for the Hopi, Navajo and Northern Paiutes.

put on a hunt, the news is passed by word of mouth rather than through a crier. This, and the fact that the shaman also lets it be known that no guns or ordinary weapons are to be used in the hunt, indicates that the pattern was set before the tribe established itself in the Plains, for the crier and gun are both cultural traits acquired after the Cheyenne had migrated into the Plains.

"As a first step the shaman raises a small medicine teepee within which he performs an all-night ritual, the details of which are not known. At certain stages, the members of a military society beat on the lodge covering over four of the lodge poles which are mystically endowed. If the hunt is going to be successful, large quantities of antelope hair fall off the lodge covering.

"The next morning the shaman leads the people out toward where his power has told him the antelope will be. The hunters are on their fastest horses, but he is afoot. At the chosen spot, he selects two exemplary virgin girls. They must be good-tempered, or the antelope will be fractious and hard to control. They should also be plump, or the antelope will be skinny and stringy. Each is given a so-called antelope arrow, a wand with a medicine wheel at one end. The shaman has already used these to draw the antelope toward the spot. Each girl begins running outward on diverging, diagonal lines so that their paths begin to describe a wide V. Two young men, supposed to be their suitors, chase after them on the fastest and longest winded horses available. The hunters on their horses tail out after them in two long lines.

"As soon as the hunters are on their way, the remaining women and children form a circle at the foot of the V, with the shaman in the center. As the two leading young men pass the pair of girls, each takes one of the wands the girls have been carrying. They continue on the diverging line for a couple of miles riding at a fast pace. Soon they are on both sides of an antelope herd which instead of running away turns toward the shaman. The men with the wands then turn in and cross behind the herd, continuing to ride back outside the lines of hunters, who have followed them and entirely surround the herd. When the two reach the shaman they return the wands. Down the V the antelope are driven at a fast pace, pall mall into

the circle of old men, women, and children who have been waving blankets close around them to form a human corral. Using his two wands as directional signals, the shaman makes the antelope rush around and around until they are utterly confused and exhausted. This is the drama that is reenacted in the crazy animal dance. Then the people set upon the befuddled beasts and kill them with clubs. For his pains and skill the shaman receives all the tongues (a choice delicacy) and his choice of two antelopes. The two girls and two young men make their choice next. After that, an even distribution is made among all the families.

"William Bent, the trader, was with the Southern Cheyenne in 1858 when such a hunt was held under the direction of Whitefaced Bull. It was so successful that every one of 600 Cheyenne lodges had an antelope, and Bent's wagon train had all it could use."

Hoebel (1960) recounted a similar ceremonial hunt, and Mooney (1898) wrote of one in which two Kiowa war chiefs, instead of virgins and their suitors, carried the magic arrows and the pronghorn were driven into a pit. Stands in Timber and Liberty (1967) also reported a ceremonial pronghorn drive, harking back to the days before the Cheyennes had horses. In that case, the exhausted animals were forced into a pit dug by four men, instead of into a human corral. Wallace and Hoebel (1952) gave an account of a magical pronghorn drive by Comanches. During that drive, if the medicine man pointed a pronghorn hoof at an exhausted pronghorn, it reportedly dropped dead. Shamans obviously knew a great deal about pronghorn behavior and how the animals would react to disturbances in a selected landscape. As for dropping an animal by pointing a hoof, Bart O'Gara captured hundreds of pronghorn in drive nets and corrals. A small percentage usually drop dead from fear or overexertion. By watching closely, imminent collapse is recognizable. The forementioned Comanche shaman apparently was especially observant.

In many claims of successful charming, the natural behavior of pronghorn—notably their consuming curiosity—played into the hands of the clever shaman. Shamanism was an effective means of developing and maintaining cooperative hunter behavior so necessary in communal hunts. Clearly, Indians of many tribes thought that shamanism was essential to assure successful hunting of the pronghorn and other game animals.

Cressman (1977:104) wrote that effective taking of pronghorn in the Great Basin was a well-organized community affair under the leadership of a shaman and that the "element of supernatural involvement in behalf of the hunters suggests that normal hunting methods had never been very successful." There is little evidence to corroborate the latter inference. More plausible is that normal hunting methods did occasionally succeed, but tended to run off other animals in the herd. Invoking spiritualism to charm pronghorn merely was an important hedge against an inadequate harvest. Furthermore, shamans had the authority to provide social order and essential timing to the undertakings.

FIGURE 14. *Despite the superb eyesight and inherent wariness of pronghorn, the animals were vulnerable to skilled Indian stalking disguised as another pronghorn. The sketch by Hidatsa Lean-Wolf shows an Indian bow hunter wearing a pronghorn mask (from Mallery 1893). Unlike as the illustration depicts, the stalk typically was made in a bent-over position.*

Stalking

There are many reports in the literature of Indians stalking (still-hunting) pronghorn with disguises (Figure 14), but few indicate which tribe was involved. Some that did name tribes or particular areas are in-

cluded in Table 9. Decoys are used today by archers, but few pronghorn hunters would choose to use or be close to a decoy during the rifle season. Such discretion was warranted as well in the 19th century: "After 18 or 20 miles east of the copper mines of Santa

TABLE 9. Reports concerning the use of masks and other disguises to stalk pronghorn during the 1800s

Tribe/Area	Remarks	Reference
Achomawi		Voegelin (1942)
Apache	Narrator nearly shot a chief's son who was hunting in a mask	Cremony (1868)
Apache		Barrett (1970)
Apache (Jicarillo and Mescalero)	Wore horns or antlers of whatever animal they hunted	Goddard (1975)
Apache (Mescalero)	Sometimes crawled long distances with just brush for a shield	Opler (1969)
	Deer mask for elk and pronghorn	Olmstead and Stewart (1978)
Apache (Lipan)	Worn by lone hunters	Opler (2001)
Assiniboine, Crow, Sioux and other tribes along the upper Yellowstone River		Hewitt (1970)
Blackfoot	Had no superiors in stalking	Grinnell (1962)
Chihuahua	Besides pronghorn head, hunter wore a white cotton shirt falling to the ground and crudely painted to imitate the animal's color	Grinnell (1925)
Costanoan	Most important method of stalking	Levy (1978)
Great Basin	Susceptible to wiles such as disguises	Ebeling (1986)
Havasupai	At times, two to four could be killed before the others fled	Spier (1928)
Modoc		Ray (1963)
Navajo (Western)	Slowly approached from downwind, mimicking a pronghorn's actions	Hill (1938)
Nomlaki		Goldschmidt (1951)
Paiute (Surprise Valley)	Enhanced disguise by applying white paint to body and using a stick the length of a pronghorn's leg as an aid in walking stooped over	Kelly (1932)
Shoshone		Lowie (1924)
Shoshone (Nevada)	Most effective method for lone hunter	Steward (1941)
Walapai		Kniffen et al. (1935)
Yavapai	Approach first over brow of hill or from behind a rock	Corbusier (1886)
Yavapai (Northeastern)		Gifford (1936)
Yavapai (Southeastern)	Hunters supposedly ignored wind direction as they were not disturbed by scent	Gifford (1932)
Zuni	Masked hunters used a snorting type call	Gifford (1940)

Head decoys were used effectively by Apache hunters to approach pronghorn within bow and arrow range. The pronghorn head skin, at left, with horns detached, was collected in Arizona before 1876. A twig was bent into a circle and lashed with leather to the base of the mask, which rested on a hunter's shoulders. The features of the skinned-out head were maintained by stuffing with grass. The head decoy, at right, features a superb set of horn sheaths. Buck head decoys would have been more noticeable to pronghorn, but somewhat more cumbersome for the stalkers. Photos courtesy of the Smithsonian Institution Anthropology Archives, Washington, DC.

Rita, is a hot spring. . . . After examining it thoroughly . . . my attention was soon after arrested by a number of antelopes feeding on the plain. . . . Crawling from bush to bush, and hiding behind every stone which offered any shelter, I got within handsome range of a fine buck, and feeling sure that the animal could not escape me, I raised to fire, when, just as I was taking aim, I was astonished to see the animal raise erect upon its hind legs, and heard it cry out, in fair Spanish 'No tiras, no tiras!'—Don't fire, don't fire! What I would have sworn was an antelope proved to be a young Indian, the son of Ponce, a chief, who, having enveloped himself in an antelope's skin, with head, horns and all complete, had gradually crept up to the herd under his disguise, until his operations were brought to an untimely end by perceiving my aim directed at him. The Apaches frequently adopt this method of hunting, and imitate the actions of the antelope so exactly as to completely mislead those animals with the belief that their deadliest enemy is one of their number" (Cremony 1868:28).

Writing of the Assiniboine, Hewitt (1970:143–144) reported that: "Accidental injury or death to a member of a tribe demands the same vengeance or propitiation as death or injury inflicted purposely. The only exculpation held to be valid is the wounding or killing of a man in the disguise of an animal skin that Indians adopt to decoy stags or antelopes. Such an accident is pardonable, because one must shoot on the instant one is aware of the slightest indication of an animal being near. For the further reason, also, there is the possibility of an enemy concealing himself under that disguise in order to play the spy." As an alternative, the Assiniboine of the upper Missouri Valley used wolf skins as disguises (Denig 1930).

The Southern Paiute sometimes stalked pronghorn using only a bunch of rabbitbrush for concealment (Kelly 1964). Deep Creek Gosiutes maintained that ducks liked pronghorn and flocked around hunters disguised as such (Stewart 1942). Presumably, the ruse provided close shots at the birds.

Seldom does the literature indicate when in daytime pronghorn were most often and successfully hunted. When noted, the times appear to be coincidental. However, Burton (1862:68) definitively stated: "The best time for 'still-hunting' is at early dawn, when the little herds of four or five are busy grazing. They disappear during the midday heat of summer, and in the evening . . . they are wild and wary."

Pursuing

Pronghorn are the fleetest of North American mammals. Thus, it may seem incredulous that one

An old hunter near Casa Grandes, Chihuahua, Mexico, disguised himself by means of a cloak of cotton cloth painted to resemble and decoy pronghorn. The cloth covered his body, arms and legs. Horn sheaths and head skin completed the disguise. According to the Mexicans, Apaches were experts at hunting pronghorn in this manner. Photo by C. H. Taylor, from Lumholtz (1902).

means of taking them before the advent of the horse was simply to pursue them to exhaustion on foot. The pronghorn is credited with bursts of speed near 60 miles per hour (96.5 km/hr) (Frison 1978), whereas the fastest human runners do not exceed 28 miles per hour (45 km/hr) (Myers 1989). Obviously, a human would be the loser in a short contest. However, using a steady deliberate pace, a well-conditioned, determined human, such as an Indian hunter, eventually could outlast a pronghorn. According to Yoakum (1978), pronghorn become exhausted after running 3 to 4 miles (4.8–6.4 km) at a speed of about 30 miles per hour (48 km/hr). In the Kalahari of South Africa, Bushmen are known to run down cheetahs, generally recognized as the swiftest of all mammals (Myers 1989). An elderly Indian told how, when he was about 24 years of age, he ran down an oddly behaving pronghorn in about 1.5 miles (2.4 km) on a hot July

day, and killed it with his knife (Botkin 1975). Thinking that the animal may have been crippled, he carefully skinned it but found no sign of injury.

The relentless pursuit strategy was used by many tribes to procure pronghorn. They included Hopi, who hunted in pairs (Beaglehole 1936), Shoshone (Lowie 1924) and Flathead (Turney-High 1937). Shoshone fathers taught their sons to run pronghorn until the animals dropped from exhaustion (Mails 1972). Shoshones might pursue one animal for two days before closing in for a kill. Running pronghorn in valleys, Flatheads kept inside the several-mile circle pronghorn were bound to run (Turney-High 1937).

Some northern tribes pursued big game during winter on snowshoes when the mobility of game was restricted by snow (Newman et al. 1957). Pronghorn occasionally were driven into deep snow where they could be approached closely. The Achomawi exploited deep snows to hunt pronghorn in the Sierra Nevada foothills. One informant said that his father once killed 200 stranded pronghorn by walking among them and "breaking their necks" (Curtis 1924 [13]:139). Haley (1997) reported that, in relays, mounted western Apache ran down pronghorn and roped and strangled the quarry. If unblemished skins were desired, the exhausted pronghorn might be slashed where skinning incisions were to be made.

Surrounding

Surrounding, also known as encircling, apparently became more common after Indians acquired horses, but large numbers of women, old men and children afoot still participated as they had before the horse culture era (Newhouse 1869). Steward (1974a) referred to collective pronghorn drives that required cooperation among prehorse Ute families. Walker (1978) reported that Northern Paiute held communal pronghorn drives during September and early spring, but neither Steward or Walker specified whether these drives were to concealed archers, surrounds, pens or pits. Tubatulabal, Yokuts and Kawaiisu gathered annually for pronghorn drives in the San Joaquin Valley (Olmsted and Stewart 1978). Without specifying the tribes, Burton (1862:68) wrote that, along the Rocky Mountain's eastern front, "the Indian savages kill them by surrounds, especially in winter."

As with pursuing pronghorn afoot, mounted hunters could set up relays to run pronghorn in large circles, gradually tiring the quarry until the hunters on horseback could approach closely and dispatch the exhausted pronghorn. Illustration by Buffalo Meat, a Cheyenne; courtesy of the Amon Carter Museum, Fort Worth, Texas.

A Northeastern Yavapai described an antelope surround that involved use of fire near the upper Verde River, Arizona. Hunters surrounded a large herd, lit fires and shouted to keep the animals encircled. The hunters gradually closed in on the animals, which milled around "just like sheep," and killed about 100 (Gifford 1936:265). Cremony (1868) provided similar detail for a pronghorn hunt by Apaches and noted that such a hunt could completely decimate a herd.

For the Lipan Apache, the discovery of a large number of pronghorn in lowlands adjoining the hilly regions of southern Texas called for a surround. "Because the antelope was not considered dangerous quarry," wrote Opler (2001:946), "the event was treated as a festive occasion and as an opportunity for women to demonstrate their riding and roping skills. Etiquette required that a man should not overtake and pass a woman who was chasing an antelope. The only weapon a woman carried was a lasso, and if she roped an antelope or merely struck it, the nearest man was obligated to shoot it for her."

Egan (1917:240–241) provided one of the better accounts of a surround: "There were ten [Gosiute hunters] on horses and five or six foot men. When they arrived at the edge of the hunting ground they divided into parties, one going to the right and the other to the left and occasionally leaving a man, and so spacing them apart that when the two ends of the line swung around they formed a very large circle.

The Yokut Indians of California captured pronghorn in surrounds and drives. They spared bucks with peculiar horns because such animals were said to sing as they ran with burrowing owls setting on their heads (Kroeber 1976). Photo by Jim Jeffress; courtesy of the Nevada Department of Wildlife, Carson City.

"We could see where the antelope were running and the plan was to keep them in the circle and on the run all the time and not allow rest. When any of them attempted to pass out they were headed off and turned back or around the circle. We could not see an antelope half way across the circle, but could see the dust they raised and the direction they were traveling.

"When, after they had been kept running back and forth till they were very tired, a man would chase one on a fast run and as he neared another man would stop to rest his horse and watch for another run. The second man could run his horse alongside the antelope easily, which I did, and wished I had brought my lariat, as I could have caught him easily, but I shot him at a distance of about eight or ten feet [2.4–3.0 m]."

Similarly, Newhouse (1869:100–101) reported: "In the winter the Indians take advantage of their congregating together and hunt them [pronghorn] by a 'surround.' The manner of doing this is as follows: A large number of Indians distribute themselves around

the antelope at such a distance as not to alarm them. Then they advance with cries and noise from all sides. The antelope, instead of endeavoring to escape, herd closer together in their fright, and suffer themselves to be beaten down with clubs. In this way great numbers are sometimes killed."

With the advent of the horse, the Northern Paiute pursued pronghorn, which typically refused to leave their normal habitat in Surprise Valley (Fowler 1989). Mounted hunters took turns, so that fresh horses and hunters were always in pursuit as the pronghorn circled the valley. By early afternoon, the pronghorn had tired and a few men easily killed the victims. Likewise, up to 50 Shoshoneans on horseback were able to surround a herd of pronghorn and take turns running them in circles until they collapsed from fatigue. By keeping inside the circling herd, the horsemen were able to

From August 1841 to May 1847, Belgian Jesuit missionary Nicolas Point assisted Father Pierre Jean DeSmet in founding the first Catholic mission in the Northwest, at a time when there was not a single permanent white settler in the northern Rockies region. Residing among the Flathead, Coeur d'Alene and Blackfeet, Father Point recorded by word and painting the ways of the people he and Father DeSmet ministered. Although the Jesuit's art is much less refined than that of Catlin, Miller, Kurz and Badmer, it nonetheless is considered equal in terms of accuracy and insight. Above is Point's image of a "small-scale" summer hunt for "antelopes" (Donnelly 1967:148). Charged and harassed, from different directions by hunters on horseback, pronghorn would either race or mill about in panicked circles until exhausted and become easy prey. Photo courtesy of the Collège Sainte-Marie, Montreal, Canada.

exercise a strategic advantage. Table 10 indicates some of the tribes that used the surround method.

Driving, Free-range

Game drives essentially are attempts to enhance game aggregation and predictability by creating an artificial herding effect, to impose artificial funneling factors or to alter the pace and direction of herded animals (Thomas 1983).

In this type of hunting, pronghorn were driven into confined areas where hidden archers killed them. Narrowing natural features, such as canyons or draws, or such artificial barriers as brush or stone fences were used to guide the harassed animals. The strategy capitalized on the natural inclinations of pronghorn to follow a lead animal.

The Shoshone-Goship (Gosiute) Indians of Deep Creek Valley, Utah, created brush fences several miles in length for the express purpose of driving pronghorn (Reagan 1922). Unlike deer, pronghorn are reluctant to bound over obstacles. These converging fences had openings, to which driven pronghorn would head for escape and where skilled archers lay in wait. An informant told Goldschmidt (1951) that the best Nomlaki marksmen concealed themselves by the gaps, while other men and boys drove the pronghorn from the valley toward the barrier. The method was used by many other tribes: Northeastern Yavapai (Gifford 1936), Northern Paiute (Fowler 1989) and Southern Paiute (Kelly 1964). Northern Shoshone hunters who hid behind brush were called *Wagadu*, while the Indians who herded game toward them were known as *Tunabonig*.

The Cahuilla of southern California used relays of pursuers to drive tired pronghorn into side canyons, where thirsty, fatigued animals overdrank or retired into dense thickets where they were easily killed (Bean 1972).

Shoshonean Indians were said to drive pronghorn to or over precipices (Lowie 1924), but whether this was to concentrate them near hunters lying in wait or to kill the animals directly by the fall is not known. The success of this method depended largely on a critical number of animals being present and their emotional state (Frison 1974). Animals do not know-

ingly plunge off precipices, but must be pressed or pushed by following animals.

At the Garnsey site in southeastern New Mexico, two butchered pronghorn were found among the remains of several dozen bison (Speth and Parry 1980); it is uncertain whether they had been driven over a "jump" with the bison or separately. Small numbers of pronghorn bones have been found at other bison jumps, but they may have been remains of food brought to the butchering sites.

In Montana, Indians intercepted and killed pronghorn while they were swimming a river or crossing a frozen lake (Davis 1986).

Driving, with Fence and Pen or Pit

"It is said that once in early times the [Blackfoot] men determined that they would use antelope skins for the women's dresses, instead of cow skins. So they found a place where antelope were plenty, and set up on the prairie long lines of rock piles, or of bushes, so as to form a chute like a V. Near the point where the lines joined, they dug deep pits, which they roofed with slender poles, and covered these with grass and a little dirt. Then the people scattered out, and while most of them hid behind the rock piles and bushes, a few started the antelope toward the mouth of the chute. As they ran by them, the people showed themselves and yelled, and the antelope ran down the chute and finally reached the pits, and falling into them were taken, when they were killed and divided among the hunters. Afterward, this was the common method of securing antelopes up to the coming of the whites" (Grinnell 1962:236). This is supported by the number of pronghorn pens or traps still recognizable in the West (Table 11). Davis (1986) reported that Montana Indians hunted pronghorn by driving them into prepared pits.

George Bird Grinnell (1923), primary ethnographer of the Cheyenne, recorded detailed information from White Bull telling how these Indians once "pitted" pronghorn. Moving west of the Missouri River toward the Black Hills, the Cheyenne found abandoned pits and trenches that had been constructed by earlier Indians. Many of these pits were near converging streams. Brush barriers or fence wings evidently guided animals to and into the pits.

Table 10. Selected references to surround hunts for pronghorn during the 1800s

Tribe or location	Remarks	Reference
Achomawi	During winter, 15 to 20 men on snowshoes surrounded with bows and arrows	Curtis (1924 [13])
Apache	An off-reservation hunt by reservation Apaches (95 men and 15 women), 87 pronghorn killed by mounted Indians	Cremony (1868)
Apache	Horseback drive to waiting hunters	Gifford (1940)
Apache (Lipan)	All who could ride, including women and children, participated	Newcomb (1961)
Apwaruge	Pronghorn charmed by all-night singing; actual surround by long, twisted buckbrush rope with small strands hanging down	Garth (1950)
Arapaho	Relays of ponies until more than 500 exhausted pronghorn were killed during autumn, 1860, in present-day Boulder County, Colorado	Bixby (1880)
Arapaho	Horseback surrounds about 1880	Kindig (1987)
California	Surrounds most practicable in open country (southern two-thirds of state)	Kroeber (1976)
Cheyenne	Few such hunts conducted during 19th century	Underhill (1948)
Comanche	Retained from their Shoshonean background the magical pronghorn surround	Wallace and Hoebel (1952)
Gosiute	Horseback surround by 16 hunters yielded three pronghorn	Egan (1917)
Hopi	Pronghorn were run down and suffocated for unblemished skins	Oswalt (1966)
Hopi	Prehistoric ancestors hunted this way and it continued through the 18th and 19th centuries	Peckham (1965)
Hopi	Pedestrian relays exhausting animals inside surround	Curtis (1922)
Kiowa	No shooting allowed, pronghorn roped or captured by hand	Newcomb (1961)
Kiowa	Horseback and pedestrian surround during winter 1848–49 along Arkansas River, Colorado	Mooney (1898)
Klamath	Surround with a large net set on stakes in a marsh area	Voegelin (1942)
Northern California	Hunters converged from at least two directions; Tubatulabal, Yokuts and Kawaiisu joined for drives in San Joaquin Valley	Olmsted and Stewart (1978)
Paiute (Northern)	Ran down on horseback	Fowler (1989)
Paiute (Southern)	Surround or driven past waiting hunters	Stewart (1942)
Patwin	Crept up and surrounded flocks	Kroeber (1932)
Pawnee	Several hundred pronghorn often killed in one surround, hides more sought after than meat	Haines (1976)
Pueblo (Santa Clara)	Frequently augmented by Spanish Americans and men from neighboring pueblos; bands of Kiowa and Comanche might join party	Arnon and Hill (1979)
San Joaquin Valley	Gregarious pronghorn ideal to victimize once or twice a year by surrounds	Ebeling (1986)
Shoshone	40 to 50 horsemen sometimes engaged for a day to obtain 2 to 3 pronghorn	Godman (1826)
Shoshone	Women and children killed some with clubs	Huntington (1904)
Shoshone	Bison were becoming scarce, so pronghorn were important	Trenholm and Carley (1964)
Shoshone (Eastern)	Surround, then run down in relays by mounted hunters; early reservation period	Murphy and Murphy (1960)
Shoshone (Northern)	Horseback chase of 10 pronghorn for two hours by 20 hunters, none killed	Thwaites (1969)
Shoshone (Northern)	Pen of sagebrush bark rope on sagebrush piles or on poles above 18-inch (46 cm) high sagebrush pen	Steward (1943)
Shoshone (Western)	Drives into pens 50 feet (14 m) to 1 mile (1.6 km) in diameter, with or without wings; some wings 3 miles (4.8 km) long; usually directed by charmers	Steward (1941)
Tiwa	Horseback chase involving 400 men from 50 pueblos about 1896	Curtis (1926)
Ute	Surround or driven past waiting hunters	Stewart (1942)
Ute	Men drove up to 200 pronghorn through V wings over low cliff into pen	Smith (1974)
Ute in North Park, Colorado	4,400 pronghorn killed in one surround during 1868	Seton (1909)
Ute and other Indians of the foothills	Late autumn when pronghorn congregated in great herds; large numbers were killed	Dodge (1877)
Ute, Eutaw and Shoshone	Directed by a shaman who ordered every man, woman and child who could lift a club to join the surround	Steward (1974b)
Unspecified valleys near the Rocky Mountains	Take advantage of winter congregations	Newhouse (1869)
	Mounted Indians surround and run pronghorn until the animals tire and large numbers can be slain	Marcy (1859)
Valleys near the Rocky Mountains	Winter concentrations, large numbers killed	Johnson (1969)
Yavapai	Fire used to encircle pronghorn	Gifford (1936)
Yokut	Only two men from each village shot (with arrows) at pronghorn within the circle for safety reasons; bucks with peculiar horns were spared; intertribal pedestrian circle several miles in diameter	Kroeber (1976)

The Cheyennes repaired the abandoned pit traps and constructed others to capture pronghorn. Two straight, tight, brush fences, each about 400 to 500 feet (121.8–160.3 m) long, were built diagonally outward from where a pit was to be dug. Between the narrow constriction, a large pit, about 5 feet (1.7 m) deep with vertical sides, was dug. The exposed brink of the pit was carefully hidden by vegetation and many killing clubs were hidden nearby. After extensive shamanistic ceremonies, hunters circled behind a herd of pronghorn and drove them between the converging wings and into the pit. Men and women quickly clubbed them to death.

Grinnell (1972) also told of a drive held in 1858 along the Arkansas River, where 600 pronghorn were

pitted. According to Curley Hair, the last Cheyenne pit drive took place along the Antelope Pit River (now the Little Missouri River) in 1865.

More often than being pitted, pronghorn were driven into pens, where they could be held and killed

TABLE 11. Probable pronghorn traps constructed by Indians

Locations	Remarks	References
Laidlaw, Alberta	115-foot (35 m) long stone V-wings leading into 23- by 10-foot (7 by 3 m) enclosure; dig revealed pronghorn and probable bison bones, which were radiocarbon dated at 3,280 years before present	Brumley (1984, 1986)
Belle Fourche, SD	Extant 16- by 8-foot (4.9 by 2.4 m) pit identified as a pronghorn trap by a Cheyenne shaman	Stands in Timber and Liberty (1967)
Missouri Buttes, WY	Three-sided, log-lined 9.8- by 9.8-foot (3 by 3 m) pit appearing like an abandoned cellar and attached juniper log V-wings	Frison (1978)
Fort Bridger, southwestern WY	Juniper debris in 656- by 492-foot (200 by 150 m) pen with 2,051-foot (625 m) circling fence	Frison (1978)
Utah	Juniper pen about 984 feet (300 m) in diameter with V-wings—one 377 feet (115 m) long—steel axe cuts on wood	Raymond (1982)
Utah	558- by 459-foot (170 by 140 m) juniper corral with 66-foot (20 m) long V-wings and steel axe cuts on wood	Raymond (1982)
Butte Valley, NV[a]	U-shaped pen about 1,641 by 656 feet (500 by 200 m)	Murphy and Frampton (1986)
Clover Valley, NV[a]	U-shaped juniper pen about 1,247 by 1,050 feet (380 by 320 m), some steel axe cuts	Murphy and Frampton (1986), Polk (1987)
Currie Hills, NV[a]	1,181- by 820-foot (360 by 250 m) juniper pen with one 203-foot (62 m) wing and one 2,576-foot (785 m) circling wing, some steel axe cuts	Murphy and Frampton (1986)
Cobre, NV[a]	1,083- by 984-foot (330 by 300 m) juniper pen incorporating posts (some standing, some axe-cut) and living trees; 150 arrowheads and three hearths on surface	Murphy and Frampton (1986), Polk (1987)
Dry Lake Flat North, NV[a]	Juniper pen about 1,312 by 984 feet (400 by 300 m)	Murphy and Frampton (1986)
Dry Lake Flat South, NV[a]	U-shaped juniper pen about 1,641 by 1,312 feet (500 by 400 m), incorporating a few living trees and some steel axe cuts	Murphy and Frampton (1986)
Five Mile Draw North, NV[a]	Juniper log and living tree pen about 1,312 by 984 feet (400 by 300 m)	Murphy and Frampton (1986)
Five Mile Draw East, NV[a]	Juniper pen about 1,312 by 984 feet (400 by 300 m)	Murphy and Frampton (1986)
Hendry's Creek, NV[a]	U-shaped pen about 591 by 525 feet (180 by 160 m), formed largely of cobbles and boulders	Rudy (1953)
Maverick Range, NV[a]	Juniper pen about 1,641 by 1,641 feet (500 by 500 m) with short V-wings	Murphy and Frampton (1986)
Ruby Wash, NV[a]	1,312- by 656-foot (400 by 200 m) pen of juniper logs	Murphy and Frampton (1986)
Toano Draw, NV[a]	Pen about 1,148 by 984 feet (350 by 300 m)	Murphy and Frampton (1986)
Tobar, NV[a]	1,411- by 1,181-foot (430 by 360 m) juniper post pen with 328-foot (100 m) V-wings and some steel axe cuts	Murphy and Frampton (1986), Polk (1987)
Wendover, NV[a]	Stone and juniper pen, about 902 by 902 feet (275 by 275 m), with attached circling wall about 1,312 feet (400 m) long and seven interior blinds; 52 arrowheads recovered from surface	Murphy and Frampton (1986)
Anchorite Pass, NV[b]	984- by 984-foot (300 by 300 m) pen of juniper, rocks and living trees; four projectile points found	Hall (1990)
Excelsior, NV[b]	705- by 541-foot (215 by 165 m) juniper, piñon and rock pen with 1,312-foot (400 m) plus long V-wings, and flagstones across entrance; possibly a deer trap	Wilke (1986)
Huntoon, NV[b]	1,099- by 853-foot (335 by 260 m) juniper and rock pen with 10,778-foot (3,285 m) drift fence and flagstones at entrance	Parr (1989)
Whisky Flat, NV[b]	1,132- by 853-foot (345 by 260 m) juniper and rock pen with 3,432-foot (1,046 m) drift fence, interior rock blinds and flagstones at entrance; 79 projectile points found inside pen	Wilke (1986)
Trap 1, CA[b]	Burnt juniper pen 745 by 656 feet (230 by 200 m) with parallel, sinuous entrance wings about 0.6 mile (1 km) long	Arkush (1995)
Trap 2, CA[b]	Burnt juniper pen 1,148 by 984 feet (350 by 300 m), with 1,641-foot (500 m) + V-wings and 164-foot (50 m) entrance	Arkush (1995)
Trap 4, CA[b]	Burnt juniper corral about 1,641 by 1,312 feet (500 by 400 m), with basalt flagstones across 197-foot (60 m) entrance and 820-foot (250 m) plus V-wings	Arkush (1995)

Source: Lubinski 1997.
[a] Northeastern part of state.
[b] Mono Basin area.

at leisure (see Raynolds (1868). Entire herds might be taken. More has been written of this Indian method of obtaining pronghorn than any other (Table 12), with the many reporters using varied terminologies. For example, the fence that guides the animals toward and into the capture structure has been variously described as barrier, chute, wing and wall; whereas the enclosure is referred to as corral, stockade, park, pen, pound and trap.

The Hidatsa reportedly drove pronghorn over cliffs into pens (Weitzner 1979). Prince Maximilian Zu Weid reported that Mandan drove pronghorn between converging brushwood fences 1 to 2 miles (1.6–3.2 km) in length, dropping sharply toward the end and into a pole corral (Thwaites 1906 [23]:347).

Steward (1938) explained how the fence-pen hunting method was used by Plateau/Great Basin Indians. In the evening preceding the hunt, young men were sent to the extreme southern end of the valley, about 20 miles (32.2 km) from the previously constructed capture pen. The following morning, they spread across the valley and worked their way northward, herding pronghorn far before them. Typically, the animals paused at knolls from which they had good visibility. Seeing nothing threatening to the north, they trotted that direction as more drivers joined from the sides of the valley.

The outer ends of the fences were about 4 miles (6.4 km) apart and marked to ensure that the pronghorn were being properly herded between them. The outermost fences consisted of intermittently uprooted sagebrush piled on growing sagebrush. Closer to the corral, the brush piles were placed closer together. A more or less continuous fence of uprooted sagebrush commenced about 2 miles (3.2 km) from the pen. As the funnel narrowed, it curved through a grove of standing junipers into a well-constructed pen. Once the pronghorn were inside, the entrance was sealed off, and the killing commenced. Sometimes, as many as 200 were taken in a single drive. Because such large numbers could not be processed quickly, some victims were kept penned for two or more days before slaughtering (Kelly 1932).

The Honey Lake Paiute employed a number of variations in their drives of pronghorn at Secret Valley (Riddell 1960). They drove during March, when the ground was muddy and the animals consequently

tired more quickly. Also, families wove lengths of sagebrush-bark rope. These were joined to other ropes, and the long rope was strung over the stone and sagebrush piles leading to the pen. Strips of sagebrush bark hung from the rope. When pronghorn approached the fence, the people shook the rope to scare them back. These sagebrush-bark ropes, the size of a man's wrist in diameter, sometimes were a mile (1.6 km) long (Stewart 1941). Particularly large brush piles were placed on each side of the corral entrance. Once the pronghorn had entered, women lit them with torches, thus blocking the pronghorn's escape. Harassed pronghorn became so exhausted that they lay down and even children could approach and kill them.

Among several excellent, detailed accounts of drive-trapping pronghorn are those of Steward (1938) for the Plateau/Great Basin Indians, and Egan (1917) for the Gosiute of eastern Nevada.

The manner of dispatching trapped pronghorn varied. The Hopi believed that "To kill antelope or deer by cutting the throat or letting blood run from a wound causes a whirlwind and sandstorm; to smother them enables their spirits to go to their home and so to live again on earth" (Beaglehole 1936). Upon throwing an exhausted pronghorn to the ground, a Hopi hunter turned the animal's head toward the village to produce rain there. Then grasping the nose and jaws with the hand, pressed the head into the sand until it was smothered.

The Modoc, however, had no compunction against killing pronghorn by clubbing (Ray 1963) and exhibited no spiritual overtures in the process. "Organization larger than the village was only temporary among the western Shoshone and their neighbors. The most common occasions for the assemblage of the members of several villages was the rabbit or antelope drive, which rarely lasted more than two or three weeks and was normally held only once a year. One group of a hundred persons could round up more game per capita than, say, five groups of twenty operating independently. Such drives were led by skilled hunters thought to possess supernatural power and to be able to attract rabbits and antelope" (Driver 1972:289–290).

Some tribes, upon corralling a large number of pronghorn, released a few alive. The Navajos released one of each sex, or sometimes four pairs, one toward

TABLE 12. Selected references to Indian drives of pronghorn to pens or pits

Tribe or area	Remarks	Reference
Achomawi	Pen of tules; ceremonial; women inside pen make the kill	Voeglin (1942)
Apache (Jicarillo and Mescalero)	Pen	Goddard (1975)
Apache	Pen 100 yards (91 m) in diameter of juniper brush; one animal released for good luck	Gifford (1940)
Arapaho	Abandoned pine log pen and attached pit observed during 1851 in present-day Converse County, WY; said to have been used about 1843	Snowden (1868)
Assiniboine	Abandoned pen observed by Lewis and Clark in present-day ND	Coues (1893)
Blackfoot	Pedestrian drive through V-wings into covered pit	Grinnell (1962)
Blood and Piegan	Elbow turn in chute to conceal pit	Wissler (1910)
Brule Sioux	Several hundred Indians drove several hundred pronghorn over a precipice into log and brush pen	Denig (1961)
Cheyenne	Pedestrian drive into partially concealed pit, about 1855; horseback drive of 600 or more pronghorn into human pen in 1858	Grinnell (1923)
Cheyenne	Ceremonial pedestrian drive through human V wings into 8- by 16-foot (2.4 by 4.9 m) pit, then killed with clubs in present-day SD before 1850; game laid out in row from largest to smallest	Stands in Timber and Liberty (1967)
Cheyenne (Southern)	Pen of old men, women and children waving blankets, more than 600 pronghorn killed	Grinnell (1923)
Cheyenne and Kiowa	Pit during spring migration	Hill (1979)
Comanche	Pen	Wallace and Hoebel (1952)
"Digger" (Paiute)	Pen	Irving (1850)
General	Brush and wood pens, much as for caribou in north	Herrick (1892)
General	Pen and chute of posts (some covered with blankets to resemble men), ceremonial, only during winters of scarcity	Mooney (1979)
Gosiute	Pen concealed by turns in chute and by trees	Egan (1917)
Gosiute	A single valley could support a drive to pens about once every 10 years; also traveled toward the Wasatch Mountains to drive pronghorn over cliffs. A rancher in Skull Valley saw a brush drive fence in 1870, but sheep herders soon used it for fuel; drives (usually during spring) necessitated more preparation and cooperative effort than any other social or economic activity	Malouf (1974)
Great Basin	A shaman would take advantage of pronghorn curiosity and lead them into a pen; "antelope was a luxury in this area"	Minor and Minor (1978:106)
Grouse Creek Valley (northwest of Great Salt Lake)	New pen built each year; hunts held during spring and autumn migrations	Steward (1938)
Hidatsa	Ceremonial drive to pen at undercut stream bank	Bowers (1965)
Hidatsa	Drive over precipice into pen	Weitzner (1979)
Hidatsa and Mandan	Horseback drive between 1- to 2-mile long wings over a low cliff into small pen, then clubbed or taken alive	Thwaites (1906)
Hopi	Pens and pits	Hodge (1907)
Hopi	Former pedestrian drives into 100- by 200-yard (91 by 182 m) pen with 15- to 20-foot (457–610 cm) opening and 800- to 1,000-yard (732–914 m) wings	Parsons (1936)
Kiowa	Drive along game trail into large pit covered with grass and shrubs	Mooney (1898)
Kiowa and Kiowa Sioux	Pen of upright logs, chute of blanket-covered scarecrows	Newcomb (1961)
Lakota	Drive over precipice into pens	Hill (1979)
Mandan	Pen	Richardson (1829)
Mandan	Yield of 100 pronghorn during two days driven into pen during November 1804, in present-day ND	Coues (1893)
Mandan	Pen; pronghorn next in importance to bison	Will and Spinden (1906)
Mandan and Minitaries	Pen	Wied (1843)
Mandan and Minitaries (Hidatsa)	Pens, used by Minitaries more frequently than by the Mandans, drive up valleys	Thomas and Ronnefeldt (1976)
Modoc	Sagebrush piles fired at entrance to pen to retain pronghorn	Ray (1963)
Navajo	12 men sufficed to drive pronghorn into brush pen; one animal released for good luck	Gifford (1940)
Navajo	20 to 50 men on horses or foot drove pronghorn into 100-yard (91 m) diameter pen of piñon and juniper with wings 400 yards to 1 mile (336 m–1.6 km) long	Hill (1938)
Nevada Shoshone	Most hunting was communal and ceremonial	Steward (1941)
Paiute (Honey Lake)	Pen, sagebrush bark rope wings, drove when muddy to slow and tire pronghorn	Riddell (1960)
Paiute (Northern)	Used sagebrush bark ropes in wings and pens	Walker (1978)
Paiute (Northern)	March drive into pen of brush and shaking rope	Riddell (1960)
Paiute (Northern)	Directed by charmer; a seasonally important source of meat	Fowler (1989)
Paiute (Northern)	Charmed pronghorn ran about inside a circle of six sagebrush piles as if there was a fence	Hopkins (1883)
Paiute (Northern)	Report of driving pronghorn into a sagebrush rope circle by six Surprise Valley Paiutes	Kelly (1932)

continued on next page

TABLE 12—*continued*

Tribe or area	Remarks	Reference
Paiute (Northern and Southern)	Pens, ceremonial; sagebrush or tule rope with suspended balls of sagebrush in circle on top of existing shrubs	Steward (1941)
Paiute (Southern)	Pen	Stewart (1942)
Paiute (Southern)	Semicircular pen with V-wings	Kelly (1964)
Pueblo Indians at Taos, Picuris and Pecos	Brush pens still in place in 1881	Goddard (1975)
Shoshone	Pens, ceremonial, perhaps once every eight years	Maxwell (1978)
Shoshone	Might take years to restore a herd after a drive to pens	Ebeling (1986)
Tribes on plains west of the Missouri	Pens most usual way of capturing pronghorn	U.S. House of Representatives (1852)
Upper Missouri River country	Caught in pens during the mid-1800s in nearly the same manner as bison, but generally dispatched with clubs by women	Audubon and Bachman (1851)
Ute	Pens, communal hunts nearly universal	Steward (1941)
Zuni	Up to 200 horsemen drive through 2- to 3-mile (3.2–4.8 km) wings into pen and close rope/blanket gate	Gifford (1940)

each cardinal point. Pollen and an herb were placed in the mouth of each before freeing, so that "they would increase in the future for men" (Hill 1938:155). Possibly these ritual releases were simply tacit recognition that a highly successful drive virtually depopulated the locale of pronghorn. It is reasonable to assume that successful pronghorn drives in some of the more barren shrublands of the West were infrequent events, depending on the rate of pioneering by pronghorn from adjacent rangelands.

At least in parts of the Great Basin, a successful communal hunt gave rise to many important social activities not practiced at other times of the year, including feasting, dancing, singing, contests, gambling, courting and visiting with neighbors who cooperated in the hunt (Stewart 1941). These contacts, in turn, served to maintain or alter friendships, leadership, hierarchy and direction of the tribe, band or family, and associated alliances. Such gatherings were made possible solely because of a large food supply. In this sense, the pronghorn was a catalyst in the social structure and welfare of some western tribes, particularly those lacking regular access to bison.

Fire Driving

Fire already has been noted as a hunting aid to driving or constraining captured animals. Uncontrolled fire, because of its often unpredictable nature—its intensity, speed, direction and magnitude—must have been an uncertain ally and an aid to be used

judiciously. Nonetheless, many accounts document the use of both controlled and uncontrolled fire by Indians in hunting big game, including pronghorn.

Use of fire in hunting apparently was more common before Indians had horses. Cabeza de Vaca (1983) told of Indians in Texas during 1542 using fire to deprive game of pasturage so the animals were forced to seek it where the Indians could trap them.

Emmitt (1954) indicated that deer, elk and pronghorn on the White River Agency west of Meeker, Colorado, were easily killed by Utes during late summer. The country had been fired, and game milled around running streams and springs.

When driving pronghorn, Navajo horsemen headed them off by igniting fires (Hill 1938). Once the pronghorn were corralled, the Navajo fired piles of brush at the corral entrance to prevent escape. A Northeastern Yavapai related how hunters lit fires around a herd of pronghorn and shouted to keep them in the constricting circle. The bewildered animals reportedly milled around "just like sheep," and more than a hundred were killed (Gifford 1936:265). Yokuts were said to set the great San Joaquin plain ablaze to drive pronghorn, deer and elk past concealed hunters (Curtis 1924, Olmsted and Stewart 1978).

Underhill (1991:59), discussing the hunting practices of the Hopi and other Pueblo people of the Southwest, noted that "Antelope were easier to get in quantity, since they travel in herds while deer feed by twos and threes. Moreover, a herd of antelope is easily stampeded and can be driven to the place where hunters are waiting. The Hopi, who lived near

"The Indians burn portions of the prairies every fall," wrote Dodge (1877:29), "setting the fires so as to burn as vast an extent of country as possible, and yet preserve unburned a good section in the vicinity where they propose to make their fall hunt. The buffalo, finding nothing to eat on the burnt ground collect on that unburnt—reducing greatly the labor of the hunt." Top scene, "Herd of Buffalo Fleeing from a Prairie Fire," is an 1888 oil on canvas painting by Meyer Strauss; photo courtesy of the Joselyn Art Museum, Omaha, Nebraska. Bottom scene, "Prairie Fire," is an 1898 oil painting by Charles M. Russell; photo courtesy of the C. M. Russell Museum, Great Falls, Montana.

open country where antelope are found, went to enormous trouble to accomplish this. They chose a place partly fenced in by hills and with trees nearby. There they built a corral of strong tree trunks with one opening. From this, long wings led out, fenced with brush for some distance and then marked by piles of brush for ten miles or so. Men stood along these wings to scare the antelope so that they would not try to leap the brush but would gallop down the open space into the corral.

"When a herd was reported nearby, the boys of the village were sent to round them up. They got behind the animals and made a fire to frighten them. Then, as they began to move, the boys closed in around them, howling like wolves to make them run and driving them toward the corral." As soon as the pronghorn entered the corral, the opening was closed with brush. Marksmen positioned outside the fence then shot the trapped animals.

Hunting Fawns

With very few exceptions, we are not aware that hunts were made specifically or systematically for pronghorn fawns. Quite likely, fawns were killed when happened upon by hunters. But in most regions where and when pronghorn fawns were found in any number, more providential and less problematic game likely was to be found. Biologists today locate fawns for capture by watching where nursing fawns bed down, then capturing the young in their beds. This is not a technique that would have been missed by Indians. Nomlaki Indians, for example, captured fawns in the early morning (Goldschmidt 1951), a time when pronghorn fawns tend to be bedded and daybreak light conditions are optimal for sneaking close.

Before reaching adulthood, Cheyenne boys spent much time learning the craft and skills of hunting. "Older boys often set out in companies of 4 or 5 and traveled across the prairies a bow shot apart and walked considerable distances. They were often very successful in this hunting. Sometimes in the spring they succeeded in killing a kid antelope or two—a great prize" (Grinnell 1972 [1]:116).

Ambush

Small, circular rock blinds, usually near game trails or springs, can be found throughout the West. Blinds made of other materials did not withstand the elements and fire. Supposed pronghorn-hunting blinds that author Reeves observed on the eastern Snake River plain of Idaho were constructed of lava rocks on the flanks of buttes above sagebrush flats. Blinds of brush were used by Mescalero Apaches, and Southern Utes constructed blinds of brush and stone (Gifford 1940).

Cheyenne Making Medicine illustrated ambush hunting of pronghorn by a concealed rifleman using crossed sticks to steady his aim. At the top of the scene lies a dead or wounded buck. The rest of the small herd travels first away from where the buck was shot, then back toward the hunter, indicating their confusion about the shooter's location. Photo courtesy of the Smithsonian Institution Anthropology Archives, Washington, DC.

The Tabeguache Utes of southwestern Colorado (chiefly around Los Piños), "having only bows and arrows and no horses or dogs, and yet trusting to the chase for subsistence, they secured all their wild game by use of the ambush" (Steward 1974b:135). Schlissel (1982) noted that Indians in the western mountains who lacked horses were experts at the ambush hunting technique.

Another form of lying in ambush was practiced by the Shoshones (Curtis 1925). They quietly herded pronghorn away from the animals' favored grazing or bedding spots and then abandoned pursuit. They then hid near the vacated areas and ambushed the returning pronghorn.

Luring

Being innately curious, pronghorn readily respond quizzically to strange objects or sounds. Assiniboines of the upper Missouri River enticed pronghorn by tying an article of clothing to a pole (Denig 1930). The hunter then lay down and raised and lowered the pole at intervals, or alternately kicked up his heels. An inquisitive individual or band of pronghorn, after making several tentative circles, often approached close enough to provide the recumbent, hidden hunter with an arrow shot.

The Ohlone of central coastal California likewise capitalized on the pronghorn's curiosity by tying

Knowing that pronghorn would attempt to elude pursuers by running along natural pathways, as few as two hunters could successfully take the animals by driving. With one or more Indians causing pronghorn to move in a predictable fashion and direction, one or more shooters, such as the Pawnee depicted, would position at passes and other places of concealment along the "flight" route, to intercept the driven quarry. Artwork by Alfred Jacob Miller; photo courtesy of the Walters Art Gallery, Baltimore, Maryland.

Luring curious pronghorn by flagging and other actions was a tactic common to Indians, who, in fact, introduced it to white hunters. In the 1830s scene above, by George Catlin, the hunter is using a staked flag and his weapon is a muzzle-loading rifle. Photo courtesy of the Smithsonian Institution Anthropology Archives, Washington, DC.

strips of hide onto their ankles and wrists, lying down on their backs and waving their arms and legs in the air (Margolin 1978). Perplexed by this odd phenomenon, the pronghorn drew closer and were shot by other hunters hidden nearby.

Hewitt (1970) wrote that some plains Indians turned summersaults, tumbled and gesticulated madly to arouse the animals' intrigue, but always kept themselves in the lee of the wind.

A Nomlaki informant told Goldschmidt (1951) that captive pronghorn does sometimes served as decoys, presumably to attract wild pronghorn to hunters.

Dozens of other references to luring pronghorn were found, but none of them gave data on numbers of animals killed or how much time was expended per animal.

Pitfalls on Trails

Few references were found to Indian use of pitfalls for pronghorn. However, Hodge (1907) and Minor and Minor (1978) reported that plains tribes and ancient Pueblos captured deer, pronghorn and wolves by means of pitfalls. Also Kroeber (1976) indicated that the Achomawi, who hunted pronghorn, caught large game in concealed pits. Mooney (1979:309) gave more details. "Antelope make regular trails . . . and the Indians [Kiowa] sometimes caught them by digging a large pitfall along such a trail—an entire band assisting in the work—and carrying the excavated earth a long distance away, so as to leave no trace on the trail, after which the pitfall was loosely covered with bushes and grass. The hunters then concealed themselves until the herd approached, when they closed in behind and drove the frightened animals forward until they fell into the pit."

Jesuit missionary Nicolas Point painted Indians (probably Blackfeet) capturing and dispatching pronghorn—and other game "less mammoth than the buffalo" (Donnelly 1967:146)—in a pit fall. Photo courtesy of the Collège Sainte-Marie, Montreal, Canada.

Impaling

A Lemhi Shoshone gave an account of impaling pronghorn during winter, when footing on snow and ice was insecure (Steward 1943). Spears 3 to 4 feet (0.9–1.2 m) long were set in game trails and angled upward where the trails sloped downward. The spears were tipped with poisoned stone points. Pronghorn, driven downhill, impaled themselves.

Techniques such as the pitfalls and impaling probably were little used after Indians acquired horses.

Calls

Few references indicated that Indians used calls in hunting pronghorn. However, the Mescalero Apache called with ocotillo leaves in their mouths. The sound imitated was not described, but one prostrate, hidden hunter was said to have been trampled by a responding buck (Gifford 1940). The Llanero

hunter also called with a leaf in his mouth. Zuni stalkers wearing pronghorn masks expelled their breath explosively, apparently imitating the snort-wheeze of bucks. Zuni also compelled captive fawns to bleat, drawing does within arrow range. A Nomlaki informant told Goldschmidt (1951) that hidden hunters imitated the cry of a pronghorn fawn, thereby enticing the mother within weapon range.

Netting

Margolin (1978) asserted that the Ohlones of west-central California drove pronghorn into nets, but he gave no other information. Klamath Indians surrounded pronghorn with a large, circular net set on stakes in an Oregon marsh (Voegelin 1942:169). Some petroglyphs appear to depict various quadrupeds being driven into nets or snares, but such images are not sufficiently distinct to conclude that pronghorn were hunted in this way.

Dogs

Dogs evidently accompanied people to North America and were used for transport of small articles, companionship and sometimes hunting. Most important, they were eaten on special occasions or when game was unavailable. Their hunting value is variously described in the literature. Special mention was made that some tribes—Arikara (de Trobriand 1951), Mandan and Hidatsa (Thomas and Ronnefeldt 1976)—did not use dogs for hunting. Others used them for trailing and attacking game (Kroeber 1976). The Northern Paiute had a small variety of dog, never eaten, that was used in pronghorn drives (Walker 1978, Fowler 1989). The Hopi occasionally used dogs to help run down animals, but the dogs were not specially trained for hunting (Beaglehole 1936). Overall, the dog appears to have been relatively unimportant in pronghorn hunting.

DISTRIBUTION, PROCESSING AND TRANSPORTING

Hunting of big game generally was a male responsibility, although Maxwell (1978:168) reported that "Hard-riding Comanche women on horseback went antelope hunting with their men, successfully competing with them in bringing down game." Almost universally, transporting and processing meat was the job of wives and older children. Also, the fruits of communal hunts typically were distributed in unprocessed form, often at the scene of the kill, but the manner of distribution varied greatly among the tribes and was firmly fixed by tradition or religious canon. The shaman of a successful hunt invariably was well rewarded, and all who participated in the hunt shared the spoils. Some tribes removed and buried the eyes of pronghorn or tied them together and hung them on trees to demonstrate respect (Hill 1938). Among the Navajos, and probably most other tribes, each step in skinning and butchering was carried out according to prescribed rules (Hill 1938, Fowler 1989).

The processing of large game into smaller, more usable or transportable portions has been studied in detail (Hill 1938, White 1952, 1954, Frison 1971, 1978, Binford 1981). Knife marks and fractures caused by pounding with hammer stones leave little doubt about the dismembering steps followed. Generally, bison,

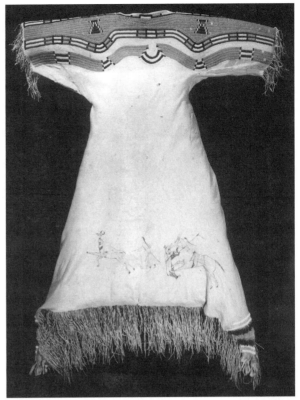

The dress (top) *of Hunkpapa Sioux Pretty White Cow Walking (Mrs. Spotted Horn Bull), niece of Sitting Bull, is rare in that it shows Pretty White Cow involved in hunting, which was traditionally and almost exclusively the domain of Indian men. However, if a woman was inclined and skilled as a hunter or warrior, she was not discouraged from those vocations and, among some tribes, held a venerated position as a result. Also, the artistic detailing of personal achievements was seldom a female prerogative. The drawing on the dress of the woman hunting pronghorn is detailed in the bottom photo. She is shown with a breechloading rifle. The images have a degree of definition that Ewers (1939) indicated was consistent with reservation artwork (ca. 1880). Those facts provide speculation about the authenticity of the drawings' actual history, but by virtue of the beadwork, fringe and art, the dress is quite spectacular.* Photos courtesy of the State Historical Society of North Dakota, Bismarck.

"The men of the tribe provided the meat for the family but their responsibility ended when the animal was killed. It was the women's job to follow the chase and bring the game back to camp—the carcasses of four antelope in this case. They also did the skinning, prepared the meat for cooking or for drying as 'jerky,' and tanned the hides. Between times they raised a family, moved camp, set up the tipi, gathered the wood, and decorated their braves' clothing with beadwork" (Renner 1974:60). This characterization of the Indian division of labor was generally true for tribes within pronghorn range, but not always and not everywhere (see Landes 1968). Oil painting, "Bringing Home the Meat," by Charles M. Russell; photo courtesy of the Amon Carter Museum, Fort Worth, Texas.

deer and pronghorn were butchered in the same basic manner, using natural disarticulations and bone fracturing. Large pieces were deboned to facilitate transportation (Yohe 1984). Inasmuch as a whole bison could be butchered within an hour by a skilled Indian using a flint knife (Turney-High 1937), several pronghorn probably could be processed within the same time frame.

The distance of the kill from camp often determined how much meat was consumed at the kill or butchering site versus how much was taken to camp for further processing and preservation. Many seminomadic hunters simply moved their camp to the kill site, often engorging themselves on the hard-

earned abundance. Pronghorn killed near a village or campsite generally were taken there for further butchering. The horseless Northern Paiute stripped back the skin a few inches from the hooves, and with this the hind and forelegs were tied so that the skin formed a tumpline that was supported by the shoulders (Fowler 1989). Each hind leg was tied to a foreleg and then all four legs were tied together and placed over the head and shoulders of the carrier. If a Hidatsa was to transport a pronghorn carcass some distance by horse, it was only partially dismembered, the parts tied together by thongs and slung over the back of the horse, which was protected by deerskin, hair side down (Weitzner 1979).

COOKING AND PRESERVING

Many writers indicated that Indians generally preferred bison meat to any other, but took pronghorn and other ruminants for their skins or for meat when bison were scarce. Among these Indians were Assiniboine (Denig 1961), Crow (Marquis 1975), Gros Ventre (Flannery 1953), Kiowa (Marriott 1968) and Mescalero Apache (Opler 1969).

Difficult to transport or unprocessable food portions, such as the liver, entrails, blood, lower legs and even heads (including brains) of freshly killed pronghorn, were eagerly consumed on the spot (Clark 1884, Fowler 1989). Leg bones were roasted and cracked to obtain the relished marrow. Final butchering began when the meat arrived at a village or camp. The pronghorn's tongue might be eaten by the successful Hopi hunter and his immediate family, then the tedious work of preserving the meat by drying in the sun or smoke-drying for several days commenced (Beaglehole 1936). Fat and tallow were dried in the shade and saved for future consumption.

Kiowas (Marriott 1963) and Surprise Valley Paiutes (Kelly 1932) roasted pronghorn meat on a green stick over an open fire or stone boiled it. Yavapai cooking methods included boiling in pots, stone boiling in a rock hole or barrel cactus, roasting in coals or ashes, cooking in an earthen oven or parching with coals in a basket (Gifford 1936).

Until they acquired copper or iron pots from traders, Comanche women cooked meat in water in bison paunches, heating by immersing hot stones in the water because a fire could not be built directly under the containers (Wallace and Hoebel 1952). Kettles were placed over open fires, and all sorts of meats were dumped in and stewed or boiled. The contents were stirred periodically with the broad rib of a bison.

The bones of large animals often were pounded into fragments and put into a big kettle for prolonged boiling. The marrow fat was skimmed off and, upon cooling and solidifying, it was cut into chunks and packed into rawhide bags. It was eaten as a cold delicacy. Taken with dried lean meat, in alternate bites, a marrow fat feast was comparable to one of roast rib or dried tongue.

Pemmican and dried meats were eaten throughout the year. The Surprise Valley Paiutes also mixed pounded dried meat with tallow, making pemmican, and stored it in tule bags beneath rocks and earth to deter animal depredations. Although such meat could be eaten without further cooking, it usually was roasted on coals or boiled with roots, grains, berries, etc. (Kelly 1932). Of game not eaten fresh, Crow Indians dried and pounded the meat into a fibrous meal, which was stuffed into intestines or parfleches (Marquis 1974).

Drying meat greatly reduced its weight and volume and, by lowering its moisture content, deterred spoilage. According to Weltfish (1977), a bison bull whose live weight was 2,000 pounds (907 kg) could be reduced to 80 pounds (36 kg) of dried meat. Dried pronghorn meat weighed only about one-tenth of its fresh weight, and an adult pronghorn yielded about 5 pounds (2.3 kg) of highly concentrated meat (Frison 1971).

INDIAN USES OF PRONGHORN

The course, brittle hair of the antelope is used for pillows, the tanned skin for the uppers of moccasins, and the shin bone is made into a pipe. The meat at certain seasons is highly prized, and the liver sprinkled with a little gall is eaten hot; i.e., before the animal heat has dissipated after the killing. The brains are usually cooked by roasting the entire head, the horns being broken off before the head is placed on the coals.
—Clark (1884:32)

Considerably smaller and somewhat less hardy than bison or elk, the pronghorn was not the Indian "commissary" that the other species, particularly bison, represented. Nevertheless, it served the natives as food and fiber and in a variety of ways nearly equal to the larger fauna. The following categories and items indicate the scope of pronghorn utilization, but neither is comprehensive (McHugh 1972:285).

Meat

As stated earlier, pronghorn meat seldom was a mainstay source of protein to Indian tribes. Where common, bison provided the bulk of Indian diets, as succinctly summarized by Barsness (1985:104): "most Plains Indians seldom ate deer, elk or pronghorn when bison meat was available." Generally, in arid areas where bison did not roam, lagomorphs provided a greater meat source than did pronghorn. In other parts of pronghorn range, other game invariably was the primary animal food (McCabe 1982, 2002). However, pronghorn meat was seasonally or locally important, besides providing dietary diversification at all times. "The flesh and other edible parts of most animals hunted . . . [on the central plains and eastern Plateau]," wrote Flannery (1953:59), "were appreciated if there happened to be a dearth of buffalo, or as a welcome change during the winter months from the dried buffalo meat. . . . So far as additional meat is concerned . . . elk, deer, and antelope were the most important."

Dodge (1885:274) wrote that "The Indian is an enormous feeder." In the course of a night of feasting, dancing and story telling, according to Dodge, an average Indian would consume from 10 to 15 pounds (4.5–6.8 kg) of meat; if he had an abundance of food and could select the parts to be eaten, he ingested not less than 20 pounds (9.1 kg). The Indian diet and reported gluttony has been examined fairly extensively. According to geography and seasonal diversity of foods, estimates of average daily rations of meat range from 2 to 10 pounds (0.9–4.5 kg) (see Irving 1835, Thompson 1916, Chittenden 1935, Phillips and Smurr 1961, Wissler 1966, McCabe 2002). For Indians within the historic range of pronghorn, the 3-pound (1.4 kg) per person daily average is accepted conservatively (see Table 1).

Skins

Many accounts concerning Indian uses of animal hides did not distinguish between articles made of deer hide versus pronghorn hide. A notable exception was that of Dodge (1877:203). "Unlike those of deer, which are so useful in thousands of ways, the skins of antelope are thin, porous, and weak. They are of little value, and are rarely preserved, except by the poorest of the pot-hunters, who, after taking the hair off, sometimes attempt to sell them as buckskins. The Indians make use of them for fringes and ornamental work."

Dodge's assessment of pronghorn skins probably is shared by most hunters today. However, his view was not necessarily held by those Indians or others beyond his familiarity, as evidenced by the widespread use of pronghorn hide for clothing and other purposes. In comparison with hides of other prominent ungulates in the West, that of pronghorn is relatively "thin, porous, and weak," as Dodge indicated. However, it also is easier to treat and ultimately softer, thinner and more supple for certain articles, particularly clothing (Table 13).

In the domestic economy of Indians in pronghorn range, skins were among the most valued and useful property, and later became principal trading assets. Hide articles constituted nearly half of their earthly possessions (Hodge 1910). Every kind of skin large enough to be stripped from any carcass was used by

TABLE 13. Selected references to Indian uses of pronghorn skin

Tribe or area	Remarks	Reference
Apache	Maternity belts from combined skins of deer, mountain lion and pronghorn because these animals bore their young easily	Curtis (1907 [1])
Apsaroke	Men's leggings with broad fringed flaps at sides; long hair of chief rolled up in a bag of pronghorn skin; moccasins	Curtis (1909 [4])
Assiniboine, Blackfoot, Crow, Gros Ventre, Mandan, Western Sioux and various plateau tribes	Men's shirts before 1840, but worn only by tribal leaders for ceremonies	Koch (1977)
Atsina	Men's shirts and leggings	Curtis (1909 [5])
Blackfoot	Head skin with ears on created odd-looking caps for men, leggings and gowns for women; the latter reached below the knees and had no sleeves but a sort of cape or flap reached the elbows; the dress of a bride was white as snow	Grinnell (1962)
Blackfoot	Soft tanned for clothing, pronghorn rawhide strings around bundle containing medicine pipe and a ceremonial dress worn by a sacred woman during the sun dance	McClintock (1968)
California Mission Indians	Pronghorn hide poncho-type shirts	Paterek (1994)
Cayuse	Main garment of women was a long dress of pronghorn or elk skin; breechclouts and early robes of pronghorn skins	Ruby and Brown (1972), Paterek (1994)
Chemehuevi	All of 40 Indians near present-day Needles, CA, wearing shirts in 1776	Euler (1972)

continued on next page

TABLE 13—*continued*

Tribe or area	Remarks	Reference
Cheyenne	Women's dresses, leggings, upper part of mocassins; skins were smoked so garments could easily be softened after being wet; war shirts trimmed along seams with scalps of enemies; covers for war shields; both sexes wore pronghorn robes	Grinnell (1972 [1]) Paterek (1994)
Cheyenne	Two skins/shirt—one front, one back	Mails (1972)
Chinook	Pronghorn hide robes	Paterek (1994)
Cochiti	Strip of gamuza (pronghorn skin) as a bow string; apparently this was for a young boy— would hardly be strong enough for a heavy bow	Lange and Riley (1966)
Comanche	Ornamented men's shirts; some of the 12 bands wore pronghorn skin garments	Wallace and Hoebel (1952), Paterek (1994)
Costanoan	Outerwear of pronghorn hide	Paterek (1994)
Crow	Artistically painted parfleche (rawhide) bags	Marquis (1975)
Dakota	Fresh skins used to disguise a hunter's approach to bison and mask human odor, used in gowns, shirts and leggings	Hill (1979)
Dakota	Whole skin used to make a "smoking sack"	Hill (1979:390)
Great Basin	The supple, tan-and-white hides were soft to the touch and had many uses	Maxwell (1978)
Great Basin	Fremont-style moccasins made from three pieces cut from foreleg of pronghorn; preferred hides were bighorn, pronghorn and deer	Paterek (1994)
Great Plains	"So worked down that they are almost as thin and white as cotton cloth"	Dodge (1885:255)
Great Plains	"Sunday-best appearance"	Koch (1977:105)
Gros Ventre	Chief wearing jacket with porcupine decorations and fringes of slashed leather and a mesh of horse or human hair	de Trobriand (1951)
Gros Ventre or Arikara	Tunic with fringes of animal hair	de Trobriand (1951)
Gros Ventre	Most clothing from deer, elk and pronghorn skins	Flannery (1953)
Gros Ventre	Preferred skin for breechclouts during warm weather, beaver skin in winter	Flannery (1953)
Havasupai	Dressed surplus skins and traded to other tribes	Goddard (1975)
Hopi	Skins especially important for ceremonial costumes, unblemished skins particularly valued	Beaglehole (1936)
Hopi	Rattle used by the Antelope Order at dances, made like a small drum covered with pronghorn skin stretched very tightly and containing dry kernels of corn	Stephen (1940)
Mandan	Chief's shirt ornamented with many-colored porcupine quills	de Trobriand (1951)
Mandan	Basket cover during certain ceremonies	Bowers (1965)
Mandan	"Maker's" apron, which fell from waist to ankles, was worn during ceremonies	Curtis (1909 [5])
Northern Plains	Daughters of the chiefs in white dresses of pronghorn skin	Parker (1842)
Oglala Sioux	Women's dresses with long fringes around bottom, drum heads	Unrau (1979)
Omaha	Ceremonial pipe with eagle plume attached by pronghorn-skin string	Parker (1954)
Paiute (Northern)	Women's dresses with long fringes around bottom	Walker (1978)
Pawnee	Too small to make dresses for women and shirts for men	Haines (1976)
Plains Apache	Light garments, containers for personal possessions and small utilitarian cases	Terrel (1975)
Plateau tribes	Pronghorn hide moccasin uppers	Paterek (1994)
San Joaquin Valley	Women's petticoats in 1776	Gifford and Schenck (1926–1928)
Shoshone	"The warrior wore a leather tunic—a sleeveless shirt made of six layers of antelope hide; between the layers was often spread a mixture of sand and glue held in place by quilting."	Paterek (1994:197)
Shoshone (Eastern)	Close-fitting legging with flaps rather than fringe; winter robes	Paterek (1994)
Shoshone (Northern)	Robes, often with hair on for ornamentation or warmth	Trenholm and Carley (1964)
Shoshone (Western)	Men wore thigh-length pronghorn hide shirts in cooler weather	Paterek (1994)
Sioux	Warriors' dress clothes included leggings of very white fringed pronghorn skin and a long, wide chemise of the same with all of its edges fringed	McDermott (1970)
Sioux (Yanktonia)	Leggings trimmed with hair locks from scalped victims	Bancroft-Hunt (1992)
Sioux (Yanktonia)	Chief's jacket ornamented with porcupine quills of different colors	de Trobriand (1951)
Ute	Skins beautifully prepared for clothing; the hair always removed; women's wrap-around skirts and dresses	Dodge (1877) Paterek (1994)
Western Woods Cree	Men's shirts hanging to about middle of the thigh	Curtis (1928 [18])

Some of these references are just to pronghorn, others are to pronghorn in combination with bighorn, deer or elk.

some tribe or another, but those in most general use were from the beaver, bison, deer, elk and pronghorn. Along the Little Bighorn River in Montana during the 1830s, Miller (1985:47) reported that: "Open stretches of prairie were dotted with fresh-killed antelope hides, pegged out to dry in the sun."

HISTORY

Apache women made maternity belts of deer, mountain lion and pronghorn skins because those animals were thought to easily give birth to their young. The women believed that by wearing such belts, their own deliveries might be eased. Photo from Edward Curtis (1907 [1]:38).

Skins were precious commodities among Indians of the Great Basin, where the infrequency of taking large game placed a premium on them (Steward 1938). Articles manufactured from skin were well cared for, mended and reused. An abundance of skin articles, especially those made into clothing, represented wealth and brought prestige to the successful hunter and his family.

Pronghorn skins usually were tanned, using animal brains, boiled or roasted, pulverized and mixed with hot water to make a sudsy liquid in which the skin was thoroughly soaked for 1 to 2 days (Fowler 1989). The skin was then hung over a tree limb and laboriously twisted with a stick to remove as much water as possible. Later, it was spread in the sun, worked by hand, dried, rubbed with a rough rock and perhaps smoked over a smoldering fire to make it pliable. Skins that were to be used with the hair on

were tanned by burying in dampened earth for 24 to 36 hours, then removed and rubbed with a concoction of brains, water and sagebrush-bark fibers. The inner surface was rubbed with stones and finally scraped in the sun.

According to Koch (1977:105), "Bison hides gave warmth [presumably as robes and tipi coverings]; antelope and mountain sheep skins produced a Sunday-best appearance; deer and elk skins provided durability for daily wear." While with Indians of the Upper Missouri River in 1843, John James Audubon received a gift of a pronghorn hide robe decorated with 56 elk tusks (Audubon and Bachman 1851).

As previously noted, pronghorn heads and skins were widely used as stalking disguises against bison and other pronghorn.

Bones

Besides providing relished marrow, pronghorn bones were made into tools and toys (Table 14). All too frequently, pronghorn bone tools found at archaeological sites were classified generally as deer. Only occasionally is further classification made.

Red-pigmented pronghorn bones have been recovered from archaeological sites. At Spring Creek Cave, Wyoming, for example, a section of rib bone, so colored, was found (Frison 1965). Such bones are thought to have had some religious significance.

Members of the Cheyenne Elk Society had an elk antler carved like a rattlesnake as their emblem. Grooves were cut about 0.5 inch (1.3 cm) apart on the snake's back. Rubbing the shin (cannon) bone of a

Pronghorn bone awls (central plains tribe), probably used to punch holes in hides being made into garments. Photo by Steve Harmon; courtesy of the Union Pacific Railroad Museum, Omaha, Nebraska.

pronghorn backward and forward over the snake's back produced a loud, raspy sound. When accompanied by ceremonial singing and dancing, the noise supposedly charmed herds of game to approach the Indians' camps (Hoebel 1960).

Hooves and Horns

Horn sheaths and their bony cores served a number of purposes (Table 15). See Table 9 concerning horn sheaths in disguises worn by hunters while stalking pronghorn. Pronghorn hooves frequently were used for decoration or other purposes (Table 16).

Hair

Hair was an extremely useful material to the Indians. It generally was more available than were vegetable fibers. Hair was obtained from many mammals, including pronghorn (Hodge 1907). Pronghorn hair is hollow and fairly long; thus, it has excellent insulating and cushioning properties. Also, it is easily plucked from the skin.

TABLE 14. Selected references to Indian uses of pronghorn bones

Tribe or area	Remarks	Reference
Arizona, near Vernon	Awl from ulna, found during dig in eastcentral part of state	Martin and Rinaldo (1960)
Blackfoot	Girls played "hiding bones" game with beautifully carved and decorated pronghorn bones	McClintock (1968)
Cheyenne	First pipes made of cannon bone, just the straight, hollow bone with hole drilled on top at one end and wrapped in sinew to prevent splitting	Stands in Timber and Liberty (1967)
Comanche and Kiowa	Straight pipes from cannon bones	Wallace and Hoebel (1952)
Dakota	"Foot bone game" using the fingerlike bone from the ankle	Hill (1979)
Flathead and Pawnee	Straight pipes from cannon bones	Clark (1884)
New Mexico, southwestern	Indians made awls from metatarsal and metapodial bones	Kidder et al. (1949)
Sioux	Straight pipes from cannon bones	Cook (1923)

TABLE 15. Indian uses of pronghorn horns

Tribe or area	Remarks	Reference
Absaroke (Crow)	A pole tipped with horn sheath used in a hoop and pole game	Curtis (1909 [4])
Baja California, Mexico	Sheaths used to make fish hooks in 1803	Bernabéu (1994) in Cancino and Reygadas (1999)
Cheyenne	Sheath with hole drilled in prong was filled with magical plants by medicine man and tied with thongs around neck of young war pony to supernaturally fortify it during training; thongs were loosened as pony grew	Grinnell (1923)
Cheyenne	Soldier band called Crazy Dogs wore bonnets ornamented with sheaths and eagle feathers	Koch (1977)
Chiricahua	Medicine cap features sheaths	Mails (1974)
Isleta, NM	Horns set into pueblo walls for hanging clothes and other things	Ellis (1979)
Point of Pines, AZ	Abundant cores suggest they were found afield and carried to village; possibly of ritualistic significance or good luck pieces	Stein (1963)
Unspecified	Sheaths cut and strung as rattles, used by dancers and singers or hung so babies could play with them	Loud and Harrington (1929)

TABLE 16. Indian uses of pronghorn hooves by tribe when tribe is given

Tribe or area	Remarks	Reference
Arapaho	Strung together as rattles and suspended in cradles as toys	Hilger (1952)
Arapaho	Ring and pin game: a pin was attached by a thong to a hoof—the object was to spear perforations in the hoof with the pin by flipping with the wrist	Marriott (1963)
Blackfoot	Hung from dress of medicine man	Catlin (1973)
Cheyenne	Elk Society revealed membership by carrying hoof or horn rattles	Hoebel (1960)
Comanche	Shaman used sticks decorated with hooves to execute communal hunts	Mails (1972)
Mandan	Shaman's staff strung with grizzly bear claws and hooves with ermine, sagebrush and bat's wings all perfumed with the odor of skunk; bison-hide shields with edges decorated with hooves	Catlin (1973)
Mandan	Women's dresses decorated with hooves	Will and Spinden (1906)
Not specified	Boiled to procure glue; one use was to bind pigments to stone	Steward (1929)

Pronghorn hooves were widely used for decoration and instruments. When removed and dried, the hooves curled and hardened. Strung together, they produced a castanet-like rattling sound. Such collection could be the primary intent, as with the Nez Perce rattle lakat (top left), a desirable secondary characteristic, as with the Lakota necklace (top right), which also includes carved deer hooves. A noise effect also was produced by the Shoshone man's eagle quill and pronghorn "toes' ornament (lower left), but whether the primary intent was musical or decorative is unknown. At lower right is an example of a Paiute woman's skirt, with fringe and pronghorn hoof beads. Top left and bottom photos courtesy of the Smithsonian Institution Department of Anthropology, Washington, DC. Top right photo courtesy of the North Dakota State Historical Society, Bismarck.

Pronghorn horn headdresses, often augmented with skins and feathers, were symbols of rank, authority or fraternal association. Wets It (top left), an Assiniboine chief, wears such a bonnet. Top right is a Chiricahua Apache warrior's headdress. A Crow (Absaroke) medicine man is depicted (bottom left) holding a number of instruments that were used one at a time to treat specific maladies. On the healer's head is a plumed headdress featuring pronghorn horns. Top left photo courtesy of the Library of Congress, Washington, DC. Top right photo courtesy of the Museum of American Indian, Heye Foundation, New York, New York. Bottom left illustration from Mails (1972).

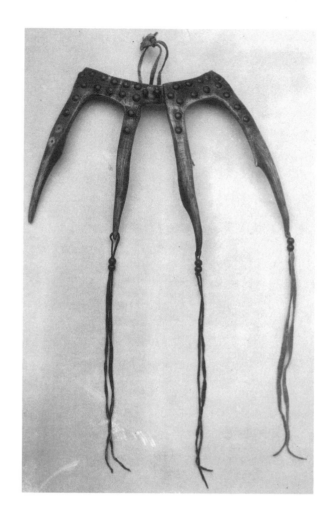

Two distinctly different uses of pronghorn by geographically distant Indians. Above is a pronghorn horn arrow straightener, used by Zia Indians, a small Keresan-speaking Pueblo on Jemez River, a Rio Grande tributary, about 30 miles (48.3 km) north of Albuquerque, New Mexico. At right is a pronghorn horn neck ornament ostensibly used in dance ceremonies by Tenino Indians around Warm Springs, Oregon. Left photo courtesy of the Smithsonian Institution Anthropology Department, Washington, DC. Right photo courtesy of the Museum of the American Indian, Heye Foundation, New York, New York.

Skin pads stuffed with pronghorn hair were used instead of saddles by some of the plains tribes when running bison and in war (Hodge 1907, Boller 1972). Hill (1979) mentioned a Dakota who stuffed a skin with pronghorn hair to make an armrest. Grinnell (1972) wrote of deerhide pillows filled with pronghorn hair being used by Cheyenne girls from puberty until marriage. One side was embroidered with porcupine quills for show during the day. When a pillow was in use, the head rested on the unornamented side. Flowers of bitter perfume, an aromatic plant, were used in the pillows to lessen the odor of the pronghorn hair.

Some Cheyenne warriors stuffed the space between their war shield and its covering—which infrequently was a well-dressed pronghorn skin—with pronghorn hair (Grinnell 1972). This cushioned the force of an arrow or bullet.

"In a game somewhat similar to modern day soccer, Crow Indian women played . . . hand-and-foot ball using a ball that was a bladder filled with antelope hair (6¾ inches in diameter) enclosed in a network of sinew. The principal object of the game apparently was to keep the ball in motion" (Marriott 1963:707, Culin 1975). Cheyenne women played a somewhat similar game with a deerskin ball filled with pronghorn hair (Miller 1985). Also, during the late 19th century, a tuft of pronghorn hair was mounted on a stick in imitation of the white man's paint brushes (Mails 1972).

Other

Besides its meat (muscle), pronghorn provided a wide array of foods for Indians. For example, even when game was plentiful, the Comanche taste for certain pronghorn organs and parts would be distasteful to most people today (Wallace and Hoebel 1952). When a pronghorn or other large animal was killed, the Comanche hunter and his family gathered about, opened its veins and drank the warm blood. Raw

PREVIOUS PAGE
"Fluehtende Rehe," watercolor by Rudolph Friedrich Kurz, painted in Germany from field sketches made by the artist during 1851 and 1852 in the American West; courtesy of the Berne Museum of Fine Art, Berne, Switzerland.

▲ "The White Castles of the Missouri," summer 1833 watercolor by Karl Bodmer; courtesy of the Joslyn Art Museum, Omaha Nebraska.

▼ "Pronghorn Antelope, Cody, Wyoming," undated oil on canvas by William Robinson Leigh; courtesy of the Thomas Gilerrase Institute of American History and Art, Tulsa, Oklahoma.

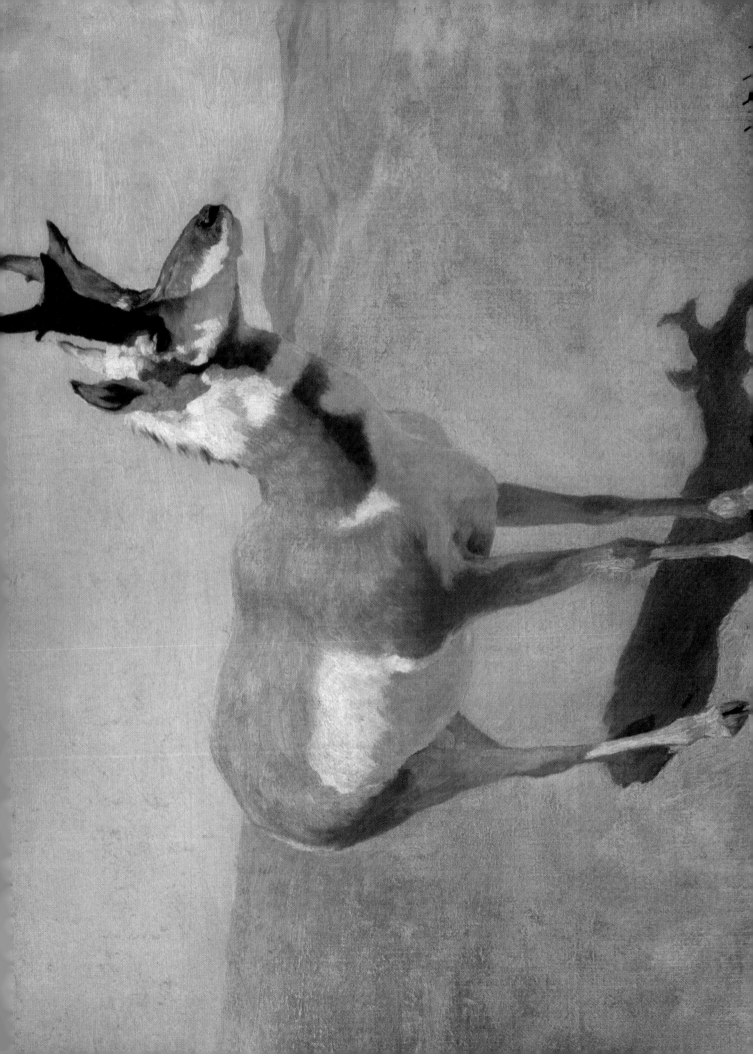

▲ "The Rocky Mountains," 1863 oil on canvas by Albert Bierstadt; courtesy of the Rogers Fund of the Metropolitan Museum of Art, New York, New York.

▼ "In the Foothills," undated oil on canvas by Carl M. Rungius; courtesy of the Buffalo Bill Historical Center, Cody, Wyoming.

▲"Confluence of the Yellowstone and Missouri Rivers," 1833 watercolor by Karl Bodmer; courtesy of the James Jerome Hill Reference Library, St. Paul, Minnesota.

▼"Children of the Sage," 1942 oil on canvas by Carl M. Rungius; courtesy of the Shelburne Museum, Shelburne, Vermont.

▲ "The Last of the Buffalo," 1891 hand-colored engraving by Albert Bierstadt; courtesy of the Amon Carter Museum, Fort Worth, Texas.

▼ "Spring on the Range," undated oil on canvas by Carl M. Rungius; courtesy of the Glenbow Museum, Calgary, Alberta.

WALTER A. WEBER

▲ Untitled, 1962 oil on canvas by F. Lee Jaques; courtesy of Mrs. Junius Bird, Bronx, New York.

▼ "Antelopes," 1892 watercolor by Charles M. Russell, featured in *The Pronghorn Antelope and its Management* (Einarsen 1948) and on loan to The White House from 1980 to 1988; courtesy of The Minneapolis Institute of Arts, Minneapolis, Minnesota.

▲ Untitled and undated oil on paper by Albert Bierstadt; courtesy of Thomas Gilcrease Institute

▼ "Male Antelope," 1890 watercolor by Ernest Thompson Seton; courtesy of the Seton

Top
"Pronghorn Antelope, Rawhide Creek, Wyoming," undated oil on canvas by William Robinson Leigh; courtesy of The Thomas Gilcrease Institute of American History and Art, Tulsa, Oklahoma.

Lower Left
"Head of an Antelope," Fall 1833 watercolor by Karl Bodmer; courtesy of the Joslyn Art Museum, Omaha, Nebraska.

Lower Right
Untitled 1897 unfinished oil painting by Ernest Thompson Seton; courtesy of the Seton Memorial Library, Philmont Scout Ranch, Boy Scouts of America, Cimarron, New Mexico.

brains and the marrow from the leg bones were stirred together on the flesh side of the hide or in a concave dish made by removing a section of the animal's ribs. All were consumed without further preparation. The fresh, warm liver covered with the contents of the gallbladder was considered one of the finest delicacies; children crowded around the butcher begging for it. Liver cooked on coals and spread with marrow also was a choice dish. Entrails stripped of their digesting contents by drawing them between the fingers, kidneys with surrounding fat and the paunch all were eaten raw while still warm and without washing. A Comanche would slash the udder of a doe and, placing his mouth on the gash, suck the warm mixture of milk and blood. Curdled milk from the stomach of a suckling fawn also was a delicacy. The heart generally was left within the skeleton, probably a ceremonial gesture to propitiate the animal's spirit. Although seemingly indelicate from the modern point of view, these pronghorn parts provided Indians with vitamins and iron in large quantities.

U.S. Army Captain James Bourke had the opportunity to dine with Pawnee scouts during the 1876 Powder River campaign. The Pawnee provided pronghorn liver, sliced thin and roasted over hot coals. They roasted pronghorn head in ashes. Bourke (unpublished:21) described the cuisine as "extremely appetizing" and "toothsome," respectively.

Mescalero Apache boys were instructed to take out the heart of their first kill and eat it raw (Opler 1969). Then, they could always kill. The Dakota harvested pronghorn does to obtain milk for motherless Indian babies (Hill 1979). Arapaho and Cheyenne also killed pronghorn does with young and gave the udders to babies to suckle (Grinnell 1972). According to tribal lore, the Kiowa were divided into two factions (Plains Kiowa and Kiowa Apache) because of a pronghorn udder (Mooney 1898). The legend told that a dispute between two headmen who coveted the delicacy grew into an angry quarrel and caused the split.

Referring to protohistoric tribes of the central and northern plains, Marquis (1975:169) wrote that "Veal meat was favored by Indians. They liked best the unborn young—buffalo, elk, deer, antelope or other animal" (see also Haley 1997).

Nearly all inedible parts of the pronghorn had utility. Pronghorn sinew served as strings for bows

An unusual pronghorn-part artifact was the above Paiute pendant, with the lower palates and teeth of young pronghorn. Photo courtesy of the Smithsonian Institution Department of Anthropology, Washington, DC.

and for sewing. Dakotas used sinews (tendons) of the long muscles along the backbones of pronghorn for sewing beads and quills on moccasins (Hill 1979), and the Assiniboine used such sinews to sew bison robes together (Hewitt 1970). Marrow from pronghorn long bones was rubbed on sunburned or chapped lips, hands, arms and legs, as well as on scratches (Fowler 1989). A Sioux doctor's medicine pouch was made of four pronghorn ears and had a buckskin top, the whole being decorated with wrapped quill bands and done in typical Sioux colors and patterns (Densmore 1918, Miller 1985). Piegan Blackfeet mixed pronghorn dung with tobacco seeds before planting them (Curtis 1911).

Cheyennes and other Indians dug pits in which to hide on high ridges and covered them with branches to catch eagles by their legs for their feathers. Usually, a deer or pronghorn fawn was tied on top as bait (Stands in Timber and Liberty 1967). It was not made clear whether the fawns were alive or dead.

Another use was inciting a rattlesnake to strike a piece of pronghorn liver, which then was allowed to putrefy (Thomas 1983). When a poisoned arrow was needed, the head was thrust into the festering green liver (Hodge 1907, Benavides 1945). Such arrowheads were specially knapped to fragment in the enemy.

This antelope altar was photographed about 1900 by Sumner W. Matteson. It had been drawn and reconstructed from memory by Fewkes (1897a, 1897b), when he was not allowed to photograph it. Antelope Society rituals were enacted before this altar, which was embellished with two pronghorn buck heads along with other religious paraphernalia. Photo from Voth (1903).

Regarding this practice by the Maidu, Kroeber (1976:417) wrote: "The septic effect of such a preparation is likely to have been much greater than the toxic." This statement seemingly could apply to most of the concoctions reported. Also for arrow poison, the Gabrielino used boiled down gall (Kroeber 1976), and Shoshones used decayed spleens (Wheeler 1923), but the sources may have been deer or pronghorn.

Pronghorn heads had a special religious significance, and hunters sometimes bestowed them as gifts. Dorsey and Voth (1901), who reported on the Soyal Ceremony at Oraibi, a Hopi pueblo in northeastern Arizona, described the display of two large buck heads on the ritualistic antelope altar.

CAPTIVE PRONGHORN

Motecuhzoma's zoo in his capital, Tenochtitlan, was one of the many marvels of the Aztec empire seen and described by Spaniards in 1520 (Loisel 1912). Its col-

lection of animals far exceeded those of any contemporary European zoo, and a staff of 300 keepers cared for its captives. It is not surprising that pronghorn, inhabitants of the Valley of Mexico, were among the animals displayed there (Fisher 1967).

Farther north, most captured pronghorn fawns probably were eaten immediately. They, like fetuses, were prized for tenderness and taste, but did not represent a significant amount of food, so their removal in springtime to camp or village from a kill site probably was unnecessary and unlikely. Indians occasionally captured very young fawns and reared them to adulthood or nearly so, at which time, the animals were killed and eaten (Goldschmidt 1951). Such custom probably was most common among sedentary tribes, such as pueblo-dwellers, and semisedentary tribes that had regular supplies of other foods and few dogs. However, there are reliable reports of pronghorn pets among tribes of the central and northern plains. In fact, Thaddeus Culbertson (1952), a trav-

Tom Lovell's painting "Comanche Moon" shows a successful Comanche war party returning home. In the village is a pronghorn fawn tethered to a tent pole. Shown, too, are dogs and youngsters with bows who, in all likelihood, would not have made the pronghorn's captivity especially lengthy or pleasant. Painting by Tom Lovell; courtesy of the Abell-Hanger Foundation and the Permian Basin Petroleum Museum, Library and Hall of Fame, Midland, Texas.

eler to the upper Missouri River in 1850, told of seeing an Indian woman suckle a pronghorn fawn. He was informed that it was quite common for Indian women, in this manner, to nourish young animals, even grizzly cubs. Hill (1979, personal communication: 1983) was told the same for the Lakota, with inference that such nursing was done not only to feed the neonates, but sometimes to ease or sustain lactation.

"The Blackfeet make pets of all kinds of birds and wild animals," wrote McClintock (1968:246). "In former days they tamed and kept in the tepees cranes, hawks, eagles, wolves, antelopes, and even grizzly bears."

PETROGLYPHS AND PICTOGRAPHS

These pictures on skin, bark, and stone, crude in execution as they often are, yet represent the first artistic records of ancient, though probably not of primitive, man. In them lies the germ of achievement which time and effort have developed into the masterpieces of modern eras.

—Hodge (1910:245)

For years researchers used what I call the "gaze and guess" approach to interpreting rock art—look at a painting and surmise what it seems to be about. Without understanding the people who made the art, that method yields predictably wrong interpretations. It's like trying to understand Shakespeare without having a firm grasp of the English language.

—Lewis-Williams (2001:119)

Animal representations in the form of petroglyphs and pictographs appear in hundreds of North American caves and rockshelters and on exposed rock cliffs and walls. In his early overview, Mallery (1893) referred to Indian rock art as "picture-writing." Petroglyphs (three-dimensional) are created by incising a design into a comparatively smooth and even rock surface, usually vertical, by pecking with a hammerstone or scratching with a scraper (Steward 1929). Pictographs (two-dimensional) are formed by painting a design onto the rock surface; pigment usually is bonded with an adhesive. Pictographs generally are sharper in outline and have more detail and color than petroglyphs. Unfortunately, they are less enduring.

FIGURE 15. *Pictographs by Cloud-Shield (left and right) and American-Horse (center), both Oglala Sioux, are separate winter count records of major, successful drives of pronghorn to corrals or pens in 1828–29 (left and center) and 1860–61 (right) (from Mallery 1893).*

Hodge (1910) believed the use of pictographic signs in the United States reached its highest development among the Kiowa and the Dakota tribes in their "calendars." These paintings on bison, deer and pronghorn skins constituted a chronology of past years (Figure 15). The "winter count" of Iron Shirt, leader of the Blackfoot clan of Grease Melters and later head chief of the Blackfeet, included "the winter, when the antelopes broke through the ice," and "the winter, when we caught antelope in the deep snow" (McClintock 1968:422–423). The exact years of these winters were not detailed.

The number of unquestionable pronghorn in Indian rock art throughout the West is small when compared with the thousands of bighorn, deer and other animals clearly portrayed. Supposed pronghorn petroglyphs have been found near The Dalles, Oregon, adjoining the Columbia River (Strong and Schenck 1925). Among California images interpreted as pronghorn are pictographs found in Pleito Canyon, Kern County, along the San Antonio River, Monterey County, and near Porterville, Kern County (Steward 1929). Likewise, a fanciful rock art image from Cimarron County, Oklahoma, is thought to depict a bounding pronghorn (Lawton 1962).

The striking petroglyphs of Dinwoody Canyon in the northeastern Wind River Mountains of western Wyoming are notable because they include bear, bighorn, elk, mountain goat, mule deer and pronghorn (Gebhard and Cahn 1950). The inclusion of the pronghorn is interesting because the species surely did not occur in those extremely rugged mountains. Its memory must have been brought from the plains to the east.

A collection of Indian rock art stretches along a 1-mile (1.6 km) segment of the Milk River in southern Alberta, within the Writing-On-Stone Provincial Park (Keyser 1977). Several pronghorn are among the likenesses of 12 species of animals made by incising, scratching, abrading and pecking of the sandstone walls (Figure 16).

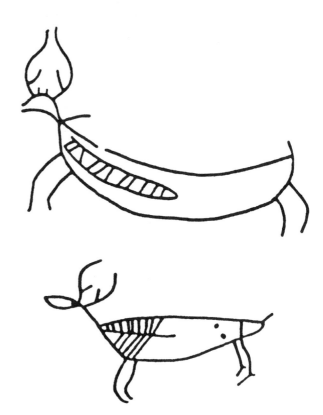

FIGURE 16. *Two of the four boat-shaped zoomorphs identified pronghorn images on sandstone in Writing-On-Stone Provincial Park, along the Milk River in southern Alberta (from Keyser 1977). Many intended pronghorn petroglyphs, at the park and elsewhere, lack or have lost their diagnostic characters.*

Plains Indians recorded major annual events by depictions on large skins (top left)*. These pictographic calendars were called winter counts. Most documented seminal events in a tribe's annual cycle, but some were individual histories and invariably were signed by the artist with his name symbol. The line attachment of the symbol to the person was a relatively primitive signature* (see Figure 17 for *symbol for an Indian named Antelope Dung*)*. The remarque-type signature figure, such as at the top right—for Hunkpapa Sioux chief Running Antelope—is characterized by artistic elements that show considerable Euro-American influence. Painted in 1873, not as a winter count but for a white benefactor, the autobiographical watercolor scene above* (1 of 11) *depicts an 1853 event, called "killed two Arikara." Alexander Gardner's 1872 photo of Running Antelope* (bottom right) *was selected as the image for the 1899 U.S. $5.00 silver certificate* (bottom left) *(see Daniel 1969). The stereotype also was used on the Indian head nickel. On the certificate, Running Antelope* (born 1821, died 1896 or 1897) *is shown wearing a plains chief's headdress that was photographed in 1899 by Thomas Smillie.* Top left photo by John A. Anderson, courtesy of the Nebraska State Historical Society, Lincoln. Top right photo from Mallery (1893), courtesy of the Smithsonian Institution Anthropological Archives, Washington, DC. Bottom photos courtesy of the Smithsonian Institution Anthropological Archives, Washington, DC.

The relative scarcity of pronghorn petroglyphs has several explanations. First, most zoomorphs are unidentifiable to species, and perhaps some were intended as pronghorn. Also, the major diagnostic character—the short bifurcated horn with the inferior forward-projecting prong, situated just anterior of rather large ears—does not lend itself to detailed portrayal on coarsely grained rock. Furthermore, some authorities believe that taboos deterred the portrayal of certain species, such as the bison (Dewdney 1964) and perhaps the pronghorn. The extraordinarily abundant and distinctive bison appears in relative scarcity when compared with bighorn and deer. Also, aboriginal drawings of big game may be related to hunting magic. In Nevada, rock paintings invariably were on game trails or near springs where ambushing and driving were possible. Beyond that, Grant (1967) expressed belief that drawings were mainly of hard-to-get animals. Easy-to-come-by game seldom was pictured. The hunter need not draw rabbits or pronghorn, both easy to procure in communal drives.

A petroglyph of undetermined age near the Desierto de Vizcaino on the Baja Peninsula, which appears to depict a pronghorn buck. The vertical line protruding from the animal may represent a spear or, more likely, indicated that the figure was a spirit animal. Photo by Jorge Cancino, Chinle, Arizona.

DECORATION

The pronghorn motif frequently is encountered in ancient Indian art, especially in the southwestern United States, where communal pueblo living and agriculture enabled religion and art to flourish.

Antelope Cave, in Canyon del Muerto of northern Arizona, is named for a procession of life-size pronghorn painted across the face of a nearly inaccessible cliff by a Navajo artist about 1805. The animals are attractively rendered in tawny red with white rumps and black horns, hooves and noses (Morris 1940).

Holmes (1884) catalogued clay artifacts collected from the Zuni in 1881 for the Smithsonian Institution. Among them were eight ollas (water jugs), each decorated with one or more pronghorn. A bowl for food storage, made by the Lagunas of northcentral New Mexico, measures 20 inches (51 cm) deep and 22 inches (56 cm) wide; a procession of painted pronghorn encircles it (Curtis 1926).

CLANS, SOCIETIES AND KACHINAS

Various tribes named bands, clans or societies for familiar animals, including the pronghorn (Table 17). Antelope was one of the larger bands of the Comanches. It was so named because it frequented the prairie country and staked plains of Texas (Wallace and Hoebel 1952). It was Quannah Parker's band—the last Comanche band to surrender, in 1874.

The Hopi were divided into social phratries (groups of clans within a tribe), consisting of numerous clans with distinct legends and ceremonies. Antelope was one of the 12 in the east mesa villages (Hodge 1907). Antelope clans or societies existed in at least eight pueblos (White 1932).

Pueblo Indians developed complex, ritualistic societies having elaborate accompanying ceremonies, including dances and songs. Many evolved around the mystical kachina. Kachinas are supernatural beings having bodies and limbs like humans but with heads of a shape and design, often imitative of animals, including bear, deer and pronghorn. According to White (1962), the kachina (formerly, katsina) complex represents a word, concept and masked im-

Antelope House (left) is a renowned cliff house of the ancient Anasazi. Located in Canyon del Muerto, within Canyon de Chelly National Monument in northeastern Arizona, the communal dwelling reportedly was named for pronghorn rock art, including the image above, on nearby walls. Photos courtesy of the U.S. National Park Service.

TABLE 17. Indian bands, clans, phratries, moieties and societies identified as antelope

Kind or group	Pueblo or tribe	Reference
Band	Arapaho	Trenholm (1986)
	Comanche	Wallace and Hoebel (1952)
	Tewa	Curtis (1926 [16])
	Zuni	Parsons (1939)
Clan or society	Acoma	Henderson and Harrington (1914)
		Curtis (1926)
	Arapaho	Bowers (1965)
	Cochiti	Henderson and Harrington (1914)
		Curtis (1926 [16])
	Comanche	Bowers (1965)
	Crow	Bowers (1965)
	Hopi	White (1932)
	Isleta	Henderson and Harrington (1914)
	Mandan	Bowers (1965)
	San Felipe	Henderson and Harrington (1914)
	San Ildefonso	Henderson and Harrington (1914)
	Santo Domingo	Curtis (1926 [16])
	Sia	Henderson and Harrington (1914)
	Zuni	Kroeber (1917)
Moiety	Miwok (waterside)	Kroeber (1976)
	Yokut (Tohelyuwish division)	Kroeber (1976)
Phratry	Hopi	Hodge (1907)

The head of a pronghorn buck is visible on this decorative water jar recovered intact from the old Santa Ana Pueblo along the Jemez River in north-central New Mexico. Such pottery was first produced in the late 18th century. Like the fanciful image of the elk ahead of the pronghorn, the artwork is acknowledged as highly specialized and skilled. Photo courtesy of the Museum of American Indian, Heye Foundation, New York, New York.

At left is a Hopi kachina doll, or tihu, *featuring pronghorn horns. Hopi kachinas are anthropomorphic beings who live in lakes, springs and mountains. There are more than 250 Hopi kachinas (Zunis have their own); they are intermediaries between the Hopi and their gods. Each has its own appearance, male or female and can represent characteristics of other Indian groups or plants or animals (Griffith 1983). Most are benevolent, but they can be dangerous if mistreated. They objectify certain truths and dynamics of life, and have the power to heal, control weather and reinforce religious and social laws by means of positive or negative sanctions (Dockstader 1954). The kachinas visit the villages at different time and, in time past, are believed to have danced in their own forms. In modern times (at least since the 1930s), the kachinas invest impersonators with their spirit (Parsons 1939). Kachina societies, dancers, masks, rituals and ceremonies are complex and highly spiritual as well as entertaining. Kachina dolls are carved figurines representing the masked, ceremonial impersonators of kachina spirits. They are given to children as educational treasures (not toys). Although not sacred objects, their possession has spiritual overtones connected with the particular kachina.* Tihu *usually are presented to females by kachina dancers, to commemorate important events and stages in their lives. Hopis, Navajos and some Zunis now also make the dolls for commercial purposes, but these kachina dolls do not represent authentic kachinas (Hirschfelder and Molin 1992).* Photo courtesy of the Smithsonian Institution Department of Anthropology, Washington, DC.

personation found among all pueblo dwellers of the Southwest. To the Hopi, kachina was the name given supernatural beings who visited the village, the name of a religious function, the name of the participants, and the dance and the mask worn by the celebrants (Dockstader 1985).

Kachinas also have been described as intercessors between man and the highest supernatural beings, thus they are subordinate to the greater gods (Fewkes 1897a). The primary purposes of the kachina and its ritual, according to some, are to bring rain and promote the growth of crops. Anthropologist Adolph Bandelier gave a broader interpretation to the kachina dance, noting that its incantations were invoked for the hunt, warfare or other works of public utility (Anderson 1955).

Kachina masks were constructed of leather, feathers, vegetation and other materials, and then painted to improve their somewhat grotesque appearance.

Pronghorn were impersonated by many Puebloans (White 1932), and the mask was readily identified by its horns. These paganistic objects and rituals were repugnant to early Spaniards, but despite 17th century Catholic missionaries' efforts to obliterate them, they persisted.

SPIRITUALISM

Spiritualism is believed to have infused virtually every aspect of Native American life, and especially their relationships with wild animals (Brown 1992, Harrod 2000). However, in our opinion, no element of aboriginal culture in North America is as fraught with misrepresentation and tendency toward overgeneralization as is native spirituality. It is not appropriate to suggest that Indians felt kinship or spiritual relationship with all animals or invested in them special powers or personifications. However, it may be said that most Indians felt so and did so with some animals, and that animals figured prominently in their amazingly diverse belief systems, including their cosmologies and mythologies (see Snow 1981, Harrod 2000).

It appears that, for many Indians within historic time, certain animals were sources of or vehicles to spirituality, spiritual inspiration, and personal and group identity. Frequently, those same venerated animals also were sources of food, clothing and other material products. At least some Indians saw killing of animals as a willing sacrifice by those animals, and perhaps even a gifting or vesting of the species' innate or symbolic power, which typically was a behavioral manifestation (Martin 1978). Not all Indians held all animals or even the same animals as sacred or in some other spiritual regard, and even of those animals commonly or almost universally accorded supernatural power—such as the coyote, elk, snake, fox, bat, spider and raven—the extent or degree of esteem differed widely among tribes, and especially among regions.

Symbolism

For many, if not most, Indians in the historic West, the pronghorn mainly personified speed, grace, vigilance and elusiveness, although some clearly saw the animal as personification of gullibility. For others, it symbolized good fortune and peace. "While the deer's power may be used for good or for evil, the power of the antelope is all good. To dream about an antelope is fortunate," wrote Grinnell (1972 [2]:104). A pronghorn vision by a Dakota dream seeker was told to represent peace (Hill 1979). To sustain their freedom and culture in the face of invading soldiers, miners and settlers, the Dakota came to believe that "Only fools dream of the pronghorn on earth where the grizzly prowls" (Hill 1979:681).

Lake-Thom (1997:76), a Karuk-Seneca healer and teacher, informed that the pronghorn "serves as a messenger and forewarns us of human behavior," including people's sexual feelings and desires.

Also among some Sioux, the pronghorn was believed to provide protective power during Indian warfare (Walker 1980). A sash worn over a warrior's right shoulder and chest, when decorated with pronghorn

Bead and quill work by plains Indian women reached its artistic zenith during the first decades of reservation life (1875 to 1900), perhaps because many of the traditional duties of women were foregone with the relatively sedentary life style. Above, a Dakota girl, wearing an elk tooth dress, exhibits a very decorative beaded bag. The top image of the bag is thought to be a pronghorn. Before reservation life, Indian women typically produced artwork consisting of abstract patterns rather than real subjects. Note the girl's elaborately beaded moccasins. Photo by Jesse H. Bratley; courtesy of the Smithsonian Institution Anthropological Archives, Washington, DC.

Painting of tepee covers was widespread among plains tribes, but it was not a common practice, at least before reservation days. Painted tepees usually signified the residence or special sanctuary of a chief or spiritual leader, and it featured some geometric design, totem, vision or event of personal significance. The tribes best known to paint tepee covers were the Blackfeet (left) and Kiowa (right), but such artistry was identified among the Assiniboine, Sarcee, Crow, Teton Sioux, Arapaho, Cheyenne and Kiowa Apache (see DeMallie 2001). To the Blackfeet, the alert manner of pronghorn was a favorable trait associated with watching for enemies. No Blackfeet could copy the design of someone else's tepee unless the privilege had been formally transferred or permission received in a dream. Otherwise, it was believed, such infringement would incur sickness or death. Of the painted tepees, there could be more than one pronghorn tepee, but each would be distinct in feature and origin. Representations of bison, beaver, eagles, elk, otter and pronghorn proclaimed the belief that those mammals and birds were endowed with power from the sun and, therefore, the owner and his family would secure from the animal protection against sickness and other misfortune. Thus, a representation of the powerful protector, painted on a tepee cover, was held sacred (McClintock 1968). Left photo taken about 1900, on the Blood Reservation in Alberta; photo courtesy of the National Museum of Canada, Ottawa. The artwork at right is from U.S. Secretary of War (1856); photo courtesy of the Smithsonian Institution Anthropological Archives, Washington, DC.

hoof prints and provided by a shaman, was thought to protect the wearer from wounds. This may account for the painted image of pronghorn on some war shields used by northern plains Indians. According to McClintock (1968), the exemplification in pronghorn of alertness to danger was especially admirable.

Near Woodland in Yoho County, California, a complete pronghorn skeleton was found with two bone basketry awls and clamshell disc beads. Of this enigmatic find, Heizer and Hewes (1940:598) commented that "The mere fact that a whole animal would be buried without being eaten seems significant." Whether it was sacrificed as a food or symbolically stood for some other form of propitiation remains a mystery.

Myths and Beliefs

Native American's myths were more than stories that chronicled the past; they projected perceived truths to prevailing circumstances and future probabilities. Myths served as substance and process of history. They were perpetuated orally through stories, songs and placenames, physically by dances, and visually through a variety of pictographic forms (Reeves and McCabe 1998, McCabe 2002). In other cultures, Native American myths may have been characterized as traditions, religious parables or folklore.

Most Indians had myths to explain the origin of the world, how humans and animals came into being and why certain natural events occurred. One

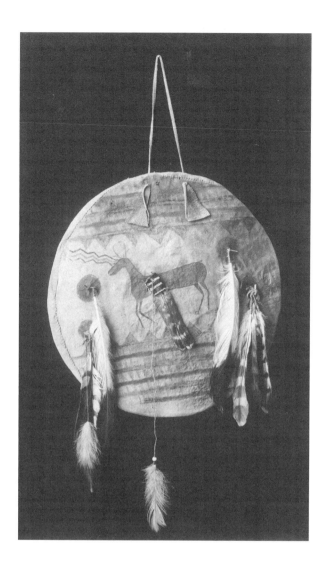

Most war shields used by western Indians were circular and made from the thick neck or chest hide of bull bison or elk. Before they lost favor when firearms became more accessible, shields served in battle to display the owner's source of power and to deflect projectiles. Mails (1972:490) observed that, among plains Indians, "the completed shield was literally infused with prayer and 'power,' and this force could be brought to bear as a wall of defense or to radiate destruction at the enemy." Shields also were widely used in ceremonies, to supplicate or patronize the owner's totem, or simply to exhibit the owner's strengths or medicines or those of his fraternity, clan or cult. The shields of horsemen typically were smaller than those of warriors who lived, traveled and fought with limited or no access to horses. Also, most warriors (such as the Blackfeet) decorated the shield itself, whereas Crow and Sioux put the ornamental designs on separate buckskin covers (Lowie 1982). At left *is a Crow shield, with buckskin cover, featuring a variety of symbolic shapes and attachments. A pronghorn is the central figure—undoubtedly the owner's spirit animal—and the wavy lines to the animal's head indicate supernatural force, probably vision. Above is a bison hide shield from the Santo Domingo Pueblo in New Mexico. It, too, is highlighted by a faded pronghorn, painted yellow. To the Indians who embraced the pronghorn totemically or in other social or personal kinship, the animal represented and shared fleetness, alertness and pertinaciousness. Left photo (#11993) courtesy of the Field Museum, Chicago, Illinois. Right photo courtesy of the Museum of the American Indian, Heye Foundation, New York, New York.*

such pronghorn creation myth of the Navajo, preserved by Franciscans, tells of the "Twelve Antelope" (O'Bryan 1956:94): "First he [Elder Brother] made a torch out of bark and then he started for the plain. When the Twelve Antelope saw him coming they all ran for him, but he lit the torch and touched off the dry grass. The Antelope circled the fire and the rising smoke, and with his weapons he was able to kill eleven of them. He caught just one. He talked to the Antelope and said: All the thoughts and spirits of your comrades have departed from you. Those thoughts will never enter you again. People will use your flesh for meat. Your head, also, will be used by the people. He let the antelope go. Your home will be the plains, he said. Later the people will use the antelope head, called bea da', when they go hunting." This myth explains to the Navajos how the feared pronghorn was reduced to a harmless source of sub-

sistence, why it was forced to live on the plains and why its head was to have both a ritualistic and practical value.

Some pueblo-dwelling Indians of the Southwest believed that the image or manifestation of an animal—captured in dreams, art, ceremony or ceremonial costume—could convey to the image owner, at least temporarily, some of that species' perceived spiritual power. In his 1985 watercolor painting, "The Magic of Her Hands," Robert A. Kercher depicted somewhat the reverse symbolic relationship. By creating the pronghorn images on an earthenware jar (a vessel to hold water), which then was exposed to air and sunlight, the Hopi woman gave her artistic subjects life, power and freedom. That suggests an origin myth (not otherwise found in the literature), but Bob Kercher (personal communication:2003) indicated that such was not his motivation or intent, although many viewers have drawn that and similar conclusions about the scene. Photo courtesy of Robert A. Kercher, Great Falls, Montana.

A second pronghorn creation myth existed among the Hopi (Beaglehole 1936:4): "The Hopi emerged from the Underworld and wandered around from place to place. At last they stopped at Burro Spring. There were many snakes here, however, which fatally bit the children, so that the people were once more obliged to move on. There was one woman in their company who was about to give birth to a child. She managed to accompany the wanderers only as far as Giant's Chair where she remained alone while the others went on to a place by Corn Rock where they decided to stay and build a village. [The n]ext day certain men went back to find out how the woman was getting on. They found that she had given birth to twins, which were like little antelopes with horns on their heads. They also found that the mother had become an antelope as well. Although the three wanted to remain where they were, the Hopi brought them back to the mesa. They were unhappy in the village so the Hopi later sent them back to the place

DIXGI GI, where they made a hole in the ground and let the animals live there. The mother the Hopi called *DIX i i WI XDI*, Mother of all Animals. They gave the antelopes prayer sticks, and have done so ever since so that the antelope and deer may increase in number and be hunted for the good of the Hopi."

Pronghorn also figured in the Mandan creation myth (Smith 1997, Will and Spinden 1906). According to legend, the tribe originally lived underground. One day, while traveling beneath the Earth's surface, the people saw daylight from a hole above and a grapevine hanging down. One of the men climbed the vine, emerged from the hole and saw prairie covered with bison and pronghorn. The man called down the hole and beckoned his tribal members to join him, and many did. Eventually, a large woman started up the vine, but it broke. As a result, half the tribe remained underground, and the Mandan call themselves *ha-a-wak-took-taes*, or "where are they—the wandering tribe" (Smith 1997:53).

The pronghorn also figured in Blackfoot mythology, including that pertaining to the Blackfoot genesis, in which the pronghorn was made out of dirt and turned loose to see how it would go. "It ran so fast that it fell over some rocks and hurt itself. He [the old man] saw that this would not do, and he took the antelope down on the prairie and turned it loose; and it ran away fast and gracefully, and he said, 'this is what you are suited to'" (Grinnell 1962:138).

Other myths featuring the pronghorn include one of the Valley Nisenan about conflicts between Grizzly-bear and Antelope sisters-in-law (Kroeber 1929). A Kamia myth explained the distribution of the bighorn, deer and pronghorn (Gifford 1931). A myth of the Tachi Yokuts explained that, as a result of a race, the antelope (winner) chose to inhabit open country, whereas the deer (loser) was relegated to brushy country (Kroeber 1906–1907). A Kutenai myth tells of a race between the frog and the antelope (Boas 1918). The pronghorn also is a character in the legend titled *Old Grizzly and Old Antelope* (Judson 1910), and it figures in the Ute myth, *A Devil Steals Pigeon-Boy* (Mason 1910). Crow Indian mythology informs that pronghorn as well as bison and deer were given by a god to the Crow for food (Clark 1884), so too for Blackfeet (Grinnell 1962). The Arapaho believed that deceased members of their tribe lived in a far off land in lodges and had "plenty of buffalo, antelope, and all kinds of game" (Clark 1884:32).

Just before reaching the south fork of the Platte River, while traveling west on the Oregon Trail in 1846, Francis Parkman noted that pronghorn were very numerous and bold as they always seemed to be when in the company of bison (Feltskog 1969). One morning, Parkman was summoned to the lodge of an old man, where the old man told a story. "He was one of a powerful family, renowned for warlike exploits. When a very young man he submitted to the singular rite to which most of the tribe subject themselves before entering upon life. He painted his face black; then seeking out a cavern in a sequestered part of the Black Hills, he lay for several days, fasting, and praying to the spirits. In the dream and visions produced by his weakened and excited state he fancied, like all Indians, that he saw a supernatural revelation. Again and again the form of an antelope appeared before him. The antelope is the graceful peace-spirit of the

Ogillallah but seldom is it that such a gentle visitor presents itself during the initiatory fasts of their young men. The terrible grizzly bear, the divinity of war, usually appears, to fire them with martial ardor and thirst for renown. At length the antelope spoke. It told the young dreamer that he was not to follow the path of war; that a life of peace and tranquility was marked out for him; that thence forward he was to guide people by his counsels and protect them from the evils of their own feuds and dissensions. Others were to gain renown by fighting the enemy; but greatness of a different kind was in store for him.

"The visions beheld during the period of this fast usually determine the whole course of the dreamer's life. From that time [the Indian] abandoned all thoughts of war, and devoted himself to the labors of peace. He told his vision to the people. They honored his commission and respected him in his novel capacity" (Parkman 1901:179–180).

Among the Pawnee folk stories was that of how the deer lost his gall (Grinnell 1961). It concerned an argument between deer and pronghorn about which was the fastest animal. They raced on the prairie and the pronghorn won, and took the deer's gall as the victory prize. The deer felt so badly that the pronghorn felt sorry for him and, to cheer him up, took off his own dewclaws and gave them to the deer. Since then, the deer has had no gall and the pronghorn no dewclaws. The Blackfoot tribes had a somewhat similar lodge tale (Grinnell 1961). In it, the pronghorn also won a race on the prairie, but feeling it was not fair, the deer decided that they also should race through timber, a race won by the deer. The pronghorn had originally won the deer's gall, but after the second race the deer took the pronghorn's dewclaws.

MUSIC
Instruments

Music played an important role in Indian life and society, particularly as an adjunct to religious ceremonies. Musical instruments included drums, flutes, whistles, gourds, rattles and notched rasps. Pronghorn skins sometimes were used for drum heads, hooves for rattles and notched scapula for rasps.

The drum was a universal musical instrument among Indians—the accompaniment to religious ceremonies and necessity to social gatherings (Dodge 1885). Primitive drums were cut from trunks of hollow trees. A thin, raw skin was then stretched tightly over one end. When it became loose from continued beating, it was restored by sprinkling water on the skin and shrinking it over a fire. For lengthy ceremonies or at social dances, a fire was always kept for tightening drum heads.

Rattles were made by placing small, smooth stones in a dry gourd (Dodge 1885) or by stringing deer or pronghorn hooves on rawhide thongs (Hilger 1952). Pronghorn horn sheaths also were cut into rattles (Loud and Harrington 1929).

Song

Indian songs tended to be personal or community evocations of love, atonement, supplication or celebration. As with songs of other cultures past and since, they were releases or provocations of emotion. Songs were important elements of shamanism and preparations for pronghorn hunts, as previously noted. At least some were passed from generation to generation. "In a solemn ceremony transferring a medicine pipe from one chief to another, the Blackfeet sang an antelope song and imitated with their hands the motions of an antelope walking while the strings of antelope rawhide were being loosened on a medicine bundle that contained an inner wrapper of elk hide that contained the medicine pipe" (McClintock 1968:262).

The first anthology of Indian songs and chants did not appear until the 20th century. From it, part of the Paiute *Songs of Life Returning*, in which the pronghorn is mentioned, is excerpted (Cronyn 1918:65).

. . . III
A slender antelope,
A slender antelope
He is wallowing upon the ground. . . .

The pronghorn also is mentioned in a hunting song of the Santa Ana Pueblo Indians (White 1942:292):

Let me go to the Yellow Land
Where the antelope fawns are born
And the clouds hover over them
And the rain descends
And the rivers begin to flow.

A Puebloan prehunt song and a pronghorn song sung only with gourd rattle accompaniment were transcribed by Densmore (1957). Blackfeet performed "The Song of the Antelope"—a form of prayer, devotion or supplication (Schultz 1957:76). Apparently referring to the same song, Grinnell (1962:280) wrote that an antelope song was used by Blackfoot healers who simultaneously "closed the hands, leaving the index finger extended and the thumb partly open, and in time to the music . . . alternately touched the wrappers with the tips of the left and right forefinger, the motions being quick and firm, and occasionally brought the hands to the side of the head, making the sign for antelope, and at the same time uttering a loud 'kuh' to represent the whistling or snorting of that

Two of the more popular instruments on the plains were rattles and bone whistles. The beaded Lakota rattle (left) features pronghorn hooves dried, curled and sewn into the leather covering of the rattle handle. These hooves produced the rattling sound. The dried pronghorn hooves on the bone whistle (right), also Lakota, probably were mainly ornamental. Photo courtesy of the Museum of the American Indian, Heye Foundation, New York, New York.

animal." Regarding the Blackfoot sun dance, McClintock (1968) referred to a ceremonial dress of mule deer and pronghorn skins worn by a sacred woman. As the sacred woman dressed, women assistants sang and made signs in imitation of those animals.

Laird (1976) reported that the Chemeuevis, curiously, had no antelope song, but did include pronghorn (as minor characters) in their myths.

Dance

One of the most fascinating North American aboriginal ceremonies was the Snake Dance performed by Hopi males of the Snake and Antelope Societies at Oraibi Pueblo and other villages in northeastern Arizona (Fewkes 1897a, 1897b, Voth 1903).

Thomas and Ronnefeldt (1976:244) considered antelope dancers to be minor characters in a Mandan penitential ceremony. The Mandan held a ritual called the Bull Dance to make atonement for the past and to ask the Great Spirit to bring bison close to their village. The four-day ceremony included dancing, fasts and self-imposed tortures that were public evidence of the Indians' sincerity and faith in the power of the Great Spirit. On the afternoon of the third day, 50 or 60 "antelope" (men and boys entirely naked and painted all over with white clay and with willow twigs bound on their heads in the shape of and to represent horns) became part of the ceremony. The darting about of these individuals among participants and spectators appeared to be a form of comic relief, but the pronghorn's presence was significant because it was widely believed that wherever pronghorn were present, bison certainly were nearby (Boller 1972).

The Rio Grande Pueblos had a bison dance that included 2 men dressed as bison, 4 or 5 dressed as deer, and 12 or more dressed as pronghorn (Strong 1979).

"The Cheyenne had three great tribal ceremonies, including the Massaum or animal dance which was intended to insure the tribe of plenty of meat" (Hoebel 1960:16–17). "In private lodges, various men who have dreamed of some animal acting in a peculiar way got a group of friends ritually to dress up in imitation of this animal. On the fourth day women build a symbolic antelope or buffalo corral—a shaded pen of upright poles with two diverging arms of brush extending out toward the opening of the camp circle.

"Two wolves are the main ritual animal, but on the fifth day other groups may join in—buffalo, elk, deer, foxes, mountain lions, horses, bears, antelope, coyotes, and cranes and blackbirds. The men of each group run, dance, and act like the animal they represent. The animals run about, 'hunted' by members of the bow string society, or contrary warriors, who do things backwards and are the bravest of the brave. In the animal dance, they clown and cut up to the delight of the people watching. Hence, the dance is called the Massaum, derived from *massa'ne*, crazy. At various points, the animals enter the corral, which is just what the Cheyenne want the animals to do when they use this method of hunting. All the mimicry and clowning which occurs on the final day, involves a great deal of high jinks and sporting fun, and is thus a great contrast to the heavy solemnity of the arrow renewal and the strenuous self sacrifice of the sun dance."

ORIENTATION

Direction

Many Indians recognized the zenith and nadir as directions. The Tusaýans (Hopi) assigned "pets" to each of the six directions, designating the pronghorn to the Tatyuka direction, or south (Fewkes 1897b).

The Zuni also used six points of orientation, each with its own color and hierarchal position (Benedict 1935, Tedlock 1972). Six game animals had directional assignments, pronghorn represented the south. These game animals were hunted by the predators of the six directions; bobcat was aligned with pronghorn (Cushing 1883, Tedlock 1979).

Time

Indians associated time with natural phenomena that reliably could be expected to recur. The Jemez pueblo dwellers called their approximate equivalent of our May the "baby antelope month" because pronghorn were born at that time each year (Harrington 1916, Cope 1919). The time count of the Surprise Valley Paiute, based on lunar periods, started in the autumn with the rutting season of deer and pronghorn (Kelly 1932).

(Top) Snake society (in line on left) and Antelope Society members at Oraibi Pueblo in Arizona, during the Snake Dance. The Snake dancers are about to be handed cleansed rattlesnakes and other snakes, which they hold in their hands and mouths. (Bottom left) Antelope dancers or priests participated in the dance, but without snakes. This public dance marked the close of a nine-day celebration held in August of even-numbered years. During the first eight days, Snake and Antelope priests perform secretly in underground kivas. (Bottom right) The entrance to the Antelope kiva of the Walapai, a Yuman-speaking group in northwestern Arizona, about 1897. Top photo by Edward S. Curtis; courtesy of the Amon Carter Museum of Western History, Fort Worth, Texas. Bottom left photo by Emily Kopta, and bottom right photo by George H. Pepper; both courtesy of the American Museum of the American Indian, Heye Foundation, New York, New York.

The Jahu (Horn Dance)—a puberty ritual—was painted on a finely tanned pronghorn hide by Chiricahua Apache chief Naiche. Elaborate and inclusive, the art is characteristically Apache, but shows considerable white artistic and religious influence. Photo courtesy of the Museum of the American Indian, Heye Foundation, New York, New York.

Cosmology

Indians named constellations for familiar objects, including animals. The Kamia (Diegueños) of the Imperial Valley gave the name *Amuh* (bighorn) to the constellation universally known now as Orion (Gifford 1931). *Amuh* consisted of three aligned stars, named Bighorn, Deer and Pronghorn, with another star, Arrow Point, to one side, and two others named Chemehuevan and Yavaipa Archers to the other. An informant said that the arrow point and the bow were held in the right hand of the celestial archer, and the arrow drawn with the left hand, with the Deer and Pronghorn being pierced by the arrow. In the beginning of the world, according to Kamia mythology, the bighorn, deer and pronghorn were killed by two archers. Their souls, with those of the archers, ascended skyward, where they are now visible as six prominent stars.

LANGUAGE

Names for the Pronghorn

Indians, being intimately familiar with wildlife species sharing their environment, developed names for each. Although the languages of the many tribes and bands may be grouped into larger linguistic groups, the tongue of each local Indian group retained certain, often subtle characteristics, and these are evident in names given the same animals. During the course of research, more than 220 published names given the pronghorn by about 100 tribes were encountered (Appendix B). Some names are errors arising from faulty phonetic interpretation or typographical transcription. Separate names for the various sex and age classes accounted for nearly twice as many names as tribes. Native Americans as far outside of pronghorn range as New Brunswick, Nova Scotia (Rand 1888) and Labrador (Peacock 1974) had names for the species. Predominating among the many names were terms that essentially imitated or characterized a pronghorn's snort.

Appendix B serves as a reminder of the number and breadth of dialects that were spoken by aboriginals in western North America. It also indicates that characterizing or stereotyping Indians and any aspect of their equally diverse cultural elements is foolhardy.

Interestingly, Clark (1884:212) indicated that "Some tribes called the hog the 'bear-antelope.'"

Personal Names

Indian children typically were named for elements or events of the natural world. For boys, names that took some form of a large or powerful animal, such as bear, bison, deer and elk, could be gifted, inherited or acquired by virtue of dramatic act, revelation or memorable event. "Antelope" apparently was not a common name, perhaps because it held relatively less heroic or other symbolic associations. Antelope appears rather infrequently. However, *Running Antelope*, a chief of the Hunkpapa Sioux, was a model for a five-dollar silver certificate printed by the U.S. Government (Fleming and Luskey 1986). We also have encountered Lakota *Antelope Dung*, who broke his neck while surrounding bison (Figure 17), *Antelope Old Man* of the Tewas (Curtis 1926), *Antelope Skin* a

FIGURE 17. *Pictographic designation of particular individuals, before Euro-American artistic influence, sometimes involved a sketch connected to the mouth with a line, representing the name both graphically and verbally. The named individual above, Antelope Dung, an Oglala Sioux, was featured in a winter count by another Oglala, Cloud-Shield (from Mallery 1893).*

Cheyenne (Grinnell 1956), *White Antelope* a Cheyenne chief friendly to whites but killed during the Sand Creek Massacre (Curtis 1911), *White Antelope* a chief of the Hunkpapa Sioux (Vestal 1957), a Piegan Blackfoot chief named *The Antelope* (Denig 1961) and a Caddo named *Antelope* (Swanton 1942). Females with "Antelope" in their name were found less frequently, primarily because female names were not often recorded. Nevertheless, Grinnell (1972) told of *Antelope Woman*, a Cheyenne.

Sign Language

As DeVoto (1947:11) wrote, "The intertribal trade of the Indians was amazingly complex." That numerous tribes with different languages could barter peaceably would seem unlikely. However, sign lan-

guage was understood among many tribal people who did not understand each other's speech, and Indians habitually accompanied their words with signs. Thus, according to Dodge (1885), sign language became a natural and instinctive habit.

No sign language was common to all North American Indians. "The Utes, the Pacific tribes . . . the Indians of the Colorado River, the Apaches, Mohaves, Moquis, Pueblos, Navajos and others, use signs, as do all men, but they do not use or understand all the sign language of the Plains. It is 'common' to all Indians between the Mississippi River and the Rocky Mountains, and from the British line to the Gulf of Mexico. . . . The Plains Indians themselves believe

The common Indian sign for pronghorn involved placement of the thumbs and forefingers extended along the sides of the head. Burton (1966) claimed that the sign simulated ears and horns, whereas Clark (1884) indicated that it represented just the pronged horns. Both Burton (1966) and Cody (1970) suggested that the signs were static; Clark (1884) observed that the hands alongside the head were tipped forward, but acknowledged that some tribes did not move the hands. Photo from Cody (1970).

that sign language was invented by the Kiowas. . . . It is certain the Kiowas are at present [1881] more universally proficient in this language than any other Plains tribe. It is also certain that the tribes furthest [*sic*] away from them, and with whom they have least intercourse, use it with least facility" (Dodge 1885: 365).

There were two visual concepts associated with sign language designation of pronghorn, according to Clark (1884). Least common were the signs for white flanks—the animal's flared rump patches. Most universal was pronged horns. "Bring the hands, palms toward and alongside of the head near base of the ears, index fingers pointing about upwards; move the hands by wrist action parallel to head from rear to front, repeating motion" (Clark 1884:33).

Placenames

Many geographical features, such as buttes, creeks, flats, springs, etc., in the western United States are named Antelope. Such names are too numerous to list here. However, using two states as examples, 108 places in Arizona and 79 in Wyoming are so named. "Pronghorn" appears twice among placenames in Arizona and three times in Wyoming.

TRADE

In the trade which took place at the Upper Missouri villages between the Plains nomads and the horticultural tribes, the nomads exchanged horses and mules, dried meat, fat, prairie-turnip flour, dressed skins, leather "tents," buffalo robes, furs, shirts and leggins of deer and antelope skin ornamented with quill work, moccasins, etc. The village tribes supplied corn, beans, melons, pumpkins, tobacco, and other plants, guns, powder, bullets, kettles, axes, knives, awls, beads, mirrors, etc.

—Jablow (1951:44–45)

In their activities as traders Indians were actively engaged in two economic systems which interpenetrated in various ways. On the one hand they functioned in the system in intertribal trade, while on the other, they were producers and traders in furs in the European mercantile system.

—Jablow (1951:12)

We found no evidence to suggest that any Indian tribe or group relied solely on one type of food or invested exclusively in a single economic practice—gathering, hunting, fishing or farming—and nearly all supplemented their diets by trade in foodstuffs with those whose primary subsistence specialization was different from their own. The economic base of the Ponca, for example, like that of most Missouri River valley tribes, was a combination of hunting, fishing, gathering and horticulture. Throughout much of pronghorn range, the principal animal hunted was the bison, but pronghorn and other large mammals were taken as opportunities to do so presented themselves (Howard 1965). Mandan Indians, as another example, were economically well off in the early 18th century because of their horticultural/hunting subsistence, their enviable geographic positions as middlemen between groups having different commodities to exchange, and their surplus garden produce (corn, beans, squash and sunflower seeds), which they traded for bison and pronghorn hides, dry meat, pemmican and prairie turnip flour (Meyer 1977).

The Santa Ana of the Rio Grande Valley in northern New Mexico practiced agriculture by irrigation and rounded out their diet with hunting and gathering: "Deer, elk, antelope, and rabbits were the most important game animals, and regular expeditions were made to the Plains for buffalo" (Strong 1979:403). The western Apache also farmed and hunted to satisfy their needs (Josephy 1981). They derived about 25% of their food from domesticated plants, about 35% from wild plants and the remainder from hunting and trade. Both irrigation and dry-farming methods were used, and men and women tilled the plots. The men hunted, usually in groups, killing pronghorn and other game, and the women gathered piñon nuts, juniper berries, mesquite beans, wild onions, mescal heads and acorns.

Apparently, none of the Great Basin tribes practiced agriculture, but neither did they have products of the hunt to trade. "Small units of people roamed on foot through limited areas, eating whatever they could gather or catch that was edible. Most groups followed a seasonal wandering routine, gathering foods that ripened or matured at various times. . . . Hunters pursued deer, antelope, and mountain sheep

Of the Indians visited by explorers and adventurers along the upper Missouri River during at least the 1830s, none was more impressive than second Mandan chief Mah-to-toh-pa. *George Catlin (1973 [I]:92) described this warrior, whose name translated to "Four Bears," as "undoubtedly the first and most popular man in the nation. Free, generous, elegant and gentlemanly in his deportment—handsome, brave and valiant. . . . This . . . is the most extraordinary man, perhaps, who lives at this day, in the atmosphere of Nature's noblemen." Catlin produced a number of portraits of Mah-to-toh-pa, including the self portrait at* left *(detail), illustrating as well Four Bears' tribesmen's awe and alarm at the artistic likeness of the chief. Artist Karl Bodmer, who followed Catlin to the region in 1832, also selected Mah-to-toh-pa as a portrait subject. Both painted the chief in a pronghorn-horned headdress decorated with ermine tails and eagle feathers. At* right *is one of the chief's tunic shirts (Catlin described and painted another, as did Bodmer), made from pronghorn hide. Such a shirt was worn only for ceremonies or during very cold weather. Mandan men usually did not wear a shirt beneath a bison robe cover.* Left photo courtesy of Rare Book Division, New York Public Library, New York, New York. Right photo courtesy of the Library of Congress, Washington, DC.

with bows and arrows, but often had poor results" (Josephy 1981:127).

Hewitt (1970:352) observed that "Although the prairie huntsman is familiar with the cultivation of native Indian corn and other cereals, a tribe turned to that employment only when, owing to the greatly reduced number of braves, it is no longer safe to wander about and make head against opposing foes in the open field, and, therefore, is forced to establish a village and settle down." Village-dwelling agrarians were active traders; they had the produce relished by the seminomadic tribes. For example, exchanges between the Cheyenne and Arikara included tobacco and moccasins and shirts of well-dressed pronghorn skins, ornamented with

multicolored porcupine quills (Abel 1939, Paterek 1994).

Although all tribes on the Great Plains participated in barter-based trading, only those situated on or near watercourses traded successfully with Europeans, according to Jablow (1951), which was a highly mixed blessing because it was those Indians who were exposed first and worst to European diseases. Unrau (1979) mentioned that the Oglala Sioux traded mostly skins, including pronghorn, plus horses and sometimes even their women in exchange for European goods. Schultz (1957:54) wrote that, during November, many Piegan and Blood Blackfeet came down from the Saskatchewan River and its tributaries to trade with white merchants: "Buffalo robes were not yet prime, but a fair trade was done in beaver, elk, deer and antelope skins."

Most references regarding intertribal trade among pronghorn hunters involve plains and plateau Indians, but Davis (1961) and Grant (1978) indicated active trade between the coastal Chumash of California and nearby tribes. They traded shell beads, clam and abalone shells, as well as dried sea urchins and starfish to the Yokuts in exchange for elk and pronghorn skins, obsidian, seeds and herbs.

Despite scanty documentation of trade before the 19th century, such trade apparently thrived. "Prior to 1600, among the Salinas Pueblos between the Rio Grande and Rio Pecos rivers was the Humanos Pueblo, which may have been inhabited by the Jumanos. This pueblo was a trading center to which Plains Indians came to trade antelope skins and other articles for maize" (Benavides 1945:249). During the 17th century, Indian trade was of considerable value to the economy of New Mexico. All classes of the white population maintained a brisk business in deer and pronghorn skins with local Indians and transient Apaches. Some skins were tanned and passed as prime trade goods. Deer and pronghorn skins were a form of currency, and private debts sometimes were paid in such skins. For more than 100 years, missionary priests were accused of profiteering in skins at the expense of their Indian wards and jealous laymen (see Weber 1968). In addition to deer and pronghorn skins, which continued to come in during the following century, bison hides and robes were received from tribes frequenting the northern fairs (Phillips and Smurr 1961).

Abel (1939) reported trade in the late 18th century between the Teton and Yankton Sioux, involving such goods as horses, bison robes, shirts and leggings of pronghorn skin, for guns, kettles, pipes and walnut bows.

Effective trade required the production of surplus materials to barter. The fur and hide trades and European manufactured goods increased the need for such production (Lewis 1942). Acquisition of horses and, later, firearms, made the harvesting of surpluses easier and more efficient. After penetrating the plains, the Cheyenne entered into trade with the tribes in horticultural villages along the upper Missouri, and horses were inextricably interwoven with that trade.

Horses helped procure food, shelter and clothing (mostly from bison) as well as surplus hides and meat for trade. They provided transportation to get those products to markets and, themselves, often were traded for European goods (Jablow 1951).

NEAR DEMISE OF BISON

For every single buffalo that roamed the Plains in 1871, there are in 1881 not less than 2, and more probably 4 or 5, of the descendents of the longhorned cattle of Texas. The destroyers of the buffalo were followed by the preservers of the cattle.
—Dodge (1885:608–609)

Trying to explain their destruction is complicated by the fact that no one knows how many buffaloes were alive when the mass dying started.
—West (2001:27)

Rhythms of natural order in the pristine West—the old West, the frontier West—immediately before the influence and presence of Euro-Americans were firmly linked to the American bison. Its many millions—perhaps 30 million (see McHugh 1972)—affected aboriginal distribution, interactions, associations, motivations and other elements of culture. For many tribes, the bison dictated lifestyle and circumstance. Economically, no other animal species within and at the periphery of the vast home range of bison was remotely as important to Indians. Strictly in terms of its food yield, for example, an adult bison provided, on average, the equivalent of that provided by nearly 22 adult pronghorn (see Table 1). The scope of material utility of bison does not appear to have been much broader than were those of elk (McCabe 2002), moose (Reeves and McCabe 1998), deer (McCabe and McCabe 1984), pronghorn and other large mammals. However, by virtue of its relative size, abundance and, consequently, the relative emphasis placed on its procurement, the comparative material utility of an adult bison was much greater on average than were those of other adult big game. The demise of bison and of the aboriginal culture and population that depended on the animal preceded by no more than a decade the near extinction of pronghorn and other native wildlife. That sequence of tragedy was not coincidental.

Trading in bison robes did not begin in earnest until about 1823, but the Columbia Fur Company's gross income for 1825 to 1827 was from $150,000 to $200,000 (1825 to 1827 dollars) annually—approximately half being from bison robes (Phillips and Smurr 1961). The cost of merchandise and supplies for those years was not more than $20,000 or $25,000 annually. Pronghorn did not escape the early trade in hides. In 1660, the embargoed belongings of the governor of New Mexico included 1,200 pronghorn skins in bundles of 100, 200 and 400 (Weber 1968).

The use of horses made killing bison easier and encouraged great squandering of that resource. In turn, this hastened the near extermination of bison and, thus, the aspects of Indian culture based on bison hunting (Ewers 1980). From 1874 through 1877, 80,000 to 100,000 bison robes and 150 tons (135 metric tons) of pronghorn skins were shipped annually from Fort Benton, Montana (Marcy 1938). With an average dried pronghorn hide weighing about 2.5 to 3.0 pounds (1.13–1.36 kg), 150 tons (135 metric tons) equates to more than 100,000 to 120,000 pronghorn hides.

With horses, and later with improved firearms, hunter's ability to kill bison far exceeded the women's capacity to tan robes; the latter determined how many were available for trade. Untanned bison hides were practically worthless to early traders. They could obtain a tanned robe from an Indian cheaper than they could have a hide tanned (McDonald 1982). Whiskey sold for $16 per gallon ($4.20/liter) during the heyday of the robe trade (Catlin 1973). Indians would strip the skin from the last bison's back, to be tanned by their women and traded for a pint (0.5 liter) of diluted alcohol. Hundreds of thousands of flayed carcasses strewed the plains and were fed upon by wolves and dogs in sight of the smoke of wigwams, where the skins were dressed for white men's luxury. "In 1846 it was estimated that 100,000 buffalo hides annually reached the Canadian and American markets. The bull hides were then regarded as worthless for commercial purposes" (Rister 1929).

Skinning a bison was laborious and time-consuming, as was the tanning process. It is not surprising that the easily taken and transported tongues became a sought-after item for the traders, and one readily supplied by Indians. Pickled or smoked by traders, bison tongue was a delicacy in Caucasian markets and restaurants (Mead 1986).

Of the Indian's increased ability to kill bison as time went on, Grinnell (1962:235) wrote that "after the Winchester repeater came in use, it seemed as if the different tribes vied with each other in wanton slaughter. Provided with one of these weapons and belts of cartridges, the hunters would run as long as their horses could keep up with the band, and literally cover the prairie with carcasses, many of which were never even skinned."

William T. Hornaday believed the Indians of the northwestern United States were harvesting bison at an unsustainable level before Euro-Americans joined in the slaughter (Hoopes 1975). For generations and perhaps centuries in Texas, Indians competed with Mexican bison hunters, *Ciboleros,* who hauled huge loads of dried meat back to Mexico. *Ciboleros* killed bison from horseback using 6- or 8-foot (1.8–2.4 m) lances, which required excellent horses and riding skills (Collinson 1963).

Before 1870, most of the trade in bison hides involved dressed robes. Then, it was discovered that the tough, thick skins made admirable belting for machinery, and dried, untanned skins began selling for $3 to $4 each (Dodge 1885). By 1872, the West had been penetrated by three railroads and, from all parts of the country, they converged hunters, excited by the prospect of a profitable bison hunt. Hundreds of thousands of skins went to market, but they scarcely indicated the slaughter. From want of skill in shooting and want of knowledge in preserving the hides of those slain, one hide sent to market represented three to five dead bison, according to Dodge (1877).

During the peak of bison hide hunting, some 20,000 hunters reportedly were involved. About five shots were fired for every bison killed (Collinson 1963). The number of animals wounded and not retrieved must have been high. Also, millions of bison cows were killed, and their calves were left to starve or be killed by wolves and coyotes. Collinson (1963) noted that skinners often had to drive calves from their mothers' carcasses before skinning the carcasses.

U.S. Army personnel apparently were nearly as wasteful as anyone when the opportunity arose. In 1872, Eighth Cavalry troops pursuing Kiowas and Comanches in Texas had been depending on pronghorn for fresh meat, but the animals were scarce, and seldom could an adequate number be secured (Koster 1980). A party was dispatched to hunt bison. A herd was located and the chase to kill 21 lasted only 15 minutes. Three bison were loaded onto a wagon and the remaining 18 were left for the coyotes.

In the badlands of the Montana Territory, shooting by market hunters stampeded 64 bison and several pronghorn over a 75-foot (23 m) precipice (Sandoz 1978). Inadvertently, the hunters had done what Indians worked for days to accomplish before the advent of horses (Sandoz 1978).

According to U.S. government statistics, 8 million bison were killed in Texas alone. In 1877, Collinson (1963) saw what was said to be more than 1 million hides at one trading post. He and a partner hunted during winter of 1876–77 and sold 11,000 hides, 6,000 tongues and 45,000 pounds (20,412 kg) of dried, salted bison beef. The Indians of the Comanche and Kiowa Agency traded the following numbers of robes during 1876 to 1879 (Hoopes 1975): 1876, 70,400; 1877, 64,500; 1878, 26,375; 1879, 5,068. This was just one of many agencies in the West. The decline in numbers of robes traded at that agency paralleled the precipitous decline of bison everywhere.

"Like buzzards waiting for an old cow to die in a boghole, hundreds of cowmen had been waiting to grab the wonderful ranch country where the buffalo had roamed. They knew that it was the finest grazing land on earth. In 1878 they realized that the buffalo were gone and the Comanches were whipped, so they began to drive in their herds" (Collinson 1963:114).

The prairies were changed forever.

NEAR DEMISE OF THE PEOPLE

The veritable horde of miners, ranchers, farmers, and speculators who rushed to the far west following the Mexican War simply could not be contained. They were determined to strike it rich or reduce the wilderness to a ranch or garden, and they saw no reason why "savage" Indians should not be required to accept more limited living space. Mostly accommodating at first, the Indians of the Great Plains and intermontane plateau regions soon challenged the new dispensation.

—Unrau (1979:23)

While 40,000 bison hides in a Dodge City, Kansas, corral awaited rail shipment to the East in 1873, 40,000 bison carcasses decomposed on the southern plains of Kansas and Texas. Hide shipments of similar number or larger were shipped from other railheads and stops that year and in other years until the southern herd was gone and the northern herd nearly so. Photo by E. A. Brininstool; courtesy of the Denver Public Library, Western History Department, Denver, Colorado.

So long as the Sioux and Cheyenne were a menace to the hunters as well as cattlemen, sheepmen, and farmers, the antelopes were safe and showed no decrease, but as soon as the Indians were subjugated and removed from the country to the reservations and agencies and the Northern Pacific Railway crossed the continent, the last great herd of buffalos disappeared, as we have seen, and soon there were few antelopes, and in large areas none.
—Huntington (1904:234)

I see no longer the curling smoke rising from our lodge poles. I hear no longer the songs of the women as they prepare the meal. The antelope have gone; the buffalo wallows are empty. . . . The white man's medicine is stronger than ours.
—Plenty Coups in Connell (1984:404)

The subordination of North American Indians did not commence with Henry Hudson initiating trade of alcohol for Indian goods, or with the "soul derby" of Jesuit and Anglican missionaries, or the sale of Manhattan by the Lenni Lenapes to the Dutch, or the Powhatan Wars, Bacon's Rebellion, King William's War, the Natchez and Pima revolts, or the French and Indian War or Pontiac's Rebellion, the Northwest Ordinance, Nootka Convention, Tecumseh's Rebellion, Creek War, Trail of Tears, Patwin Resistance, Treaty of Guadalupe Hidalgo, Chumash and Pomo resistances, Winnebago Uprising, Treaty of Laramie, Black Hawk War, Taos Rebellion, the Long Walk, Spirit Lake Uprising, the Yakima, Paiute and Coeur D'Alene wars, Treaties of Medicine Lodge, Sand Creek, Red Cloud's War, Baker's Massacre, Modoc and Red River wars, General Allotment Act, Geronimo's Surrender, or Wounded Knee, among other defining circumstances, events and policies. In a more allegorical sense, its metastasis began in 1512, with the Law of Burgos, which gave the right to Spanish land grantees to enslave Indians under the *encomienda* system. Through that same system, Pueblo Indians eventually were obligated to pay a tax or tribute to the New Mexico governors. "A monthly collection at Pecos Pueblo, in 1662, for example, yielded 66 antelope skins, twenty-one white buckskins, eighteen buffalo hides, and sixteen large buckskins" (Weber 1968:18). One governor accumulated a stock of 1,200 pronghorn skins.

By the time the Voyage of Discovery ventured up the Missouri River in 1803, and into the range of the pronghorn, Native Americans east of the Mississippi River were mainly gone or subjugated. But, these "children of the forest" left a legacy with the continentally surging Euro-Americans. That legacy was a sense that other Indians were dangerous obstacles to the glories of manifest destiny (Billington 1985).

Lewis and Clark encountered many Indians on their journey; they befriended some and attempted peaceful relations with nearly all (Ronda 1984). They experienced petty problems with a few, but had only two or three potentially serious confrontations (Ambrose 1996). In the years that followed, as fur traders and missionaries pressed into the West, many Indians came to resent the wanton intrusions of whites. Others were resignedly or indignantly tolerant. And, some readily embraced the newcomers and their seductive possessions and odd proclivities and, in so doing, prompted heightened factionalism among tribes whose alliances were few and fragile in the first place (Goetzmann 1966, Utley 1984). Cultural differences and misunderstandings between whites and Indians catered to distrust. Disparate economies proved incompatible. Expansionist motives of the new Americans and land "ownership" or territorial ambiguity among the Native Americans fostered resentments (Hoopes 1975). Provocations of hostilities were a matter of viewpoint and, occasionally, convenience. Retaliation invariably was a matter of indignant rage. Savagery was unique to neither.

The contest for supremacy of the West was protracted by bad treaties, the Civil War and unconventional warfare. Its outcome was made inevitable by firearms, racism, greed, imperial tenacity and numerical superiority. It was hastened by disease, inclement weather and, as previously noted, collapse of the buffalo economy. The road to ruin for Indians and for bison and the Wild West actually was a series of trails—Oregon, Bozeman, Mormon, California, Santa Fe and others. In the eyes of the Indians, they were "thieves" roads (Matthiessen 1983:6), soon followed by iron roads—the Union, Northern and Southern Pacific, and others (see Brown 1977). In the land of the pronghorn, Native Americans were not perceived by Euro-Americans as having legitimate or permanent claim to the country. The real problem for the invaders was not only that Indians were dangerous obstacles to progress, but they were dangerous ob-

"By 1850, Indians across the Plains had become integrated into the capitalist economy. Indian-produced furs, robes, pemmican, and other commodities of the hunt were fed into staple industries in the United States and abroad. As the economies of the tribes became inextricably linked to the fur trade, changes in social organization resulted. When the production of buffalo robes increased to an average of 100,000 robes annually . . . the demand for hides far outstripped Indian ability to supply them" (Swagerty 2001:277, see also Sunder 1965). Dependency was followed by dispossession, followed by dislocation. The erstwhile "lords of the plains"—reduced to bartering for elk and pronghorn once the bison disappeared—were pauperized of culture, identity and social options. Left photo of two Sans Arc Sioux with two bundles of pronghorn hides near Fort Keogh in Montana in 1879, by L. A. Huffman; courtesy of the Montana State Historical Society, Helena. Above watercolor artwork, "The Wolfer's Camp," by Charles M. Russell; photo courtesy of the Amon Carter Museum of Western Art, Fort Worth, Texas.

stacles to rapid progress (see Mattes 1969, Weems 1976, Mitchell 1981, Udall 2002).

The wresting of the West from the indigenous people is a sad story, not necessarily because a soci-ety was overwhelmed, subjugated and displaced (a mirroring of human history nearly everywhere), but because it was accomplished deceptively and ruthlessly piecemeal. It is a story told repeatedly, and each

"When it was first completed in 1861, the mystified Indians variously referred to the [transcontinental] telegraph as the 'talking wire,' the 'singing wire,' or the 'humming messenger wire,'" (Unrau 1979:12). They soon came to understand that the lines of poles tethered together at the top were to their great disadvantage. At risk were their food, their land and their culture. Attacking the talking wires merely brought more soldiers to protect the lines, and more soldiers meant more travelers and settlers could and would invade the West. Artwork, "Song of the Talking Wire," by Henry Farney; photo courtesy of the Taft Museum, Cincinnati, Ohio.

new, predominantly Anglo-American generation appears to be more apologetic than the last about that historical chapter, yet more detached from the continuing issue of Indians' limited neocultural coping skills.

For most Americans, then and now, the Battle of the Little Bighorn was the defining moment of the so-called Indian Wars—the occasion when the Indians won the battle and, in so doing, lost the war. That episode and its principals will long serve as a metaphor for aggressive, blundering, Euro-American attempts to exploit the West, and for Native American defiance, simultaneously heroic and tragic. The central figure in the drama was George Armstrong Custer.

On the Trail to the Little Bighorn

The West to which U.S. Army officer Custer was posted after his Civil War exploits was still mainly wilderness, except along its watercourses. By virtue of a series of disingenuous and dubious treaties with tribes of the northern and central plains, primarily the powerful Lakota, the U.S. government had stirred

enmity to the boiling point. Massacres, such as at Sand Creek (Brown 1994), Fort Kearney (Brown 1971a), Cheyenne Hole (Monnett 1999) and along the Washita (Hoig 1979), were ugly byplays of war, exacerbating mutual contempt (Chittenden 1935, Welch 1994) and staging for a decisive confrontation. Goad and gold were found in the Black Hills, *Paha Sapa*, a land sacred to the Lakota and previously the Crow. At the head of an 1874 expedition to the Black Hills region, ostensibly a military reconnaissance and to explore its geography, was Custer. The expedition's penetration into the region heightened tension among the Indians, for whom the audacious action validated their long-held suspicion of whites' intention to ignore their own treaty sanctions and usurp what relatively little of Indian territory was still reserved and unspoiled.

On one occasion, Custer was about to fire at a pronghorn buck when his Indian scouts shot it. Custer retaliated by shooting over the scouts heads, sending them diving for cover.

By the time the reconnaissance "summer excursion" retreated (Connell 1984:236), Custer himself had downed 16 pronghorn. They and other items in the Lieutenant Colonel's "collection of curiosities" were conveyed in an ambulance driven by teamster Antelope Fred (Frost 1979:31).

Pronghorn had provided sport, food and folly for Custer and his troops as they cheerily reconnoitered the region. On July 27, 1874, expedition miner Horatio Nelson Ross found gold in a meadow near French Creek at the base of Calamity Peak, just east of what is now Custer, South Dakota, and in the Black Hills National Forest (see Progulske 1974). When first revealing his discovery to several other members of the expedition, Ross said simply, "I reckon the white people are coming, all right" (Connell 1984:246).

The prospector's prophecy was indeed true. The whites who surged (illegally) into the region also found pronghorn a source of food, but only for a brief time. Without the support of 1,200 troopers and civilians, as Custer had with him, pronghorn shooting sport and folly were minimized in the heart of a landscape deemed holy by very agitated Sioux. The Black Hills discovery and reporting opened a virtual floodgate of ambition and trespassing in the West, to gold fields of the Dakota Territory and beyond. The Old West was on the clock. So was Custer.

As did many Army contingents in the West, the Seventh Cavalry, Custer's regiment, routinely supplemented its field rations with pronghorn. At stations in Texas, Kansas and Nebraska, "Antelope were very plentiful, and the men were encouraged by troop commanders to hunt" (Godfrey 1991:361). Once, while in the field with the Seventh, DuBray (1890) participated in a hunt that bagged 40 to 50 pronghorn and provided the entire command with meat for days. Nevertheless, soldier hunting efficiency was notably poor; many pronghorn were wounded and lost. On the other hand, DuBray and a column of the Seventh Cavalry witnessed a young Crow scout creep within 50 yards (46 m) of five pronghorn and kill them all with seven shots.

Among his other characteristics, good and bad, Custer had an affinity for pets, which he took or collected on campaigns. These included hounds (sometimes used by Custer to course pronghorn), a pelican, a young bobcat and half-grown pronghorn. One time, while encamped near Fort McPherson in central Nebraska, Custer was visited by Sioux chief Pawnee-Killer and six warriors. "While the talk was going on," reported Davis (1868:301), "'Little Bill,' one of

Lieutenant Colonel Custer with Indian scouts on the 1874 Black Hills Expedition. Custer is seated in the chair, and his chief scout Bloody Knife is pointing at the map. On the fifth day of the expedition into "a region of country as yet unseen by human eyes except those of the Indian—a country described by the latter as abounding in game of all varieties, rich in scientific interest, and of surpassing beauty in natural scenery," Custer (1952:609) shot two pronghorn, and 15 to 20 were brought into camp. "Some of the soldiers were very careless in shooting across the column. Antelope were plentiful. Some came within 25 yards [23 m] of the command, and the soldiers were firing in all directions" (Frost 1979:25). This led to prohibition of shooting without an officer's permission and, with permission, it had to be done away from the column. Even so, the pronghorn skirmishes of the Keystone cavalry continued. A driver of a four-horse limber carrying a Gatling gun excitedly jumped from the wagon to fire at pronghorn with his revolver. The horses bolted, careened about a meadow and became mired in a slough. Also, at three o'clock one morning, the camp was rudely awakened by gunfire when a guard mistook a pronghorn for a lurking Indian (Krause and Olson 1974). Photo by William H. Illingsworth, from the, original, direct-contact albumen print; courtesy of the Little Bighorn National Monument, Crow Agency, Montana.

the pet antelopes, was making a careful investigation of the bead-work on the clothing of the Indians, dividing his attention between them and a pail of water. . . . The tameness of the antelope seemed to strike the Indians as peculiar; but when they saw the little fellow attack one of the dogs that came into the tent their astonishment was too great to be contained. . . ."

Three pronghorn heads adorned the walls of Lt. Colonel George and Elizabeth Custer's Fort Abraham Lincoln, Dakota Territory, headquarters (Frost 1984); two are shown here in his study. On May 17, 1876, Custer and his Seventh Cavalry circled once around the Fort Lincoln parade ground before ascending a bluff and heading to a fateful confrontation with the Sioux, approximately 350 miles (563 km) to the west. "Watch for our return, Bess," were Custer's parting words to his wife (Connell 1984:253). Photo courtesy of the Little Bighorn Battlefield National Monument, Crow Agency, Montana.

Greasy Grass Convergence

The 1876 campaign to locate, capture, punish and return the so-called renegade Indians to their reservations, involved General Alfred Terry and Custer moving a force from Fort Abraham Lincoln (near modern-day Bismarck, North Dakota) to and up the Yellowstone River. Colonel John Gibbon advanced a column of infantry down the Yellowstone. General George Crook moved troops northward from Fort Laramie in Wyoming toward the Powder River country east of the Bighorn Mountains. The pincer movement was a formidable commitment of military personnel and materiel. Into this fateful scene raced the pronghorn.

Chief of the Crow scouts for General Terry was civilian Thomas Lafarge. Ten days before the battle, Lafarge was thrown from his horse and injured (broken collarbone) when a pronghorn suddenly jumped up from hiding (Marquis 1974). As a result, six Crow scouts transferred to Custer's Seventh Cavalry were led by Mitch Bouyer (reportedly a protégé of Jim Bridger) who warned Custer that the troopers faced the largest congregation of Indians Bouyer had ever seen (Connell 1984). However, had Lafarge gone with Custer to search along Rosebud Creek for the ren-

egades, might not the scouts have been more direct with Lafarge or Lafarge with Custer concerning the strength of the encampment found along the Little Bighorn? Probably not, but one thing is certain—Bouyer died from his injuries and Lafarge did not from his.

Custer's scouts located the quarry west of a divide between the Rosebud and Little Bighorn. There, to the scouts' grave consternation was an encampment extending for 1.5 miles (2.4 km) or more, and containing 12,000 or so AWOL and restive Hunkpapa, Oglala, Sans Arc, Minneconjou and Blackfeet Sioux, plus Northern Cheyenne and some Arapaho. The alliance along the narrow serepentine river was one borne of desperation and wishful thinking, to defend against the Army, to escape the drudgery and meager charity of reservation life, and to embrace again their traditional, relatively carefree, drifting hunter/gatherer mode of living. The temporary confederation was one of the largest assembly of Indians ever on the Great Plains, as scout Bouyer had suggested (Welch 1994, Michno 2000).

Twelve thousand people and their horses represented a logistical nightmare (Ambrose 1986). They needed an abundance of fresh food, water and forage. A week before the battle, the Indians moved into the Little Bighorn Valley in hopes of finding bison. Despite initial plans to relocate, they camped along the Little Bighorn River on June 22, 1876, from which site hunters rode west to hunt pronghorn (Marquis 1967). And, it was that site where Custer found them.

By noon on June 25, 1876, as the Indians were about to prepare to move their camp farther down the valley toward juncture with the Bighorn River (Marquis 1967), Custer had divided and deployed his forces. By the charge of a battalion of three troops under Major Marcus Reno, the battle was joined at the south end of the sprawling encampment.

Taps

The death of Custer and his Seventh Cavalry troopers stunned eastern society. The news was nearly as unthinkable as the fact of defeat. Public indignation raised a hue and cry to avenge the fallen soldiers. And the military retaliation that followed was swift, bumbling and relentless, for national pride and the hubris of manifest destiny were at stake.

Indian skirmishes in the West were fought for approximately another decade—futile and final acts of resistance by small numbers of Indians. The war unofficially concluded in 1890, following an outrage at a place called Wounded Knee in South Dakota (Brown 1971b, Jensen et al. 1991).

Custer's Last Stand did not cause the downfall of traditional Indian life; it merely climaxed and hastened the inevitable. Perhaps its most significant consequence, besides the speed with which the Indian "problem" was subsequently dispatched, was the fear it elevated and wrath it evoked among the white population.

Whatever sympathy and tolerance there had been for the Indians' predicament of the mid-1800s quickly dissolved with the echoes of gunfire and screams above Greasy Grass. Whatever opportunity there otherwise might have been for the North American Indian to assimilate gradually and gracefully into the mainstream of the occupying civilization was lost. Whatever chance there otherwise might have been for mitigation of important vestiges of Indian culture, including their relationships to wildlife, was denied. In the end, the Indian spirit and vitality were the real victims. And the Indians themselves were summarily confined to arid reservations, given the tacit status of

prisoners of war, and treated as indigent curiosities and a collective reminder of a less-than-humanitarian episode in the nation's expansionist history.

It cannot be said with certainty that Indian life and prosperity would have been better if Sioux and Northern Cheyenne and Arapaho had not encamped along the Little Bighorn River to feed their livestock and hunt pronghorn. Indians throughout North America generally had not been treated with equity or even honest charity before 1876, and it was this malfeasance that presumably led to the Little Bighorn. The foundations of Indian life—the land and its living resources—already had been exploited and fragmented by the time George Armstrong Custer died in frontier Montana.

One year before the battle, the last significant Indian resistance on the southern plains—by the Quahadas (Kwahadi) Comanches under the leadership of Isatai and Quanah Parker—was ended. On the band's "surrender" journey from the vicinity of what is now Gail, Texas, to Fort Sill in the Indian Territory (Oklahoma), "the trip was filled with nostalgia" (Exley 2001). As they traveled, knowing they would have to "abandon their roving life" forever, they hunted bison, pronghorn and wild horses along the way, feasted on fresh meat, and held "the last Medicine dance they ever expect to have [on] these broad Plains" (Wallace 1978:238–241).

One year after the battle, a military post, Fort Custer, was established near the confluence of the Little Bighorn and Bighorn rivers. The post's road-building crew subsisted on bison and pronghorn (Marquis 1974).

Grave Reservations

Reservation life was frustrating and depressing for the formerly independent and seminomadic people of the West. Most injurious of their freedom losses was that of subsistence habits. "[Annuity] rations were supposed to be enough to last each family for two weeks," an Arapaho told Bass (1966:52), "but it was hard for any Indian to learn to divide what he had on hand and make it last 14 days." The rations purportedly simulated an Anglo-American diet, including no more than 4 pounds (1.8 kg) of meat per Indian per week. Indians (and whites in the West) were accustomed to average consumption of meat in excess of 4 pounds per person *per day*, as noted earlier. Furthermore, annuities often were tardy and shorted.

The Indian Bureau in Washington was told that the reservation Piegan Blackfeet were mostly self-supporting (Grinnell 1962). The tribe had subsisted by hunting bison, but there were no more bison by 1883. So the Indians killed most of the available elk, deer and pronghorn, which failed to provide much in the way of winter stores. With little to depend on during the winter of 1883–84 except annuities from the government, more than 25% of the 2,600-member tribe starved to death.

By about 1870, bison had been extirpated from what is now Caddo County, Oklahoma, so Kiowa Apache, to subsist, learned to run down deer and pronghorn on fast horses (Brant 1969). Eight years later, also on the southern plains of the Indian Territory, Comanches, tired of confinement and pernicious government handouts, left the Fort Sill reservation en masse for a communal bison hunt to procure adequate winter meat (Wallace and Hoebel 1952). They traveled a great distance and found no bison, just bison bones, and were saved from starvation only by killing pronghorn. When winter came, the Indians returned to Fort Sill and scanty rations, their former way of life immutably ended.

For the Zunis of western New Mexico, kachinas are spiritual links to natural forces. They emerge from the underworld attached back to back with a person from an alien world. This deformity condemns the two to an eternal union in which neither can see or fully comprehend the other (see Brown 1976). It serves, as well, as a compelling metaphor for the relationship of Native and nonnative North Americans.

NEAR DEMISE OF PRONGHORN

I know of no species of plant, bird, or animal that were exterminated until the coming of the white man. For some years after the buffalo disappeared there still remained huge herds of antelope, but the hunter's work was no sooner done in the destruction of the buffalo than his attention was attracted toward the deer.

—Standing Bear (1978:165)

In 1877, a year after the Battle of Little Bighorn, Fort Custer was established at the confluence of the Little Bighorn and Bighorn rivers. Its road-building crew subsisted mainly on bison and pronghorn. Photo courtesy of the Wyoming State Archives, Museum and Historical Department, Cheyenne.

Pronghorn still were numerous when bison were nearly exterminated on the Great Plains. It then required year-round hunting by those Indians who depended on the smaller animals for subsistence. These Sioux U.S. Army scouts were camped at Belle Fourche in the Black Hills during 1877, just one year after the Battle of the Little Bighorn. They were preparing for the Powder River campaign to force Lakota, Northern Cheyenne and Arapaho onto reservations. Photo by F. Jay Haynes; courtesy of the Montana State Historical Society, Helena.

Despite the fact that the antelope is a very wary animal, and owing to the character of the grounds which it inhabits, it is very difficult to approach, they are daily diminishing very rapidly. The sportsman, therefore, who desires to kill this variety of game should as soon as possible anticipate its certain extinction.

—Satterwarte (1889:877)

With a few notable exceptions, Euro-Americans generally harvested pronghorn lightly, before 1870, because bison, elk and deer provided more meat and larger hides and were easier to hunt (see Huntington 1904). Of early trappers, Healy (1982:113) wrote: "His food and clothing all came from his gun. The deer, elk and antelope furnished his choicest food and the hides were tanned and made into leggins, breeches and shirts." Many frontiersmen adopted the Indian's buckskins, much of it from pronghorn, because it was more available than cloth, tough, soft and of a good color for camouflage.

Collinson (1963) wondered what the hunters, skinners, campmen, freighters, hide buyers and cooks would do after the bison were gone. Some remained

on the plains to hunt pronghorn or buy or sell their meat and hides. Others became ranchers or homesteaders. The latter two completed the destruction that the former began.

After rifles were widely available, pronghorn was common fare throughout the West. During 1859, drought in southern California forced pronghorn to concentrate at water sources. One hunter slaughtered approximately 5,000 from a blind at a waterhole, taking only the hides, according to Van Wormer (1969).

Great numbers of pronghorn were slaughtered for their skins, which generally were dried and sold by the pound. Like the Indians before them, hide hunters sought concentrations of animals, mostly on winter ranges. Before the Black Hills were settled, they were famous wintering grounds for pronghorn. Once hide hunters discovered these dense concentrations, they killed practically entire herds because the starved and weak animals were less shy and reluctant to leave (Roosevelt 1885).

In 1867, metís along the Missouri River cut wood for steamboats during part of the year and hunted

The first wagon train across the American West carried Jesuit missionaries and settlers to California in 1841. Among the travelers was Belgian Jesuit priest and artist, Father Nicolas Point. On July 31, 1841, along the banks of the Green River in western Wyoming, Father Point sketched the emigrants' leader, Thomas Fitzpatrick, shooting a pronghorn and then carrying it back to camp. Fitzpatrick, known to the Indians as Broken Hand, was a famous mountain man, fur trader, explorer and Indian agent in the unchartered West (see Hafen 1931). Photo courtesy of the Washington State University Library, Pullman.

pronghorn and other game in winter. This supplied their larders and brought additional income from the sale of hides. Also, miners in Montana wore coats trimmed with pronghorn skins during the 1860s (de Trobriand 1951).

When Lieutenant Gustavus Doan entered the Yellowstone Valley in 1870, it was swarming with pronghorn. Within the next five years, most of the large game had been slaughtered for their skins (Strong 1876). Nearly 2,000 pronghorn skins were taken out of what now is Yellowstone National Park during spring 1875 (Norris 1877), and 53,000 were shipped down the Yellowstone River in 1881 (Blair 1982). "Buffalo, elk, mule deer and antelope are being slaughtered by thousands each year [written in 1875], without regard to age or sex, and at all seasons. Of the vast majority of the animals killed, the hide only is taken. Females of all these species are as eagerly pursued in the spring, when just about to bring forth their young, as at any other time" (Grinnell 1925:217).

In 1873, the *Sioux City Journal* reported that, during one year, Durfee and Peck of Iowa shipped 40 tons (36 metric tons) of deer and pronghorn skins. On average, these skins (dried) weighed 2.5 pounds (1.1 kg) each, which makes a total of 32,000 skins worth at least $40,000. The hide business was lucrative, and the report further commented that a score of other companies were shipping hides (Taylor 1975).

Palatability of pronghorn meat during frontier days depended on the taste buds of the consumer. Lewis Henry Morgan (1959:154), arguably the leading American Indian ethnologist and linguist in the mid-19th century, observed of pronghorn, during travel up the Missouri River in 1862, "They are said to be superior for eating to the buffalo, as the latter is to our beef." Army officer and dilettante Dodge (1877:201) wrote: "In September and October the flesh of the antelope is no better for food than that of the black- or white-tailed deer, nor so good as that of the mountain sheep, but it has the unusual advantage of being most excellent all the year round. At the season when the other large game animals are poor, tough, stringy, and unfit for food, antelope meat, however poor, is always tender, juicy, and most delicious." Ruxton (1861) agreed and Herrick (1892:289) claimed: "The antelope is assiduously pursued both by Indians and white hunters. For, though somewhat dry, the flesh is highly esteemed and even finds its way in considerable quantities to Minneapolis markets."

In 1860, Sir Richard Burton, English explorer and author, made an overland trip to California. He assiduously documented the experience, including his view that "Like other wild meats . . . antelope will disagree with a stranger; it is, however, juicy, fat . . . and the hunter and trapper, like the Indian, are loud in its praise" (Burton 1862:67–68).

John James Audubon, in 1843, voiced a different opinion: "The flesh of the Antelope is not comparable with that of Deer, being dry and unusually tough. It is very rarely indeed that a fat Antelope is killed" (Audubon 1897 [II]:114). Josiah Gregg (1954:378), who traveled the Santa Fe Trail from 1831 to 1840, similarly opined: "The flesh of the antelope is, like that of the goat, rather coarse, and but little esteemed. . . ." Faced with starvation conditions in Nevada in December 1828, Peter Skene Ogden recorded in his diary that "we are wretched reduced to skin and bone. Hunters killed 3 antelope. This will assist, tho' poor food at this season, but far preferable to horse flesh that die of disease" (Hafen 1966 [III]; 226–227).

In 1880, James H. Cook (1923) was hired by a Cheyenne businessman to secure a bighorn saddle for his Christmas dinner. Cook could not find a bighorn, so he shot a pronghorn, dressed it and picked all the hair from the meat. He then sawed the legs off short, sacked the meat and shipped it on the Union Pacific Railroad. Returning to Cheyenne shortly after Christmas, Cook met the businessman who ecstatically exclaimed that friends said it was the finest meat they ever tasted. The businessman added: "I have lived here a long time and eaten all kinds of game. I can tell by the taste what kind of meat it is. Believe me, nothing can compare with that bighorn you sent me" (Cook 1923:144).

Of the many references to sighting, shooting and eating pronghorn by overland travelers, perhaps none is more retrospectively ironic than that of Virginia Reed Murphy (1891:415), who wrote: "The meat of the young buffalo is excellent and so is that of the antelope. . . . Antelope and buffalo steaks were the main article on our bill-of-fare for weeks, and no tonic was needed to give zest for the food. . . ." These passages chronicle travel in early summer 1846 on the

Great Platte River Road of the Oregon Trail, before Murphy and others, since collectively known as the Donner Party, made an ill-fated decision to follow the new and unproven "Hastings Cutoff" en route to California. Murphy survived; others did not.

Enormous herds of pronghorn and tule elk roamed the Sacramento and San Joaquin valleys of California. After the arrival of miners, beginning in 1849, market hunters drove feral cattle and horses as well as elk and pronghorn by the thousands along fences miles in length into corrals. Meat was sold fresh in the mining camps and preserved for shipment or later use. Bands of 2,000 to 3,000 pronghorn commonly were seen on the plains of California during the 19th century (Seton 1909), and pronghorn meat sold for less than did beef in San Francisco (Bryant 1929). By 1875, tule elk were nearly extinct and pronghorn were greatly reduced in numbers (Millais 1915). Miners in the Black Hills relied heavily on commercial hunters for a steady supply of meat. One of those hunters was Johnny T. Spaulding, of Deadwood, South Dakota. Spaulding was said to take an enormous toll of big game in the region, including on one occasion 15 pronghorn with 15 shots from a single stand (Hughes 1957).

During the 1850s, great herds of pronghorn roamed the Great Basin, and thousands were killed annually for the market (Hittel 1863). Burton (1862) wrote that, in 1860, a tanned pronghorn hide was worth $300. During 1868 to 1881, pronghorn meat was in demand, and saddles sold by the thousands for $0.25 each according to Young (1946). During the winter of 1868–69, Major Pond traveled on the new railroad from Denver to Cheyenne. Pronghorn had left the plains for shelter among the foothills, and their numbers reportedly changed the color of the country. That winter, many wagonloads were hauled to Denver and sold, three or four carcasses for $0.25 (Warren 1942).

Time, supply and demand worked together to increase the market value of pronghorn. In 1873, pronghorn meat sold to butchers in Kansas for $0.02 to $0.03 per pound (5.6–6.7 cents/kg) (Fleharty 1995). During 1876, Cook (1923) and his partner hunted pronghorn approximately 35 miles (56 km) southeast of Cheyenne. They received $0.05 to $0.08 per pound (11–18 cents/kg) for saddles and $0.16 to $0.25 per pound (36–56 cents/kg) for dry hides. Those

Fort Laramie was the site of many treaty negotiations and the town was an important hub for white traders in and travelers to and through the Wyoming Territory during the mid–19th century. In all, frontier communities before refrigeration, the transport and commerce in wild game was an open and everyday occurrence. Meat, typically, was hung outside the general store or butcher shop to age and stay cool, to keep flies outside, and to advertise availability. This photo was taken in 1868, the year the Laramie Treaty was signed. Photo by A. G. Hull; courtesy of E. A. Miller.

hides were shipped to Chicago. The pronghorn hides Vic Smith (1997) collected near Forth Keough and Miles City, Montana, in 1877, were worth $0.90 each.

Jim Hamlin lived 25 miles (40 km) from Colorado Springs and sent pronghorn saddles to market by the wagonload. In 1879 and later, T. S. Bingham had a meat market there and bought saddles from Hamlin, for $0.10 per pound (22 cents/kg). Thus, saddles brought $2.50 to $3.00 each. Hamlin also got about $0.50 per hide. Bingham recalled buying more than 2,000 saddles from Hamlin (Warren 1942).

The coming of the Texas and Pacific Railroad to El Paso opened up new markets. During winters, pronghorn saddles were shipped east by the thousands from Midland, Odessa and Stanton, Texas (Collinson 1963). When the Union Pacific was being built across Wyoming, pronghorn formed a large part of the workers' diet (Allred 1943). At a later date, one Texas bison hunter was known as Antelope Jack because he had furnished pronghorn to those workers (Collinson 1963).

At brief, periodic stops, early passengers on trains west of Saint Louis were fed antelope steak, which "might be anything a cook could get his hands on" (Loeffelbein 1994:32). General Sheridan rode the Kan-

sas Pacific in 1868 and stopped at Ellsworth, Kansas, for the night. There he dined on bison steak and pronghorn ham (Johnson 1969). The pronghorn ham was what currently would be called corned meat. Cook (1923:130), who was selling pronghorn meat during the 1880s, described its preparation: "In camp we took all the meat from the bones of the animals, cutting it as little as possible, opening the partings between the muscles and leaving each group of muscles as near their proper form as possible. The meat was then placed in barrels and brine poured over it until covered. It remained in this brine for 9 or 10 days; then it was taken out and hung up, each piece by itself, in the smokehouse. . . . All the meat which we dried was carefully sacked, then hauled to the railroad and shipped, to Cheyenne, then forwarded to eastern cities. . . . Meat thus prepared brought a good price."

"Although antelope might, at one time on the plains of Kansas, during the 1870s have been nearly as common as buffalo, they were more wary and traveled in small herds; consequently, there were no 'grand' antelope hunts in the same sense as buffalo hunts. Apparently antelope were never taken in large numbers on a single hunt. Rather, they were taken

Bill of Fare.

Union Pacific Rail Road Excursion.

PLATTE CITY, NEBRASKA.
Hoxie House, October 25, 1866.

ROAST.

Beef	Mutton	Lamb with green peas.
Brazen Ox	Tongue	Maccaroni a la Italian.

BOILED

Mutton	Tongue	Ham	Corn Beef.

GAME

Antelope roasted.   Sardine Salid.
Roman Goose, Chineese Duck

VEGETABLES

Peas   Tomatoes   Asparagus   mashed potatoes.

RELISHES

London Club Sauce		Wostershire Sauce
Horrey Sauce.	Pickles	Pine Apple Cheese
	Swiss Cheese.	

PASTRY

Pies,	Strawberries,	Damson
	Peach	Cherry.

FRUITS

Apples   Pine Apples.

BEN SHEPLEY, Cook.

The railroad was not the cause of the demise of the bison, pronghorn or Native American culture in the West, but it was both literally and figuratively the foremost vehicle of accommodation for the notion, doctrine and national mindset of manifest destiny. That mindset did not allow for wild animals and wild people. The railroad boosted American progress westward, and it conveyed the spoils of progress to eastern hubs. Although the transcontinental railways did not homogenize the country, it availed the halves conveniently of each other. Along many segments of the railroads in the West, pronghorn briefly thrived in new grasses following prairie first ignited by ashes from the engine fireboxes and smokestacks. Conversely, pronghorn were targets of railway passengers shooting away the monotony of travel. And just as at waystops for stagecoaches, rail depots that served food invariably featured antelope steak, which, now and then, actually was pronghorn venison. Top photo *shows an 1890s lithograph entitled "A Prairie Fire In Nebraska," artist unknown.* Left photo *features the October 25, 1866, menu of the Hoxie House in Platte City, Nebraska, including, perhaps, roasted pronghorn. Both photos courtesy of the Union Pacific Railroad Museum, Omaha, Nebraska.*

singly, or by twos and threes. No news articles mentioned large numbers of antelope killed, but reports were often made if even one was taken by a local hunter" (Fleharty 1995:32).

Little seems to have been written concerning the techniques of the professional pronghorn hunters. They were not pursuing beasts that would stand to be shot, as had the bison. However, repeating rifles were an advantage and, with practice, professional hunters became crack shots. Murphy (1879) reported that some mounted market hunters approached a herd as closely as possible before charging at it, firing away until several pronghorn were hit. The frightened animals supposedly bunched and circled about for some time, presenting additional targets. Murphy added that it took a skillful eye. Surely this method wasted much ammunition, crippled animals and ruined meat.

We suspect that some of the big kills reported were made during severe winters, when pronghorn were "caught by hunters provided with snowshoes, and they are in this manner killed, even in sight of Fort Union, from time to time" (Audubon and Bachman 1851:198). During the winter of 1840, when snow had drifted into ravines, a Mr. Laidlaw followed pronghorn on horseback and forced them into the drifts. By placing nooses, fixed on the end of a long pole, around their necks, he brought them back to Fort Union, where they all died.

Reputedly the best shot and one of the more prolific killers of big game was "Yellowstone" Vic Smith. One winter day in 1877, near Fort Keough in Montana, when the snow was deep and pronghorn were bunched together, Smith reputedly killed six with a single shot. "They took off all the hides . . . and left the meat for the wolves. A present day [ca. 1909] hunter would stagger at what he would denominate as hoggishness when he hears of such slaughter, but he must remember there were thousands of antelope, buffalo, deer, and elk then. A man who was an expert with the rifle in those days and able to stand at the head of the class with his gun was looked upon as 'Big Medicine' by both whites and Indians" (Smith 1997:79).

Blizzards during the 1880s and 1890s resulted in the deaths of countless pronghorn as far south as Texas (Simpson and Leftwich 1978). Livestock- and pronghorn-killing blizzards during those years were reported from Colorado (Collinson 1963) and Montana (Munson 1897b, 1897c). Also, drift fences were being built across the plains to control livestock. In 1882, settlers killed 1,500 pronghorn trapped by a drift fence in the Texas panhandle (Haley 1949). Market hunters probably were quick to take advantage of such traps and likely constructed some, as was reported for meat hunters in California who used fences and corrals to capture pronghorn (Millais 1915).

As previously noted, Army officers and enlisted men stationed in the West looked upon hunting as a sporting way to improve their sometimes monotonous duties and tiresome diets (Custer 1885, Forsythe 1900, Roe 1909, Midden 1930, Hull 1938, Hoekman 1953, Mattison 1965). For military pots and pot shooting on the Great Plains after the Civil War, pronghorn seems to have been the most commonly taken big game. From a stockade on the Yellowstone River during 1873, Custer (1885) wrote that he had shot 41 pronghorn, 7 deer and 4 each bison and elk on the expedition that took him to Montana. During June 1868, Second Lieutenant Belden traveled with a party from Fort Steele on the Platte River to Fort Fetterman along the Bozeman Trail in Wyoming Territory. En route, they killed 43 pronghorn, 5 elk and 3 deer. Military weapons probably were not well suited to pronghorn hunting, and many soldiers apparently were not experienced at stalking in open country. Despite the braggart's lists of pronghorn killed on particular outings, bagging (shooting and retrieving) any pronghorn was only occasional even in the presence of numerous pronghorn (see Unrau 1979, Koster 1980). Plenty of ammunition was expended at animals out of range or too fleet for proper aiming. Undoubtedly, many pronghorn were wounded and unretrieved.

At some times and places, all hunting by white men was considered poaching by red men (Carrington 1868). The Utes resented soldiers in Colorado and Wyoming because "They took their rifles and rode out to hunt in the hills" (Emmitt 1954:104). "The coursing of antelopes with a good pack of greyhounds and stag hounds on the open plains was the best sport offered to the officers stationed at the military garrisons of the far west" (Huntington 1904:244). Besides Custer, other high-ranking officers brought hounds with them to their duty stations. Some hounds were capable of catching a pronghorn, many were

Horses were considered essential for pronghorn hunting by most early hunters, even those who did not course them. "To hunt antelope successfully one must be well mounted; indeed, I have never seen anyone try it on foot, as the circuits necessary to be taken to circumvent a band are sometimes of such a radius that would take hours to go round on foot" (DuBray 1890:330). Before settlement of the Great Plains, horses were as vital for securing fresh food and other staples as are automobiles to the lifestyle of suburbanites today. Left photo courtesy of the Wyoming State Archives, Museum and Historical Department, Cheyenne. Photo above from Cook (1923).

not (Davies 1871, Custer 1885, Dodge 1885, Seton 1909).

As the West was being traversed and settled, nearly everyone who had the opportunity seems to have shot at or otherwise harassed pronghorn for food or entertainment. Most immigrants crossing the Great Plains lacked proper firearms, shooting skill or enough knowledge of pronghorn to harvest many. Pioneer Murphy's (1891) comment—"the antelope are so fleet of foot it is difficult to get a shot at one"—is typical. Also typical is the journal notation by Overland Trail traveler Elisha Douglas Perkins, written within a few miles of Fort Kearney (Nebraska) on June 14, 1849: "This morning antelope are running round us on all directions and such running! Without apparently any effort they glide over the Prairie at a bird's wing pace that scorns the effort of the fleetest horse to come up with them. We have not yet succeeded in killing though two of our party have snapped caps at them" (Clark 1967:28). Some travelers were able to pick up neonates for food (Sanford 1959), but by the time most pioneers ventured into pronghorn range, fawns were older and too elusive.

Generally, pronghorn were an undependable source of food for pioneers, especially for the inexperienced hunters (Blair 1982). Also, areas along immigrant trails probably became overhunted or depleted of game by diseases introduced by livestock. For instance, Stansbury (1852:28) wrote of an overland expedition in 1849 to 1850: "Yesterday, being Sunday was devoted to rest [somewhere between Fort Leavenworth and Fort Phil Kearney]. Most of the people, however, availed themselves of the opportunity to take a hunt, as we had killed no game up to this time. In fact, we had had no opportunity, the game having been driven from the vicinity of the traveled route by the unintermitted stream of immigration which had already passed over the road. The result of their efforts was accordingly not very magnificent, the whole party bringing in only a duck, a musk-rat, a large snapping-turtle, and 1 miserably poor little antelope" (see also Johnson 1969).

On a steamboat going down the Missouri River during October 1867, de Trobriand (1951) reported that passengers frequently disembarked to hunt and supplement their provisions. On one occasion, 100 to

150 pronghorn were noticed on a point where their retreat could be cut off. Passengers and crew landed, spread out across the peninsula with their carbines and killed a dozen animals.

Beginning about 1865, "Railroad and shipping companies recruited families from the depressed agricultural regions of Scandinavia to populate the prairies of the Midwest and southern Canada" (Tanner 1995:118). Newspaper articles of the time indicated that early settlers hunted throughout the year, suggesting that people were in need of, or at least desired, a continual supply of fresh meat (Fleharty 1995). Homesteaders thus orphaned many fawns. The waifs sometimes followed their mothers' carcasses being carried or hauled back to a homestead (Trimm 1983).

Some pioneers, especially those with children, took fawns for pets. "Saw a little girl by the name of Virginia," wrote emigrant John Markle on June 4, 1849, "and her father could hardly get her to leave it [a pronghorn]" (Clark 1967:28). *The Stockton* (Kansas) *News* of July 2, 1879, reported that a young pronghorn in a wagon attracted much admiration, and the pretty creature was perfectly tame, showing the liveliest sense of affection when petted. "Frequently the pioneers captured the young of antelope and offered them for sale, and at least two were shipped by rail to Boston. In other cases, the owners simply appeared to appreciate the animals and wanted them about" (Fleharty 1995:144). *The Pawnee County* (Kansas) *Herald* of March 31, 1877, reported that those two sold for $90.00. More often than not, however, captive pronghorn were short-lived (see Brown 1971a, Stratton 1981).

Many people living on the land hunted to feed their families and dogs. Little has been written concerning the impact of homesteaders on pronghorn numbers during the late 19th century, but Ligon (1927:85) expressed his opinion: "Homesteaders, often confronted with extreme poverty but with an excess of idleness, managed to remain on merely grasslands long enough to exterminate most of the antelope." If one visited what was considered a medium-sized ranch in prime pronghorn habitat at the end of the 20th century, a cursory examination usually would reveal 5 to 10 wells, old foundations, etc., indicating the same number of homesteader families once lived there. Practically all of them starved out, so it is easy to imagine

Three steamboats bearing the name Antelope *figure in U.S. history. This one, operated by the California Steam Navigation Company, made daily runs between Sacramento and San Francisco during gold rush days. Besides passengers, she carried mail from the Sacramento Pony Express depot to San Francisco. On the first Express run, rider William Hamilton trotted his horse aboard so that he could deliver his packet personally in the city. Later relay riders entrusted their saddlebags to the skipper (Nevin 1974). Earlier, another* Antelope, *of the American Fur Company, was among the first steamboats navigating the Missouri River, carrying trade goods upriver to trading posts and forts (Sunder 1965). However, she was not designed for use on such a shallow, unforgiving river, and was retired after the second year. The third* Antelope *was assigned to the West Gulf Blockading Squadron, and sunk on September 23, 1864, in the Mississippi River by Confederate forces (U.S. Navy 1959). Yet another* Antelope *vessel figured significantly in U.S. History. It was the two-masted, 69-foot (21 m) slave ship that, in late June 1820, was intercepted off the northern coast of Florida, near St. Augustine, by a U.S. Treasury cutter. For 8 years, the disposition and status of the* Antelope's *cargo—280 Africans—was debated in American courts. Involved were two U.S. presidents (John Quincy Adams and James Monroe), lawyer Francis Scott Key and Chief Justice of the Supreme Court John Marshall. The* Antelope *incident was a low point in the murky relationship between law, morality and justice pertaining to the slavery issue (Noonan 1977). One might speculate that the names for these various ships were chosen because of the pronghorn's renowned swiftness. Photo courtesy of the Wells Fargo Bank History Room, San Francisco, California.*

As pets, pronghorn fawns provided explorers and settlers with a great deal of amusement. During an expedition across the Rocky Mountains to the Columbia River in 1834, one of the expeditioners captured a pronghorn fawn (Townsend 1978). In a few days, it became tame and learned to drink from a cup. The men named it Zip Coon. The fawn soon became familiar with its name and would come running when called. It exhibited many other evidences of affection and attachment. A pannier of willow branches was woven for Zip and packed on a mule. When the column was assembled to march, the fawn would run to his long-eared mount, bleating with impatience until someone placed him in the pannier. Near the Snake River, the mule fell in lava rocks and Zip was so injured that, out of mercy, he was killed. Usually, pronghorn pets increasingly became a nuisance and even dangerous. Documentation of their survival to adulthood is rare. Injury, predation, and dispatch for food or nuisance elimination were the causes of loss more often than cited. Top left photo taken in 1871 by William H. Jackson, shows hide sheds on the ranch of the notorious Boettler brothers, in southern Montana Territory, near the Yellowstone River; courtesy of the U.S. Geological Survey, Herndon, Virginia. Top right photo courtesy of the U.S. National Archives, Washington, DC. Center and bottom left photos courtesy of the South Pass State Historic Site, South Pass, Wyoming. Bottom right photo courtesy of Doris Whithorn and the Park County Museum, Cody, Wyoming.

how many pronghorn were killed during year-around hunting by the "wrinkle bellies"—a term still applied by some old timers to homesteaders.

One way that wrinkle bellies and scoundrels dealt with food shortage was shooting a "big antelope"— the name given to a knowingly poached cow (Adams 1944).

On a cattle drive from Texas to Fort Robinson in Nebraska during 1873, the cowboys were able to kill pronghorn whenever they wanted fresh meat (Collinson 1963). The animals were easily taken because many ran up to or through the cattle, probably

much as they had behaved around bison herds, which had served pronghorn by deterring wolves and other predators. Within a few years, with increased trail drives and other influences on pronghorn numbers and wariness, successful shooting of pronghorn by cowboys became somewhat more problematic (see Fletcher 1966).

Trail driving cattle was not the more insidious impact of livestock on pronghorn in the settling West. Referring to declining pronghorn numbers as early as 1866, Colonel R. B. March opined that "its haunts are now being occupied so rapidly by stock-raisers

As they did with other game animals, settlers in the West tended to kill pronghorn when the opportunities to do so availed themselves. Homesteading for most was an exercise of survival; there was little time to hunt profitably and rarely for sport. As settler numbers increased and farming and ranching practices altered the landscape, most wildlife species and especially big game either retreated or were simply extirpated. Limitations of travel as well as time tended to preclude active hunting for settlers. Even when opportunity existed to kill a large number of pronghorn or other big game, settlers rarely did so. Lack of refrigeration or immediate market access made large kills in warm weather improvident not only from the standpoint of sheer wastefulness, but because it reduced or eliminated the wildlife population within reasonable proximity. On the other hand, where there was ready access to a market, some settlers, as above, supplemented their meager income by selling whatever meat and hides they could acquire. For a brief period in the 1870s and 1880s, mainly after bison herds had been depleted, professional gunners killed pronghorn for Army posts, railroad construction crews, railway passengers, and a limited hide market. However, declining pronghorn numbers and a changing economy could not sustain the unregulated taking. Photo from the A. B. Campbell Art Company; courtesy of the Library of Congress, Washington, DC.

By 1886, cattle and horse rustling had reached nearly epidemic proportions in remote regions of the Great Plains. It was countered by aggressive and nearly as lawless vigilantism. In late March of that year, neophyte rancher Theodore Roosevelt discovered that a boat he used to cross the Little Missouri River, north of Medora, North Dakota, had been stolen. He suspected a neighbor named Finnegan and several confederates of pilfering the "clinker-built" craft, to escape lynching-inclined cattlemen who believed the "three hard characters" to be cattle killers and horse stealers (Roosevelt 1888:114–115). Rather than submit to the seemingly minor offense, and the prospect that it "invited almost certain repetition," Roosevelt went in pursuit, with two ranch hands who quickly built another boat. After three days, the quarry was captured without the expected difficulty. However, rather than meting out "justice" as was the common vigilante practice, Roosevelt and his men chose to take the men to the law in Dickinson. Low on provisions, unable to move the boats up the river against the current and an ice jam, and forced to keep guard on the prisoners around the clock in mostly freezing weather, the 27-year-old rancher completed his mission after more than a week and 300 miles (483 km) traveled. The photo above shows Roosevelt, seated at left and in front of a pronghorn carcass, standing watch over the thieves. Finnegan is the middle prisoner, seated closest to Roosevelt. The photo has been credited to famous western photographer Laton Alton Huffman of Miles City, Montana (Huffman made no such claim), but actually was taken by one of Roosevelt's ranch hands, with a camera Roosevelt took along on the chase (Brown and Felton 1956). The pronghorn in the scene is not accounted for in Roosevelt's narrative of the adventure. He and his hands killed several deer before the capture. Afterward, all the men were famished before reaching Dickinson. It is assumed that the thieves had killed the animal before being captured at their campsite along the river, and that is where the photograph was taken. Photo courtesy of the Sagamore Hill National Historic Site, Oyster Bay, New York.

that these herds and flocks are pushing it [the pronghorn] further into wild and inhospitable places" (Murphy 1879:325). By the 1880s, fencing to enclose or exclude livestock herds fragmented the western landscape and greatly restricted pronghorn range and movements; many pronghorn were killed or chased away by ranchers unwilling to let them compete for forage with sheep and cattle (Dary 1989). Between August 1, 1885, and January 1886, the Barthol

brothers of Colorado killed 1,080 pronghorn because they were thought to compete with domestic livestock for forage on the brothers' rangeland (see Milner et al. 1994). Ranchers also resorted to protecting their livestock from coyote predation by shooting pronghorn and poisoning the carcasses, which coyotes would scavenge (Van Wormer 1969). Farmers likewise mounted lethal campaigns against pronghorn that ate and trampled crops (Fleharty 1995), such as the

Hunting and chasing pronghorn were popular diversions for western cowboys (Laycock 1990). These activities provided adventuresome breaks from the monotony of trail riding, offered opportunity for practicing and demonstrating horsemanship, facilitated competition or teamwork, and held promise of meat that was different from and "Better than Bacon," which Charles M. Russell titled his 1905 watercolor painting that is the bottom scene. Murphy (1879:313) observed that "some exciting fun can be enjoyed by lassoing fawns, for if a person is mounted on a good horse he can run down the latter in a mile or two." Top left is "Stalking Antelope" (detail) by Carl Rungius; from Roosevelt et al. (1902). Top right scene is an illustration by Frederick Remington; photo courtesy of the Library of Congress, Washington, DC. Left center is "Hunting Antelope"—an oil painting (detail) by Carl Rungius; photo courtesy of the Glenbow Museum, Calgary, Alberta. "Better than Bacon" photo courtesy of the Thomas Gilcrease Institute of American History and Art, Tulsa, Oklahoma.

Pronghorn were more alarmed by people afoot or even on horseback than those conveyed by wagon, according to U.S. Army Lieutenant William Johnston (1890). Accordingly, it was Army custom to hunt pronghorn from spring wagons drawn by four or six mules. During the late 1880s, parties of two or more soldiers, armed with government-issue Springfield rifles, well provisioned with ammunition and aboard a spring wagon, would leave their post near the southern limit of the Staked Plains of Texas almost daily in autumn to search for pronghorn. When the animals were sighted, the driver reportedly was exhorted by every expectant hunter to drive directly at them. When the pronghorn bunched together to run, they momentarily presented a stationary target, albeit at 500 to 1,000 yards (457–914 m). "At a signal by one [of the soldiers], all would fire at the bunch and dust would fly from the prairie at distances varying from one hundred to one thousand yards [91–914 m] from the antelope, so variously had the guns been held" (Johnston 1890:6). Sketch by J. Dalziel, in Johnston 1890; photo courtesy of The Huntington Library, San Marino, California.

droves of pronghorn that daily invaded Kansas wheat fields, as reported by the *Smith County Pioneer* on July 27, 1876. Disease also was a factor. During the early to mid-1800s, anthrax, tuberculosis, a variety of parasites (West 2001), rinderpest (Sandoz 1978) and Texas cattle fever (Stratton 1981) were introduced to the plains by livestock. All had potential to decimate pronghorn herds, especially the huge winter concentrations. But, even in other seasons, damage could occur, such as summer 1873, during which 75% to 90% of the pronghorn between the Missouri and Yellowstone rivers died, possibly from bluetongue (Allen 1874, Murphy 1879).

In addition to conveying settlers, prospectors and soldiers to the West, and taking livestock and other products eastward, the railroad transported "sports." English visitors riding on the Kansas Pacific were astonished to see pronghorn shot from cars and the

train stop to pick them up, according to the *Denver Daily Tribune* of December 20, 1875 (Fleharty 1995). Not uncommonly, passengers shot "impotently" with pistols at pronghorn running alongside trains (Reinhardt 1967:33).

During the late 1870s, hunting destinations in Nebraska, accessible via the Union Pacific Railroad, advertised hunting for pronghorn and other plains game (Hallock 1879). Selected prices for services included: guides $2.00 per day and teams $4.00 per day in Antelope County; or board $5.00 per week, teams with drivers $3.00 per day and hotel $4.00 per week in Buffalo County. At the same time, entrepreneurs in Albany County, Wyoming, also reached by the "UP," mostly specified that camping was necessary. The daily listed prices included: board $1.00 to $3.00, guides $2.00 to $4.00, teams $5.00 to $7.00 and saddle or pack horses $4.00. Some outfitters provided

Pointless shooting at game apparently was exciting recreation for some railroad and stagecoach travelers in the West. The same was true for soldiers and wagon train members, who were somewhat more likely to retrieve animals wounded or killed. It is clear from the literature that much ammunition was expended by travelers pop shooting, or potting, at pronghorn (see Lang 1926, Brown and Felton 1956). No doubt a good many pronghorn were hit and unrecovered. Featured in the May 29, 1875, issue of Harper's Weekly *was a depiction of a Kansas-Pacific train stopped near Kit Carson, Colorado, so its passengers could "amuse themselves shooting at a small herd of pronghorn" (Grafton 1992:105). While riding the Pacific Express westward in 1883, Lang (1926) witnessed other train passengers shoot at pronghorn running parallel to the train several hundred yards away. Before the train pulled away from the animals, Lang counted five pronghorn killed outright and at least ten others wounded. When the train's conductor was asked by passengers other than the shooters to stop the train and retrieve the dead pronghorn, he refused, saying tersely, "What in hell do they amount to anyhow?" The concept and slightest notion of wildlife conservation were decades away.* Illustration by unknown artist; photo courtesy of The Huntington Library, San Marino, California. Illustration credited to Frenzeny and Taverier; courtesy of the Library of Congress, Washington, DC.

camping gear, others had it for sale. Pronghorn was a featured species in all hunts. Advertisements from California and Colorado indicated roughly similar prices, but hunters needed to get permission from landowners to hunt in the former. Colorado owners reportedly seldom objected. One Colorado outfitter noted that a single hunter brought in 35 pronghorn in a day (Harris 1888).

"The system of still hunting is the one most in vogue among the Indians and pioneers, but it lacks all the spirit and excitement of the chase, and is in reality only fit for pot hunters" (Murphy 1879:324). Others echoed Murphy's sentiments (e.g., Custer 1885, Allison 1890, Huntington 1904), but many subscribed to the sentiments of Governor Saint John of Kansas, who reportedly said that it takes a mighty good greyhound to catch a mighty poor pronghorn (Seton 1909). Some who tried coursing did not believe a hound could catch a healthy, adult pronghorn (Dodge 1877). During January 1879, Mayor Kelly of Dodge City, Kansas, with his party and greyhounds, brought down 6 of a band of 12 pronghorn running on crusty snow.

Northwestern Pacific and Union Pacific railroad tracks had hardly been laid and their ties hammered before wealthy eastern "sports" made hunting trips in late summer and autumn to the Dakota and Montana Territories in hopes of bagging bison and whatever other quarry of fin, fur and feather was readily available. The wealthiest owners leased cars with sleeping quarters for the entire party, which often included family members. Above is the "City of Worcester," a Northern Pacific hunting car, and a hunting party in North Dakota in 1878. Photo by F. Jay Haynes; courtesy of the Haynes Foundation Collection, Montana Historical Society, Helena.

During warm weather, greyhounds sometimes died from the exertion of coursing pronghorn (Fleharty 1995).

More references to yesteryear sport hunting of pronghorn reported on the animal's curiosity, eyesight and vulnerability to luring to bow or gun by use of flags, hats, bandannas, etc., than to other aspects of pronghorn behavior, physiology or huntability. Burton (1862:67) observed, for example, that pronghorn were gifted "with truly feminine curiosity." Gregg (1954:378) wrote, "Being as wild as fleet, the hunting of them [pronghorn] is very difficult, except they be entrapped by their curiosity. Meeting a stranger, they seem loth [*sic*] to leave until they have fully found him out. They will often take a circuit around the object of their curiosity, usually approach-

ing nearer and nearer, until within rifle-shot. . . ." Wolfer Charlie held that "they can see everything, but their eyes don't tell um much" (Browne 1939:343). Perhaps therein lies the explanations for the claims of success of luring by some hunters—a skill reportedly learned from Indians (Huntington 1904).

Early reports indicated that the technique was effective (e.g., U.S. House of Representatives 1852, Greeley 1964, Newhouse 1869). Conversely, DuBray (1890:331), who claimed to have killed 240 pronghorn in 1878 and 1879, wrote: "I have never had much success flagging Antelope; in fact, I don't think I ever killed one that way. Although I have tried this ruse, never could I lure them within reach. The scheme doubtless worked all right in early days, before the game of the prairies became educated to the seductive wiles and sly ways of the white man." Dodge (1877), Roosevelt et al. (1902) and Seton (1909) reached similar conclusions. Also, supporting that experience and perspective was the famed guide, trapper, scout, hunter and infamous Indian hunter, Liver-Eating Johnson, a "thoroughly educated and equipped frontiersman at every point, graduate at the head of his class in prairie lore—withal, a long-headed, cool, and calculating man—once said to me while hunting: 'What a live Antelope don't see between dawn and dark isn't visible from his stand-point; and while you're a gawkin' at him thro' that 'ere glass to make out whether he's a rock or a Goat, he's a countin' your cartridges and fixin's, and makin' up his mind which way he'll scoot when you disappear in the draw for to sneak on 'im—and don't you forget it'" (DuBray 1890:316).

Commonly described in detail in the literature, luring—or flagging—involved a hunter concealed behind an object or in vegetation and waving something. When the quarry approached to well within range, the hunter or a nearby concealed companion rose and fired quickly. There were variations on the technique, such as used during the mid-1800s by neophyte pronghorn hunters Audubon and Bachman (1851). By lying on their backs and kicking their legs in the air, they brought a buck from at least 300 yards away (270 m) to within 60 yards (54 m) in about 60 minutes. The hunters then missed.

Nevertheless, unregulated killing of pronghorn for market, sport, subsistence and agriculture protection

Coursing pronghorn with greyhounds, wrote Allison (1890:333), is "one of the grandest sports that this continent affords. . . . For a merry party of sportsmen to mount their spirited horses, on a clear, cold, frosty, winter morning; to bring out the eager hounds; to speed away over the prairies for ten or twenty miles; to sight a band of Antelope, slip the dogs, and follow them through such a grand race as must ensue; to watch the startled game in its efforts to escape, and the efforts of the hounds to come up with it; to head it off at every turn; to follow and encourage the dogs, and at last to come to their aid, after they have pulled down the largest and fleetest buck in the bunch—all these afford grander and more exhilarating sport than any I have ever indulged in." Top illustration from the July 7, 1877, *Harper's Weekly* supplement. Bottom painting, "End of the Course," by William Holbrook Beard, from Roosevelt (1893); photo courtesy of the Library of Congress, Washington, DC.

"Antelope often suffer from such freaks of apathetic indifference to danger, which are doubly curious in an animal as wary as that wildest of game, the mountain sheep," observed Theodore Roosevelt (1888:138–139). Pronghorn curiosity—Roosevelt's "freaks of apathetic indifference to danger"—was well known to Indian hunters and often the animals' undoing. Successful flagging, or tolling, of pronghorn was cited frequently in period reports (e.g., U.S. House of Representatives 1852, Greeley 1964 [written in 1859], Newhouse 1869), however, many who tried luring had little or no luck (e.g., Dodge 1877, Roosevelt et al. 1902, Seton 1909). For patient, skilled hunters, the ruse still works in the 21st century . . . sometimes. Top scene opposite is a painting, "Tolling Up Antelope," by Bob Kuhn; photo courtesy of the Elman Pictorial Archive, Stewartsville, New Jersey. Bottom scene opposite, from *Harper's Weekly*, May 23, 1874, drawn by W. M. Cary; photo courtesy of the Library of Congress, Washington, DC.

caused the pronghorn population to plummet from millions to thousands. "The rifles of the miners, ranchmen, and settlers, and the destruction of the food by great flocks of sheep, soon proved to be too much for the antelopes of California, as well as those of the Great Plains" (Huntington 1904:235). And, there were other influences.

Weather seldom is considered to have been a contributor to the catastrophic decline in pronghorn during the late 1800s. However, drought conditions on the Staked Plains of Texas were said to have caused a significant decline in 1877 (Carlson 1998), as did drought in California 20 years earlier. And, as previously noted, the 1880s and 1890s witnessed especially severe blizzards and cold weather that impacted already depleted pronghorn herds (Munson 1897a, 1897b, 1897c, Collinson 1963, Simpson and Leftwich 1978). Drift fences had been built across the prairie (Haley 1949) and homesteaders had plowed or fenced much of the most fertile land. Cadieux (1986) noted that removal of bison from the South Dakota prairies was thought by some to have impaired the pronghorn's ability to travel and forage when snow was deep.

Pronghorn in Mexico were depleted in much the same manner as those farther north. According to Leopold (1959), the animals originally were abundant in northern Mexico. Lumholtz (1902) found them still abundant near Casas Grandes, Chihuahua, in 1891. However, during the late 1800s, after the Apaches and Comanches had been subjugated and settlement resumed, pronghorn were rapidly depleted. By the end of the 19th century, they had become scarce.

Pronghorn in Canada fared no better. Seton (1909) reported what generally is considered to be the last record of pronghorn in Manitoba; J. T. Brondgeest told that, when he settled near Whitewater, Manitoba, in 1879, pronghorn were plentiful, but the last one Brondgeest saw was killed by his father in 1881. By the 1890s, only a remnant of the once numerous herds remained in southern Alberta and Saskatchewan (Foster 1978).

For Hopi-Tewa Indians, pronghorn had always been an important source of food and clothing (Stanislawski 1979). By 1890, they told reservation agents that there were too few pronghorn in northeastern Arizona to hunt. It was a refrain heard throughout the West.

PRAIRIE WRAITH AND THE GENESIS OF CONSERVATION

The dainty pronghorn persisted in dwindling numbers in secluded prairies that were being taken up by ranchers and settlers almost as rapidly as they could be located. . . . Meat hunting, market hunting, night shooting, and dogging were accepted practices; poaching and eluding game wardens were secondary "sports" where any protective laws existed at all. . . . To a less optimistic group than the early members of the Boone and Crockett Club, the prospects of preserving big-game hunting in the face of these facts would have appeared hopeless.

—Trefethen (1961:62)

"Within fifty years of the journey of Lewis and Clark, no more than a long course of seasons in the Indians' unwritten time, the din of civilization had resounded from behind the forest horizon [the East]" (Matthiessen 1959:148). That din echoed loudly for the next 50 years—a period characterized as North America's wildlife "exploitation era" (McCabe and McCabe 1984:60). The end of that era, flanking the outset of the 20th century, had little to do with social or ecological conscience. It occurred mainly because the exploitable species and populations had essentially bottomed out, that is, there was not much more accessible to exploit. Some of the hue and cry of concern came initially from enterprises that needed an unlimited supply to sustain themselves, ranging from milliners and miners to whalers and loggers. Some came from officials of a government that not only condoned resource rapaciousness, but often grandly subsidized it (Trefethen 1961).

All was lost. All was done, save hand-wringing, finger-pointing and lamenting. The laments tended to be eloquent. "Those mustangs and graceful antelope made a picture that will never be seen again upon the plains," eulogized erstwhile Texas bison hunter Collinson (1963:109–110). "Now that once virgin range is fenced, and bountiful crops of cotton and maize replace the mesquite grass. The bones of the buffalo and mustangs are gone and not an antelope is left." The laments also were premature.

Of all the human elements that contributed to the "black cloud of extermination" (Trefethen 1961:62), only one stepped forward to salvage and try to restore decimated game populations. Indeed, one of the least significant elements, the emerging "order of 'true sportsmen'" took initiative (Reiger 1975:21–22). To be very certain, however, the gauntlet was taken up by only a few such hunters and anglers, but they were a very capable, energetic and ambitious few.

George Bird Grinnell, editor of the national magazine *Forest and Stream*, realized the need for an effective national sportsmen's society to do for large mammals what the Audubon Society—founded by him in 1886—was doing for birds. Grinnell's friend, and a protégé of sorts, Theodore Roosevelt, agreed and invited a number of his colleagues to a dinner party in Manhattan during December 1887, at which he suggested formation of such an association—The Boone and Crockett Club (Ward and McCabe 1988). The club took, as a basic approach, Grinnell's idea that all renewable resources benefited from efficient administration. This concept, taken from the ideology of the scientific and business worlds, was reinforced by a code of ethics, with its emphasis on the use, without

waste, of all game killed (Reiger 1975). Grinnell maintained that, with the exception of market gunners, the greatest destroyers of western wildlife had been upperclass pseudosportsmen. As a result of the club's influence, Grinnell's editorials and protestations by an irascible William T. Hornaday (1889, 1913), many hunters who had boasted of their wanton killing of game became more circumspect and contrite—the mindset of the fledgling conservation movement.

"All of the early members of the club who had experience in the frontier West—and this was by far, the majority—had a strong affection for the pronghorn antelope, and none held that wraith of the prairies in higher esteem than Theodore Roosevelt" (Trefethen 1961:145). In Roosevelt, the West, conservation and the wraith of the prairie found a champion. The road to recovery for pronghorn would take more than a champion, even one who was President of the United States, but a champion it needed for the journey to begin.

Pronghorn on a bench overlooking (eastward) the Elkhorn Ranch, along the Little Missouri River, north of Medora, in western North Dakota, in the 1880s. This was the ranch that an ambitious eastern dude named Roosevelt bought and operated unprofitably from 1884 to 1890 (sold in 1898). But, it was at the Elkhorn Ranch and from its surroundings that the young, neophyte ranchman would gain particular appreciation for the western landscape and habitats of big game populations staggering from unregulated killing—an appreciation turned conviction that would foster the conservation movement. Photo of diorama courtesy of the American Museum of Natural History, New York, New York.

Appendix A

SELECT EYEWITNESS, HISTORIC ACCOUNTS OF PRONGHORN ABUNDANCE IN THE WEST

Dates	Places	Abundance	Source/*Eyewitness*
April 17, 1540	Cibola (AZ and NM)	Great abundance	Winship (1896:550)/ *Antonio de Mendoza*
ca 1569	Northern Mexico or coastal Texas	Great plenty	Wright (1965:59)/ *David Ingram*
December 6, 1738	Vicinity of Bismarck, ND	Many	Smith (1980:59)/ *Pierre Gaultier de Varennes, the Sieur de la Vérendrye*
ca 1752	"towards the head of the river Missouris"	Very common at certain seasons	Forster (1771:356)/ *Jean-Bernard Bossu*
1769	San Joaquin Valley, CA	Many	Priestley (1937:77)/ *Pedro Fages*
June 1776	San Jose Valley, CA	In abundance	Hittel (1898:400)/ *Francisco Palou*
November 1776	Vicinity of Rainbow Bridge National Monument in Utah	Spoor as thick as that of great flocks of domestic sheep	Briggs (1976:149)/ *Frs. Francisco Atanasio Dominguez and Silvestre Velez de Escalante*
1777	Near Durango City, Mexico	Abound in the provinces	Leopold (1959:520)/ *Juan Augustin Morfi*
July 14, 1806	Vicinity of Souris, Manitoba	Herds . . . always in sight	Coues (1897 [I]:305)/ *Alexander Henry*
August 4, 1806	North of Towner, ND	Numerous herds	Coues (1897 [I]:410)/ *Alexander Henry*
June 11, 1811	Above the confluence of Cheyenne and Missouri rivers in SD	In abundance	Thwaites (1904 [6(1)]:110)/ *Henry M. Brackenridge*
September 16, 1812	Star Valley, WY	A multitude	Spaulding (1953:99)/ *Robert Stuart*
October 12, 1812	Vicinity of South Pass, WY	Many	Spaulding (1953:118)/ *Robert Stuart*
June 5, 1814	Along the Saskatchewan River in west-central Saskatchewan	Herds of light-limbed antelopes	Thwaites (1904 [6(2)]:372)/ *G. Franchere*
August 5, 1820	Vicinity of Tascosa, TX	Considerable numbers	Thwaites (1905 [16(3)]:98)/ *Edwin James*

. . . .

continued on next page

Dates	Places	Abundance	Source/*Eyewitness*
August 19, 1820	Vicinity of Antelope Hills in western OK	Astonishing numbers	Thwaites (1905 [16(3)]:140)/*Edwin James*
Autumn 1820s	Rio Grande River Valley in northwestern NM	Innumerable droves	Thwaites (1905 [18(2)]:341)/*Dr. Willard*
October 4, 1821	Vicinity of Bowring, OK	Some	Coues (1898:12)/*Jacob Fowler*
Summer 1824	Along Santa Fe Trail	Abundant	Duffus (1934:87)/*Augustus Storrs*
ca 1825	"on the plains betwixt the Saskatchewan and Missouri rivers"	A common animal	Richardson (1829:262)/*John Richardson*
February 1825	Vicinity of Fort Collins, CO	Valleys . . . filled with numerous herds	Dale (1918:129)/*William Henry Ashley*
March 16, 1825	Vicinity of Rock River, WY	Innumerable herds	Dale (1918:131)/*William Henry Ashley*
December 1826	Vicinity of Lemoore, CA	In abundance	Dale (1918:191)/*Jedediah Strong Smith*
September 4, 1827	Kit Carson County, CO	Innumerable herds	Thwaites (1905 [18(1)]:56)/*James O. Pattie*
1828	Along Santa Fe Trail east of Ellinwood, KS	Innumerable	Inman (1897:68)/*Mr. Bryant*
1830s	Nodaway County, MO	Plentiful	Anonymous (1910 [1]:233)/*Unknown*
1832	Mandan, ND	Great numbers sporting and playing about the hills and dales . . . often in flocks of 50 or 100	Catlin (1973 [I]:76)/*George Catlin*
April 15, 1932	Northeast of Carter, WY	Hundreds	Phillips (1940:141)/*Warren A. Ferris*
July 5–7, 1832	Vicinity of Glenda, WY	Plentitude . . . the plains literally covered with them	Wagner (1904:95)/*Zenas Leonard*
December 12, 1832	Vicinity of Marysville, CA	Plenty	Maloney (1945:21)/*John Work*
March 8, 1833	West of Williams, CA	Very numerous	Maloney (1945:34)/*John Work*
April 2, 1833	Between the Galiuro and Pinaleno ranges, AZ	Signs of antelope were abundant. . . . From the numbers of these animals, we called the place Antelope Plain.	Pattie (1833:69)/*James Ohio Pattie*
May 19, 1833	Near Paxton, NE	Very numerous. . . . There is not half an hour during the day in which they are not seen	Thwaites (1905 [21(2)]:159)/*John Kirk Townsend*
May 28, 1833	Big Bend area along Missouri River, SD	Very numerous in winter	Thomas and Ronnefeldt (1976:28)/*Alexander Philip Maximilian*
July 2, 1833	Near Hams Fork in WY	Abundant in vicinity	Thwaites (1905 [21(2)]:194)/*John Kirk Townsend*
July 15, 1833	Vicinity of Stockton, CA	Great numbers	Maloney (1945:65)/*John Work*
September 5, 1833	Along Missouri River in Choteau County, MT, approaching the Gate of the Stone Walls	Numerous herds	Thwaites (1906 [23]:170) *Alexander Philip Maximilian*
October 30, 1833	Vicinity of El Portal, CA	Remarkably plenty	Wagner (1904:180)/*Zenas Leonard*
June 1834	Alluvial bottomlands of country adjacent to Hams Fork of Green River, WY	abounds with . . . antelope	Russell (1965:3)/*Osborne Russell*
June 1835	Teton Valley, ID	Abounds with . . . antelope	Russell (1965:15)/*Osborne Russell*
1835–1837	Region of the Platte and Upper Kansas rivers, NE and KS	In abundance	Clark (1884:284)/*Messrs. Dunbar, Allis and Satterlee*
Winter 1835	Valley of the Grand River, SD	In large bands cover the hills	Denig (1961:10)/*Edwin Thompson Denig*

continued on next page

Dates	Places	Abundance	Source/*Eyewitness*
July 16, 1839	West of Pueblo, CO	A great many	Hafen and Hafen (1955:52)/ *Obadiah A. Oakley*
July 16, 1839	West of Pueblo, CO	Plenty	Hafen and Hafen (1955:72)/*Sidney Smith*
July 20, 1840	Vicinity of Morris, OK	Great abundance	McDermott (1940:248)/*Victor Tixier*
November 15, 1840	Near Thatcher, ID	thousands . . . travelling towards their winter quarters in Green River Valley	Russell (1965:112)/*Osborne Russell*
March 1841	On Antelope Island in Great Salt Lake, UT	Large numbers	Russell (1965:122)/*Osborne Russell*
September 1841	Along the Yellowstone River, MT	Clouds of antelopes were flying before us	Thwaites (1906 [27]:183)/*Pierre Jean DeSmet*
October 16, 1841	Vicinity of Sutter, CA	Plenty but shy	Poesch (1961:195)/*Titian Ramsey Peale*
October 17, 1841	Vicinity of Nicolaus, CA	Many small herds	Poesch (1961:195)/*Titian Ramsey Peale*
June 22, 1842	Near Hastings, NE	Seen frequently	Fremont (1843:16)/*John C. Fremont*
December 19, 1842	Denver, CO	Congregated from all parts, and covered the country in one almost unbroken band	Sage (1857:290)/*Rufus B. Sage*
1843	Along the Upper Missouri River, ND	Sometimes . . . several hundred . . . in a herd	Cahalane (1967:290)/*John James Audubon*
July 19, 1845	Vicinity of South Pass, WY	We daily see hundreds	Thwaites (1906 [30]:72)/*Joel Palmer*
February 1846	Vicinity of Cimarron, NM	Droves of gamboling . . . antelope	Garrard (1850:166)/*Lewis H. Garrard*
May 27–June 2, 1846	Vicinity of North Platte, NE	Hundreds . . . in great abundance	Thwaites (1906 [30]:248)/*Joel Palmer*
Summer 1846	Vicinity of Ogden, UT	Large flocks . . . as many as five hundred [per flock]	Bryant (1936:128)/*Edwin Bryant*
Summer 1846	Vicinity of Cobre, NV	During the day's march, we have seen not less than three or four hundred	Bryant (1936:162)/*Edwin Bryant*
June 6, 1846	Near Paxton, NE	Very numerous	Parkman (1892:82)/*Francis Parkman*
July 1846	Along Sweetwater River in Freemont County, WY	Several numerous flocks	Bryant (1936:108)/*Edwin Bryant*
September 1846	Between Fort Carlton and Fort Pitt, Saskatchewan	An immense number	Kane (1846:85)/*Paul Kane*
October 12, 1846	Vicinity of Penon Blanca, Durango, Mexico	Abundant in the plains	Ruxton (1861:111)/*George Frederick Ruxton*
November 1846	Animas Valley in Hidalgo County, NM	Hardly ever out of sight of antelope	Bigler (1932:46)/*Henry Bigler*
December 1846	San Bernadino Valley, in Cochise County, AZ	Plenty	Whitworth (1965:149)/*Robert Whitworth*
December 10, 1846	Vicinity of Charleston, AZ	Plenty	Standage (1928:191–192)/*Henry Standage*
1847	Along Vermilion Creek, north of Greystone, CO	Abundance of	Ruxton (1887:86)/*George Frederick Ruxton*
May 26, 1847	North of Chimney Rock, NE	Plentiful	Little (1946:86)/*Lorenzo Dow Young*
ca 1848	Vicinity of Park City, UT	Valley full of antelope	Alter (1942:168)/*Priddie Meeks*
November 7, 1848	Vicinity of Dodge City, KS	Bands . . . plenty	Hafen and Hafen (1960:85)/ *Benjamin Kern*
1849	North end of Great Salt Lake, UT	A herd numbering about 100	Stansbury (1852:105)/*Howard Stansbury*
1849	Vicinity of North Platte, NE	Plenty and in great droves	Manly (1894:104)/*William Lewis Manly*

continued on next page

Dates	Places	Abundance	Source/*Eyewitness*
May 27, 1849	Southeast of Kearney, NE	A great many	Potter (1945:86)/*Vincent E. Geiger*
June 12, 1849	South of Ogallala, NE	In great numbers	Settle (1989:86)/*Osborne Cross*
June 17, 1849	Near Glendo, WY	Immense numbers	Potter (1945:110)/*Vincent E. Geiger*
July 18–21, 1849	On Oregon-Mormon Trail between South Pass and Green River in WY	In large numbers	Settle (1989:145)/*Osborne Cross*
June 27, 1849	20–50 miles east of South Pass in the Wind River Mountains, WY	Plenty	Delano (1854:109)/*Alonzo Delano*
July 1849	East of Salt Lake City, UT	Abundance	Hafen and Hafen (1961c:20)/ *William C. Randolph*
September 10, 1849	Sacramento Valley, CA	Numerous in bottomland	Delano (1854:223)/*Alonzo Delano*
September 29, 1849	Santa Cruz Valley south of Tucson, AZ	Abounds	Robrock (1992:149)/ *William W. Hunter*
Mid-1800s	"Plains of California"	Bands of 2,000 or 3,000 were seen commonly	Seton (1909 [I]:219)/*J. C. Hoxie, J. S. Drury, S. F. Dickenson and others*
Mid-1800s	Klamath Valley and in other valleys in lower Klamath County, OR	Plentiful	Bailey (1936:71)/*Mr. Reams*
ca 1850	Yellowstone River Valley, MT	Seen in thousands on the neighboring hills	Denig (1961:93–94)/*Edwin Thompson Denig*
1850	East of San Jose, CA	Droves	Manly (1894:391)/*William Lewis Manly*
August 1850	Santa Rosa Valley, CA	Here and there a drove	Marryat (1855:58)/*Frank Marryat*
ca 1851	"entire plains [of California] . . . including desert"	So abundant that antelope meat in San Francisco cheaper than beef	Bryant (1929:277–278)/*Harold C. Bryant*
1851	"on plains of Red River in MN"	Abundant	U.S. House of Representatives (1852:121)/*Spencer F. Baird*
1851	Western TX, NM and CA	Exceedingly abundant	Woodhouse (1853:56)/*Samuel W. Woodhouse*
Spring 1851	Southwestern NM/northern Mexico	An occasional herd of antelope—unapproachable	Bartlett (1854 [1]:248)/*John Bartlett*
September 13, 1851	Vicinity of Elgin, AZ	Great many	Graham (1852:37)/*James D. Graham*
October 8, 1851	East of San Francisco Mountain in AZ	Abound	Sitgreaves (1853:37)/*Samuel W. Woodhouse*
October 11, 1851	Near the north side of San Francisco Mountain, AZ	Herds . . . seen in all directions	Sitgreaves (1853:10)/*Lorenzo Sitgreaves*
1852	"Bayou Salado" (South Park), CO	Abounded	Inman (1897:254)/*Henry Inman*
January 1, 1853	West of Corpus Christi, TX	Thousands . . . usually in herds from ten to fifty	Bartlett (1854:[2]:526)/*John R. Bartlett*
July 3, 1853	Vicinity of Cedar City, UT	These mountains teem with antelope	Hafen and Hafen (1957:173)/*Gwen Harris Heap*
September 17, 1853	West of Tascosa, TX	A very large number . . . a dozen or twenty with the [wagon] train all [along] the route	Sherburne (1988:97)/*John Pitts Sherburne*
November 1853	Near Zuni, NM	Grassy valleys, abounding in . . . antelopes	Kennerly (1856:6)/*C. B. R. Kennerly*
December 1853	Vicinity of Leupp, AZ	Abundant	Whipple (1941:167)/*Amiel Weeks Whipple*
December 2, 1853	Vicinity of Joseph City, AZ	Large quantity	Sherburne (1988:137)/*John Pitts Sherburne*
ca 1854	Llano Estacado or Staked Plains, TX	Seldom out of sight	Gray (1856:12)/*Andrew B. Gray*
January 1854	Vicinity of Wikieup, AZ	Abounds	Whipple (1941:213)/*Amiel Weeks Whipple*

· ·

continued on next page

Dates	Places	Abundance	Source/*Eyewitness*
July 29, 1854	Vicinity Red Springs, TX	The largest herd . . . yet met . . . more than 30 [pronghorn] in one spot	Parker (1984:143)/*W. B. Parker*
1855	Near Pozo Verde, in northern Sonora, Mexico	Many	Michler (1857:121)/*Nathaniel Michler*
1855	On plains and valleys west of the Pecos River, TX	In all directions large herds are often seen. The number . . . composing a herd vary from eight or ten to several hundred	Emory (1857 [2]:52)/*C. B. R. Kennerly*
1855	North of Fort Pierre, SD	The most abundant animal in the Sioux Country	Warren (1856:79)/*Kimble Warren*
1857	San Joaquin Valley, CA	Though found in nearly all parts of the territory of the United States west of the Mississippi, it probably is most numerous in the valley . . . found in herds literally of thousands	Newberry (1857:71)/*John S. Newberry*
September 7, 1857	Vicinity of Winslow, AZ	In large numbers	Beale (1858:45)/*Edward F. Beale*
September 29, 1857	Southwest of Seligman, AZ	Abundance . . . constantly in sight	Beale (1858:63)/*Edward F. Beale*
1858	Klamath Basin, OR	Abundant through [the] basin	*The Oregonian* (1886)/*Unknown*
1858	Along the Qu'Appelle River, Saskatchewan	Used to abound	Hind (1859:48)/*Henry Youle Hind*
May 1858	Vicinity of San Francisco Mountain in AZ	Constantly seen	Ives (1861:114)/*Joseph C. Ives*
May 1858	Cherry Creek Valley [Denver], CO	Great abundance	Marcy (1859:301)/*Randolph B. Marcy*
October 7, 1858	Vicinity of Fort Atkinson, ND	An abundance	Boller (1972:163)/*Bull Bear*
1859	Vicinity of Lincoln, KS	Unnumbered	Mead (1986:182)/*James R. Mead*
July 18, 1859	East of Empress, Alberta	Many	Spry (1963:412)/*John Palliser*
August 27, 1859	Vicinity of Englewood, CO	Very plenty	Hafen and Hafen (1961a:162)/*Augustus Wildman*
1860–1880	Black Hills of SD	Hundreds of thousands in a single herd	Humfreville (1897:648)/*J. Lee Humfreville*
1860	Tulare Valley and in the Great Basin near the Coast mountains, CA	Herds seen every day . . . thousands . . . killed yearly for the market	Hittel (1863:123)/*J. S. Hittel*
Spring 1860	Vicinity of Wichita, KS	Thousands	Mead (1986:142)/*William Ross*
July 1862	Near Oatman Mountain, east of Agua Caliente, AZ	Great droves	Hand (1862:17)/*George O. Hand*
1863	Vicinity of Roxbury, KS	Quite a number	Mead (1986:138)/*James R. Mead*
1863	In Nueces County, TX	Worlds of . . . antelope	Didear (1969:74)/*D. J. Campbell*
January 1863	Vicinity of Woodston, KS	Numerous	Mead (1986:120)/*James R. Mead*
1864	Vicinity of San Angelo, TX	In droves of thousands	Bitner (1943:99)/*R. F. Tankersley*
May 12, 1864	Along the Arkansas River on the Santa Fe Trail	Lots of antelope	Huning (1973:74)/*Ernestine Huning*
July 10, 1864	Vicinity of Glenrock, WY	A great many on the Plains	Unrau (1979:144)/*Hervey Johnson*
Autumn 1864	Gallatin Valley, MT	Aplenty . . . ten, fifteen, twenty in a band	Dickson (1929:194)/*Arthur Jerome Dickson*
November 25, 1864	Vicinity of Independence Rock in Natrona County, WY	Thousands	Unrau (1979:196)/*Hervey Johnson*

continued on next page

Dates	Places	Abundance	Source/*Eyewitness*
July 14, 1865	Vicinity of Chadron, NE	In great numbers	Hafen and Hafen (1961b:242)/ *James A. Sawyers*
August 4, 1865	Vicinity of Bill, WY	Great many	Hafen and Hafen (1961b:172)/ *B. F. Rockafellow*
August 7, 1865	Between Sand and Brown Spring creeks, Converse County, WY	Any quantity . . . on both flanks	Rogers (1938:176)/*Henry E. Palmer*
September 14, 1865	Along foothills of mountains west of Fort Laramie, WY	Plentiful	Unrau (1979:290)/*Hervey Johnson*
September 21, 1865	SE of Billings, MT	Thousands . . . seen during the day	Hafen and Hafen (1961b:266)/ *James A. Sawyers*
October 21, 1865	Vicinity of Alcova, WY	Great number	Hafen and Hafen (1961b:198)/ *B. F. Rockafellow*
1866	NE of Sheridan, WY	Ever present	Carrington (1868:32)/ *Margaret Sullivant Carrington*
May 21, 1866	Vicinity of Lexington, NE	Never a day without sight of leaping antelopes	Carrington (1929:71)/*James B. Carrington*
Winter, ca 1866	Fort Dodge, KS	Heart of . . . antelope Territory . . . 2,000 . . . in a single bunch	Garretson (1938:64)/*Mr. Wright*
July 20, 1867	Vicinity of Wheatland Reservoir in WY	Very plenty	Hafen and Hafen (1959:197)/ *William Henry Jackson*
October 24, 1867	Fort Stevenson, ND	A band of from one hundred to one hundred and fifty	de Trobriand (1951:151)/*Phillipe Regis de Trobriand*
1868	Saskatchewan	Large and small flocks	McDougall (1898:249)/*John McDougall*
1868	"Concho River Country" of southwest TX	One herd . . . estimated to contain 100,000	Rister (1938:16)/*Unknown*
1868	North Park, CO	4,400 killed	Seton (1909 [I]:220)/*W. N. Byers*
Winter 1868–69	Cache la Poudre Valley between Denver, CO and Cheyenne, WY	For 10 to 12 miles . . . one long band of antelope, 20–40 rods wide, practically continuous	Seton (1909 [I]:221)/*James B. Pond*
1870s	Vicinity of Big Springs, TX	As thick as jackrabbits	Hutto (1932:79)/*Unknown*
ca 1870	Near Old Fort Steel, WY	There was a pass where many thousands . . . crossed each autumn going south to certain wintering grounds in Colorado	Grinnell (1911:582)/*George Bird Grinnell*
ca 1870	Colorado Springs, CO	A thousand or more	Warren (1942:291)/*T. S. Brigham*
1870	Between Medicine Bow Station and the foothills of the Laramie Mountains along the Medicine Bow–Fort Fetterman freight road, WY	Almost never out of sight . . . in some cases . . . several thousand to a herd	Allred (1943:117)/*"Pizen Bill" Hooker*
1870	Yellowstone Valley, WY	Swarming with antelope	Strong (1876:80)/*William E. Strong*
1870s	Between Fort Sumner in NM and Yellow House Canyon in the south-central TX panhandle	In herds of from five hundred to two or three thousand	Biggers (1991:27)/*Don Hampton Biggers*
Early 1870s	On the "playas" of AZ	Quite large herds	Bourke (1891:129)/*John G. Bourke*
January 1871	Between Sheridan, CO and Wallace, KS	The [rail] road was lined with them all day	*Rocky Mountain News* (1871:1)/ *Jay G. Kay*
July 27, 1871	Southwest of Ouray, UT	Without number	Darrah (1949:209)/*John F. Steward*
ca 1872	Indian Territory [OK]	May be found and hunted to the heart's content	Webb (1872:462)/*W. E. Webb*
August 11, 1872	Staked Plains of TX	As plentiful as flies at harvest time	Koster (1980:101)/*Eddie Matthews*
August 13, 1872	Near Amarillo, TX	Saw at least 500	Koster (1980:101)/*Eddie Matthews*

. . . .

continued on next page

Dates	Places	Abundance	Source/*Eyewitness*
December 1872	Vicinity of Wallace, KS	Quite a number	Wheeler (1923:63)/*Homer W. Wheeler*
1873	From Fort Abraham Lincoln west to the Little Missouri River, ND	The most abundant game animal . . . almost constantly in sight	Allen (1874:40)/*J. A. Allen*
Summer 1873	Near Abilene, KS	Thousands . . . bands of hundreds as far as the eye could survey	H. B. (1911:177)/*Unknown*
1874	North Park, CO	The country . . . almost covered with Antelope of all sizes and ages	Grinnell (1911:582)/*George Bird Grinnell*
1874	In foothills and river bottoms of Blackfeet country, Alberta	Often seen in bands of many hundreds	Denny (1938:28)/*Cecil E. Denny*
August 1875	Wyoming	Saw daily from 500 to 3,000 Antelope in bands numbering 100 or 200 each	Seton (1909 [I]:219–220)/*Charles H. Stonebridge*
Late 1800s	WY and MT grasslands	Antelope millions	Hornaday (1914:86)/*William T. Hornaday*
Summer 1876	North Park, CO	Nowhere [else] . . . so abundant . . . almost continually in view, and thousands must breed in that locality	Dartt (1879)/*Elliot Coues*
1876	Along Little Crow Creek, 35 miles southeast of Cheyenne, WY	Plenty	Cook (1923:125)/*James H. Cook*
May 3, 1876	Vicinity of Whitney, NE	Seen at intervals from . . . the North Platte [River] . . . now . . . in great numbers	Hughes (1957:50)/*Richard B. Hughes*
1877	Between Valley City and Jamestown, ND	A herd of 3,000	Bailey (1926:29)/*J. S. Weiser*
August 1877	Pryor's Pass in WY	A band which looked to be five thousand in number	Allen (1903:84)/*William A. Allen*
October 1877	Yellowstone National Park, WY	Thousands	Norris (1877:843)/*Philetus W. Norris*
1877–1879	"In the big bend of the Yellowstone [River]," MT	Hundreds of thousands in one band	Allen (1903:245)/*William A. Allen*
1878–1880	Vicinity of Valley City, ND	Common, . . . as many as 200 in a . . . bunch	Bailey (1926:29)/*John Hailand*
1879	In Crosby County, TX	Before it [prairie fire] fled and swarmed countless thousands	Haley (1929:29)/*Hank Smith*
1879	Vicinity of Whitewater, Manitoba	Plenty	Seton (1909:215–216)/*J. T. Brondgeest*
1879	Western Cass County, ND	Lots	Bailey (1926:29)/*Mr. Holes*
Fall 1879	Vicinity of Flatwillow, MT	Very abundant . . . bands seen almost daily	Jackson (1982:180)/*William Jackson*
1880s	Near Jamestown, ND	Lots . . . in this country	Umber and Bihrle (1989:8)/*Bernard J. Baenen*
Autumn 1880s	Along Little Missouri River, north of Medora, ND	Gather . . . in great bands . . . sometimes so numerous they can hardly be stalked	Roosevelt (1888:132–133)/*Theodore Roosevelt*
1883	Vicinity of San Francisco Mountain in AZ	Very abundant	Grinnell (1897:6)/*Ripley Hitchcock*
May 1883	Four Lakes Region of Panhandle, TX	Thousands	Collinson (1963:74)/*Frank Collinson*
1883–1896	Along Little Missouri River, north of Medora, ND	Hundreds and thousands [some springs]	Roosevelt et al. (1902:104)/*Theodore Roosevelt*

continued on next page

Dates	Places	Abundance	Source/*Eyewitness*
1884	West of Flagstaff, AZ	Thousands killed annually around the San Francisco and Bill Williams mountains	Mearns (1907:226)/*Edgar A. Mearns*
1884	Dakota Badlands	As many as 8,000 and 9,000 a day	Seton (1909 [I]:220)/*Howard Eaton*
1884–1890	Near Belfield, ND	Thick . . . as many as 1,000 . . . in one herd	Umber and Bihrle (1989:8)/*Arthur H. Anderson*
1885	Along the Big Sandy River, WY	About 30,000	Allred (1943:117)/*Unknown*
July 1885	Near Medicine Bow, WY	Heaps	Wister (1958:31)/*Owen Wister*
Winter 1885	North Park, CO	A band estimated to contain 5,000	Warren (1942:291)/*E. N. Butler*
1886	Vicinity of Big Lake, TX	100 to 300 not unusual and . . . once . . . a herd of at least 2,000	Kupper (1951:32)/*Robert Maudslay*
August 1886	Yellowstone National Park, WY	In large bands	Wear (1886:1,072)/*David W. Wear*
Spring 1890	West side of Green River, WY	Large bands	Seton (1909 [I]:218)/*H. W. Skinner*
1891	Casa Grandes, Chihuahua, Mexico	Abundant	Lumholtz (1902:83)/*C. Lumholtz*
1895	Vicinity of Fort Yates, ND	Reasonably plenty	Munson (1897a:164)/*Edward L. Munson*
July 1896	East of Black Butte in MT	A considerable number	Grinnell (1897:5)/*L. V. Pirsson*
Summer 1896	South of Diamond Peak in OR	Quite plenty	Grinnell (1897:6)/*Lester B. Hartman*
December 1896	"between Havre and Glasgow" MT	Probably 40,000 . . . Indians killing them by the thousands	Munson (1897b:7)/*Unknown*
December 1896	Western MT	In large numbers	McClintock (1968:155)/*Walter McClintock*

Appendix B

SELECT NATIVE AMERICAN NAMES FOR PRONGHORN

Tribe	General location	Name for pronghorn[a]	Reference
Achomawi	NC California	chě-ka-va-wí	Curtis (1924 [13]:254)
		jā'-kah-kow'-we	Merriam (1979:64)
		jexkakoy (old form)	Olmsted (1966:64)
		jeqa-rarawi (modern)	
Apache		jaagé/jaadé	Perry et al. (1972:3)
		já-gĕ	Curtis (1907 [1]:139)
Apsaroke	SC Montana	úh-ka-shĕ	Curtis (1909 [4]:190)
(Crow)		u'ᵘxkacè	Lowie (1960:187)
		o-hot-du-sha	Hodge (1907:111)
Apwurakei	NE California	wahs'-te	Merriam (1979:76)
		wasti	Garth (1950:133)
Arapaho	EC Colorado/	nĭ-sī-cha	Curtis (1910 [6]:167)
	NW Kansas		
Arikara	SC North Dakota/	annoo notche	Catlin (1973 [II]:264)
	NE South Dakota	hká-ū	Curtis (1909 [5]:170)
		axkaá'	Parks et al. (1979:41)
		chk'a	Bailey (1926:27)
Assiniboine	SE Saskatchewan/	tahto'kanah	Denig (1961:63)
(Stoney)	NE Montana/	ta-tó-gŭna	Curtis (1908 [3]:153)
	NW North Dakota	tahtogan	Coues (1897 [2]:535)
		tatogana	Thwaites (1906 [III]:217)
		tah-tee-un'	Barker (1960:166)
Astakawi	NE California	chā'-kah kow'-we	Merriam (1979:66)
Atsugeuii	NE California	wahs'-te	Merriam (1979:74, 76)
Atsina	NC Montana/	na-sī-tya	Curtis (1909 [5]:170)
(Gros Ventre)	SE Saskatchewan		
Atwumwe	NE California	tsā'-ah-kah-koí	Merriam (1979:68)

continued on next page

APPENDIX B

Tribe	General location	Name for pronghorn[a]	Reference
Aztec (Nahuatl)	SC Mexico	teuthlalmacame temamacame	Richardson (1829 [I]:261)
Bankalachi	C California	soi'-yōl	Merriam (1979:196)
Bannock	EC Idaho	tin'-nah	Merriam (1979:204)
		tuna'	Steward (1938:274)
		tina	Kroeber (1906–07a:82)
Beaver		yathóne, tápi	Roe (1951:688)
Blackfeet	NC Montana/ SE Alberta S Alberta		
Blood		áuakàsi áuakàsiks (pl.)	Uhlenbeck and Van Gulik (1930:17)
		ah-wah-cous	McDowell (1985:87)
Piegan		tatogan	Denig (1961:79)
		sâ-ki-ō-wa-ka-si	Curtis (1910 [6]:167)
		saw-kee-owa-kasee	Catlin (1973 [II]:264)
		sauki awakos	Chamberlain (1901:669)
Siksika		áuakàsi áuakàsiks (pl.)	Uhlenbeck and Van Gulik (1930:17)
		auokáhs	Thwaites (1906 [III]:220)
		muchcataiwanououish	Coues (1897 [II]:535)
		cikittisso	Coues (1965 [2]:535)
Cahuilla	S California	ten-nēl	Merriam (1979:189)
		ténil ténl-am (pl.)	Seiler and Hioki (1979:209, 259)
		tĕ-nil	Curtis (1926 [15]:174)
		tenily	Bean (1972:57)
Agua Calienta		donil	Kroeber (1906–07a:82)
Chemehuevi		wahn'ts	Merriam (1979:184)
		wa'nc(i)	Press (1979:159)
		wantsi	Laird (1976:251)
Cheyenne	EC Wyoming/ SW South Dakota	vó-ka-e	Curtis (1910 [6]:167)
		dóh-do-e-wo-ka	Curtis (1930 [19]:230)
		voāe, voāeo (pl.) (large antelope)	Petter (1915:45)
		vokā, vokāeo (pl.) (small antelope)	
		vokaesson (young antelope)	
		hotoavoā (antelope buck)	
		wóh-ka	Thwaites (1906 [III]:221)
Cheyenne, Northern		vóˡkaaˡe vóˡkaaˡe-ho	Northern Cheyenne Language and Culture Center (1976:3)
Chumash			
Ventureno	SW California	kahk'	Merriam (1979:104)
Ynezeno	SW California	choo'-loo	Merriam (1979:103)
Comanche	NW Texas	kwʒharɛn' (clan)	Wallace and Hoebel (1952:68)
		qá-ha-di	Curtis (1930 [19]:230)
		kwahari (pl.)	Hodge (1907:328)
Comecrudo	EC Mexico	icnako	Swanton (1940:107)

continued on next page

144

Tribe	General location	Name for pronghorn[a]	Reference
Costanoan			
Mutsen	WC California	tew-yen	Merriam (1979:115)
Rumsen	WC California	te'-wen	Merriam (1979:114)
Santa Cruz	WC California	tĭ-yu-yĕn	Henshaw *in* Heizer (1955:165)
Soledad	WC California	tu-yĕ	Henshaw *in* Heizer (1955:165)
Cree (Plains)	EC Saskatchewan	ah-pi-chee ahtik	Van Wormer (1968:14)
		apestat-jehkus	Thwaites (1906 [III]:232)
		ahpisemoosecuse	Coues (1897 [II]:535)
		kwa' skwûti,	Watkins (1938:9)
		-a' chikosis	
		ah-pi-chee-ah-tik'	Seton (1909 [I]:209)
	SC Alberta	upista'chéckos	Anderson (1975:6)
		apeestat-choekoos	Richardson (1829 [I]:261)
		my-atlehk (sing.)	
		my-attekwuck (pl.)	
		wawakesio	Roe (1951:71)
		apeestatchoekoos	Franklin (1823:667)
		apistatikkus	Chamberlain (1901:669)
Creek [sic, Cree]	EC Saskatchewan	apestachoekoos	Godman (1826:324)
Cupeño	SC California	tun'-nil	Merriam (1979:191)
		tán-lam	Curtis (1926 [15]:174)
Dakota	South Dakota/	tatokadaŋ	Williamson (1886:8)
(Sioux)	S North Dakota/	tatókana	Bailey (1926:27)
	W Minnesota	ta'toka	Minor and Minor (1978:376)
		ta-to'-ka-daŋ	Riggs (1890:463)
		tah-kehah'-sohn-lah (generic)	Hyer (1968:2)
		tah-kehah'-sohn-bel-loh-kak (buck)	
		tah-kehah'-sohn-wee-yahn-lah (doe)	
		tah-kehah'-sohn-mah-kee'-chec-mah-sah (fawn)	
		tah to ka no	Catlin (1973 [II]:264)
Lakota		hetóŋ cík'ala	Karol and Rozman (1971:111)
Oglala		tah-keen-cha sanal	Van Wormer (1968:14)
		(little pale deer)	
		tah-heen-cha-san'-la	Seton (1909:209)
Teton		tá-licha-saⁿ-la	Curtis (1908 [3]:153)
Yankton		pah-chia-chris-teen-ah (small deer)	Van Wormer (1968:14)
Yanktonai		nigesaŋ	Williamson (1886:8)
		ni-'ghé-saⁿ	Curtis (1908 [3]:153)
Diegueno	SW California	ŭ-múïl	Curtis (1926 [15]:179)
Eskimo Labrador		tuktungajok	Peacock (1974:23)
Flathead	WC Montana	sta-án	Curtis (1911 [7]:180)
		ǐkaélstcʊn (male)	Turney-High (1937:159)
		sta:n (female)	
		kels' stá:n (kid)	
Flathead		choo ool le	Coues (1897 [II]:715)
(Salish)			
Gabrielino	SW California	to-nar"	Merriam (1979:193)
Gosiute	NW Utah/	kwah'-rah	Merriam (1979:207)
(Shoshone)	NE Nevada		
Deep Creek		kwahadu	Steward (1938:278)
Skull Valley		kwahadu	Steward (1938:278)
		kwah´-rah	Merriam (1979:206)
Gros Ventres		hottewianinay	Thwaites (1906 [III]:226)
Hammawi	NE California	chā-kah-kah'-we	Merriam (1979:70)

continued on next page

Tribe	General location	Name for pronghorn[a]	Reference
Hidatsa			
(Minnetaree)	C North Dakota	ú-ḣi	Curtis (1909 [4]:190)
		uḣi	Matthews (1874:149)
		úhchi	Bailey (1926:27)
		ōhchikihdapi	Maximilian (1906 [III]:73)
Iowa/Oto	SC Iowa	tato	Robinson (1972:41)
Jicarilla	NE New Mexico/	tá-ga-t.	Curtis (1907 [1]:139)
(Apache)	SE Colorado		
Kalispel	W Montana	Īkaèlschin (male)	Giorda (1879:13)
		staan (female)	
Kamia (Tipai)	S California/	ă-mó-[ch]-lā	Merriam (1979:107)
	Baja California/		
	Mexico		
Kasmia		kamuL	Gifford (1931:81)
Kawaiisu	SC California	wad'-ze	Merriam (1979:180)
Panamint Valley		wań'zi	Steward (1938:274)
Keres			
Eastern	NC New Mexico	k·u·uts	White (1935:203)
Kiliwa	Northern Baja	xpar	Mixco (1985:249)
Kiowa	W Oklahoma/	t'a, täp	Mooney (1979:430)
	SC Kansas/	tH-p	Harrington (1928:206)
	N Texas	ťa-seidl (herd)	
Kitanemuk	SC California	too'-moo-nats	Merriam (1979:186)
Klamath	SC Oregon	čew	Barker (1963:480)
		cha-oo	Van Wormer (1968:28)
		cha-o	Bailey (1936:70)
		ch.u	Curtis (1924 [13]:272)
			Einarsen (1948:229)
		tc'u	Spier (1930:156)
Klickitat	SC Washington	chat-wi-lí	Curtis (1911 [7]:173)
Konkow	NE California	nah'-wim	Merriam (1979:133)
Kutenai	SE British Columbia	n'ihĪ-to-kup	Curtis (1911 [7]:173)
		nilt-too-koop	Tolmie and Dawson (1884:106)
		ŋ'Ītuk!ᵘp	Boas (1918:352)
		nestukp	Thwaites (1906 [III]:233)
Luiseño	SW California	tón-la	Curtis (1926 [15]:174)
		tun'-lah	Merriam (1979:192)
		tonla	Kroeber (1906–07:82)
Mahdesi	NE California	chā'-kah kah'-we	Merriam (1979:72)
Maidu	NE California	káma	Shipley (1963:212)
Northern		kah'-t.	Merriam (1979:129, 131)
		kah'-mah	
Northwestern		ná-wim	Curtis (1924 [14]:230)
Southern		now'-o	Merriam (1979:136)
Valley		ká't-	Curtis (1924 [14]:230)
Concow Maidu		naḣ-wim	Merriam (1979:133)
Mandan	SC South Dakota	ko ka	Catlin (1973 [II]:264)
		kok	Curtis (1909 [5]:170)
		koka	Bailey (1926:27)
		kockeberokā (male)	Thwaites (1906[III]:247)
		koka	Will and Spinden (1906:209)
		kokberoke (male)	
Micmac	Nova Scotia/PEI/	tabu'lch kuloo'sil	Rand (1888:16)
	E New Brunswick	tanoosoomoo'	
		mimŭndoobĕga' dasilije	

continued on next page

Tribe	General location	Name for pronghorn[a]	Reference
Missouri		tam	Roe (1951:674)
Miwok			
Plains	C California	haí-loo	Merriam (1979:140)
Northern		hal'-loo-zoo	Merriam (1979:138)
Southern		há-lu	Curtis (1924 [14]:237)
Mohave		ma-ŭl-ya	Curtis (1908 [2]:124)
Molala		mú-yak	Curtis (1911[8]:196)
Monache		soi-yoń	Merriam (1979:169)
Entimbich	EC California	soi-yo'-de	Merriam (1979:172)
Western Mono		so'-yōn	Merriam (1979:166)
Wuksachi		soi-yo'-te	Merriam (1979:175)
Navaho	NW New Mexico/	ju-dĭ	Curtis (1907 [1]:139)
	NE Arizona	jádí	Goossen (1967:xiii)
		jadi	Young and Morgan (1980:488)
Nez Perce	C Idaho	lakáligk (buck)	Morvillo (1895:6)
		zukuláinin (doe)	
		t'su-ko-laí-ni'n	Curtis (1911 [8]:191)
Nomlaki	NC California	too-rep'	Merriam (1979:118)
		too-děp	Curtis (1924 [14]:221)
Ojibway, Plains	SW Manitoba	muchcataiwanououish	Coues (1897 [II]:535)
Okwanuchu	N California	e'-wit	Merriam (1979:63)
Omaha	NE Nebraska	tachu'ge	Fletcher and La Flesche (1972 [1]:103)
		tachu ge	Swetland (1977:6)
Osage	NE Arkansas/	ta-tsu'-ge	La Fleshche (1932:231)
	E Oklahoma/	tatóhka	Thwaites (1906 [III]:299)
	SE Kansas		
Oto	SE Nebraska	tá-to	Curtis (1930 [19]:230)
		tato	Robinson (1922:41)
Paiute	Oregon	te-na	Bailey (1936:70)
Surprise Valley	NE California	dü'ná	Kelly (1932:81)
Northern		tuna	Fowler (1989:158)
Mill City	NW Nevada	duna´, wadzĬ	Steward (1938:274)
Walker Lake	WC Nevada	tin´-nah	Merriam (1979:202)
Paviotso		tú-na	Curtis (1926 [15]:182)
Mono Lake	EC California	tin´-nah	Merriam (1979:164)
		qa-há-r.	Curtis (1926 [15]:182)
		wá-dzi	
Bridgeport	EC California	wahd'-ze	Merriam (1979:176)
Unspecified subgroup		te-na´	Bailey (1936:70)
Owens Valley		w'dzi	Steward (1938:253)
George's Creek	EC California	kwaha´du	Steward (1938:274)
Southern		wanc	Kelly (1964:156)
Chemehuevi	SE California	wahn'ts	Merriam (1979:184)
		wa'nc(i)	Press (1979:159)
		wan<u>ts</u>i	Laird (1976:251)
Las Vegas	SE California/	wantsi'	Steward (1938:276)
	S Nevada	wakńch	Merriam (1979:182)
Kaibab	NW Arizona	wahntz'	Merriam (1979:208)
Ash Meadows	SE California/	hwa:ns	Steward (1938:274)
	S Nevada		
Shivwits	NW Arizona	wahn-ze'	Merriam (1979:188)
Unspecified subgroup		wongs	Merriam (1979:210)

continued on next page

147

Tribe	General location	Name for pronghorn[a]	Reference
Papago	SW Arizona/	kóvīt	Curtis (1908 [2]:119)
	NW Sonora,	kuhwid	Saxton and Saxton (1969:54)
	Mexico	kukuwid (pl.)	
Patwin	NC California	kaĥ	Merriam (1979:124)
Hill	NC California	ka'	Curtis (1924 [14]:221)
Koru	NC California	kah'-kah"	Merriam (1979:127)
Southern	NC California	kah'-oo	Merriam (1979:128)
Valley		ka	Curtis (1924 [14]:221)
Pawnee	C Nebraska/	a'-di-ka'-tus (buck)	Hayden (1868)
	NC Kansas	u's-ka (doe)	
Pima	SW Arizona/	kó-vīt	Curtis (1908 [2]:119)
	NW Sonora,	kuhwid	Saxton and Saxton (1969:54)
	Mexico	kukuwid (pl.)	
Pomo	WC California		
Salt		sho	Merriam (1979:99)
Makahma		bo'-o	Merriam (1979:94)
Lower Lake		ko'-boo	Merriam (1979:101)
Pueblo			
Acoma	Arizona/	kurts	Hodge (1907:736)
	SE New Mexico		
Cochiti	NC New Mexico	kût's	Curtis (1926 [16]:275)
		kurts	Hodge (1907:318, 736)
Hopi	NE Arizona	t'sō-vi-o-ŭ	Curtis (1922 [12]:245)
		chöövio	Waters (1963)
		tsööviw	Albert and Shaul (1985:116)
		chubia	Hodge (1907:562)
Isleta	C New Mexico	t!a-í-d.	Curtis (1926 [16]:267)
		t!lamnin (pl.)	
		tam	Hodge (1910:680)
Jemez	NC New Mexico	t's!âh	Curtis (1926 [16]:267)
Laguna	C New Mexico	kurtsi	Hodge (1907:752)
		ku'-ts^i	Curtis (1926 [16]:275)
Pecos		alu	Hodge (1910:221)
San Felipe		kurts, kuuts	Hodge (1907:736)
San Ildefonso		ton	Hodge (1910:440)
Sia		kuts, kurts	Hodge (1907:736)
Taos	NC New Mexico	ta'-na	Curtis (1926 [16]:267)
		ta'namu^n (pl.)	
		tah ah-nah	Bailey (1931:22)
Tewa	NC New Mexico	t!loun	Curtis (1926 [17]:200)
		tong	Hodge (1910:777)
		toņ	Henderson and Harrington (1914:15)
Tigua		tam	Hodge (1910:680)
Walapai	W Arizona	u-moo	Corbusier (1923:8)
Zuni	EC Arizona/	má'-wi	Curtis (1926 [17]:204)
	WC New Mexico		
Quechan	SW Arizona	ma-úl	Curtis (1908 [2]:124)
Salinan	WC California	móe'	Merriam (1979:111)
Miguelino		lowe'c^{a}t' (small antelope)	Mason (1918:123–125)
		mu'í' (antelope)	
		notc' (young antelope)	
		tepcé (male antelope)	
Sarsi	WC Alberta	na-il-k!i-'shá	Curtis (1928 [18]:210)

continued on next page

Tribe	General location	Name for pronghorn[a]	Reference
Serrano	SC California	tŭ-mertz	Merriam (1979:188)
Shasta	NC California	e'-yú-hit[h]	Merriam (1979:61)
		e'-o-whit	Merriam (1979:63)
		í-yu-hi*r*	Curtis (1924 [13]:254)
Shoshone	SE Idaho/ W Wyoming	kwahaten, wantsi (antelope)	Miller (1972:155)
		kwahari	Kroeber (1906–07a:82)
Idaho	S Idaho	tin-nah'	Merriam (1979:204)
Northern Lemhi	C Idaho	kwahadu	Steward (1938:276)
Lower Snake River	SC Idaho	kwahad:	Steward (1938:278)
Pohogwe (Fort Hall)	SE Idaho	kwahadü	Steward (1938:276)
Unspecified		kwahaten, wantsi tepaisin, wantsi (fawn)	Miller (1972:155)
Western			
Big Smokey Valley	C Nevada	wahn'-ze	Merriam (1979:200)
Deep Creek Gosiute	EC Nevada	kwahadu	Steward (1938:278)
Egan Canyon	EC Nevada	kwahad:[u]	Steward (1938:282)
Elko	NE Nevada	kwahadu	Steward (1938:282)
Grouse Creek (Pine Nut Eaters)	NW Utah	kwaadu	Steward (1938:278)
Kawich	SC Nevada	wanzitci[ʔi]	Steward (1938:280)
Lida	SW Nevada	wanzi	Steward (1938:280)
Little Lake	SE California	wanzi	Steward (1938:280)
Little Smokey Valley (Morey)	C Nevada	kwahadü	Steward (1938:280)
Panamint	SE California	wünzi	Steward (1938:280)
Promontory Point (Huki Eaters)	N Utah	kwahadu	Steward (1938:278)
Railroad Valley	C Nevada	kwadunzi	Steward (1938:120)
Reese River	WC Nevada	wahn-ze´	Merriam (1979:201)
Ruby Valley	NE Nevada	wahn´-ze	Merriam (1979:199)
Smith Creek Valley	C Nevada	kwahada	Steward (1938:282)
White Knife (Battle Mountain)	NC Nevada	kwahadu	Steward (1938:282)
Spokan	EC Washington	'shtan	Curtis (1911 [7]:180)
Tubatulabal		macat	Kroeber (1906–07:82)
		yïtá batal	Voegelin (1938:12)
	SC California	mah-suɫ-too-nal	Merriam (1979:197)
Tuscarora	NE North Carolina	ojiruk	Catlin (1973 [II]:264)
Ute		wandjidj	Kroeber (1906–07:82)
Pahvant	W Colorado/ E Utah	wants	Steward (1938:276)
Southern	SE Utah/ SW Colorado	watsyts	Harrington (1911:217)
Utah Lake		wanz	Steward (1938:276)

continued on next page

Tribe	General location	Name for pronghorn[a]	Reference
Valley Nisenan	NC California	na'u	Kroeber (1929)
Walapai	W Arizona	ŭ-moo	Corbusier (1923:8)
		im'úl, um'úl or mu'úl	Kroeber (1935:61)
Wappo	C California	moo'-oo	Merriam (1979:57)
Washoe	EC California/	i-yus	Merriam (1979:109)
	W Nevada	á-yĭs	Curtis (1926 [15]:189)
Winnebago	S Wisconsin/	cas-k'as-ka-ra	Hayden (1868:415)
	N Illinois		
Wintu	NC California	too-rep'	Merriam (1979:117)
		tu-rĕp	Curtis (1924 [14]:221)
Wintun			
Nomlaki	NC California	too-heṕ	Merriam (1979:118)
Central	NC California	tu-dĕp	Curtis (1924 [14]:221)
Northern	NC California	tu-rĕp	Curtis (1924 [14]:221)
Ladogo	Colusa County	kaḱ	Merriam (1979:120, 122, 124)
Wishham	SC Washington/	i-'shpo-hi-á-tīn	Curtis (1911 [8]:198)
	NC Oregon		
Yakima	SC Washington	chat-wi-lí	Curtis (1911 [7]:173)
Yana	NC California	ah-poẃ-choo-se	Merriam (1979:83)
Yavapai	WC Arizona	mu-ul'	Corbusier (1873:45)
		mŭ-ŭl"	Corbusier (1921:6)
		mŭ-ŭl'	Corbusier (1922:10)
Southeastern	C Arizona	moula	Gifford (1932:215)
Yokut	C California	coyod	Kroeber (1907:242)
Chosnimni		soi-yul'	Merriam (1979:149)
Chukshansi		soi-yōl	Merriam (1979:145)
		sú-yūl	Curtis (1924 [14]:244)
Chunut	C California	soi-yōl	Merriam (1979:157)
Gashowu	C California	soo'-yūl	Merriam (1979:148)
Nutunutu	C California	soi-yōl	Merriam (1979:151)
Paleuyami	C California	mo'-ket'	Merriam (1979:160)
Tachi	C California	soi-yōl	Merriam (1979:153)
Tinlini	C California	soi-yōl	Merriam (1979:161)
Tulamni	C California	mo'-ho[ch]tan'-ne-i[ch]	Merriam (1979:162)
Wikchumni	C California	soi-ut	Merriam (1979:154)
Yauelmani	C California	soi´-yul	Merriam (1979:159)
Various dialects		mû'xotani	Kroeber (1963:200)
Yona	NC California	ah-pow'-choo-se	Merriam (1979)
Yuma		ma-úl	Curtis (1908 [2]:124)
		mo'ū'l	Forde (1931:118)

[a] Readers are encouraged to review the specified sources for particular names, because some diacritical marks are too unique or difficult to reproduce with original precision.

References

Abel, A. H., ed. 1939. Tabeau's narrative of Loisel's expedition to the Upper Missouri. Translated from French by R. A. Wright. Univ. Oklahoma Press, Norman. 272 pp.

Adams, R. F. 1944. Western words: A dictionary of the range. Univ. Oklahoma Press, Norman. 355 pp.

Aikens, C. M. 1970. Hogup Cave. Univ. Utah Anthropol. Pap. 93. Univ. Utah Press, Salt Lake City. 212 pp.

Aikens, C. M. and R. L. Greenspan. 1988. Ancient lakeside culture in the northern Great Basin: Malheur Lake, Oregon. J. California and Great Basin Anthropol. 10(1): 32–61.

Aikens, C. M., D. L. Cole and R. Stuckenrath. 1986. Introduction. Pages 1–18 *in* R. L. Andrews, J. M. Anovasio and R. C. Carlisle, eds., Perishable industries from Dirty Shame Rock Shelter, Malheur County, Oregon. Univ. Oregon Anthropol. Pap. 34. 233 pp.

Albert, R. and D. L. Shaul. 1985. A concise Hopi and English lexicon. John Benjamins Publ. Co., Philadelphia, Pennsylvania. 204 pp.

Allen, D. L. 1967. The life of prairies and plains. McGraw-Hill Book Co., New York, New York. 232 pp.

Allen, J. A. 1874. Notes on the natural history of portions of Dakota and Montana territories. Proc. Boston Soc. Nat. Hist. 17:33–85.

Allen, W. A. 1903. Adventures with Indians and game or twenty years in the Rocky Mountains. A. W. Bowen and Co., Chicago, Illinois. 302 pp.

Allison, M. E. 1890. Coursing the antelope. Pages 333–340 *in* G. O. Shields, ed., The big game of North America. Rand, McNally and Co., Chicago, Illinois. 581 pp.

Allred, W. J. 1943. Wyoming antelope—history and wartime management. Trans. N. Am. Wildl. Conf. 8:117–121.

Alter, J. C., ed. 1942. Journal of Priddie Meeks. Utah Hist. Quart. X:145+.

Ambrose, S. E. 1986. Crazy Horse and Custer. Penguin Books, New York, New York. 527 pp.

———. 1996. Undaunted courage. Simon and Schuster, New York, New York. 511 pp.

Amsden, Charles. 1931. Man-hunting: Sidelights on a symposium on "The antiquity of man in America." The Masterkey 5(2):36–47.

Anderson, A. 1975. Plains Cree dictionary in the "y" dialect. Author published, Edmonton, Alberta. 257 pp.

Anderson, F. G. 1955. The Pueblo kachina cult, a historical reconstruction. Southwest J. Anthropol. 1:404–419.

Anonymous. 1910. Past and present of Nodaway County, Missouri. 2 vols. B. F. Bowen and Co., Indianapolis, Indiana.

Appleman, R. E. 1975. Lewis and Clark: Historic places associated with their transcontinental exploration (1804–06). U.S. Natl. Park Serv. U.S. Govt. Print. Off., Washington, DC. 429 pp.

Arkush, B. S. 1995. The archaeology of CA-MNO–2122: A study of pre-contact and post-contact lifeways among the Mono Basin Paiute. Anthropol. Rec. 31. Univ. California, Berkeley. 199 pp.

Arnon, N. S. and W. W. Hill. 1979. Santa Clara Pueblo. Pages 296–307 *in* A. Ortiz, ed., Southwest. Handbook of North American Indians. Vol. 9. Smithsonian Inst., Washington, DC. 717 pp.

Arroyo-Cabrales, J., O. J. Polacio and E. Johnson. 2001. La Mastofauna del Cuaternario Tardio de Mexico (Conabio G–012), Laboratorio de Paleozoologia, INAH, México, D. F.

Audubon, J. J. and J. Bachman. 1851. The viviparous quadrupeds of North America. Vol. 2. V. G. Audubon, New York, New York. 334 pp.

Audubon, M. R. 1897. Audubon and his journals. 2 vols. Charles Scribners' Sons, New York, New York. Vol. 1, 532 pp. Vol. 2, 554 pp.

Bailey, R. J. 1978. Description of the ecoregions of the United States. U.S. For. Serv., Intermtn. Region, Ogden, Utah. 77 pp. + map.

———. 1995. Description of the ecoregions of the United States. 2nd ed. U. S. For. Serv., Washington, DC. 108 pp. + map.

Bailey, V. 1926. A biological survey of North Dakota. North American Fauna No. 49. U. S. Bur. Biol. Surv., Washington, DC. 226 pp.

———. 1931. Mammals of New Mexico. North American Fauna No. 53. U. S. Bur. Biol. Surv., Washington, DC. 412+ pp.

———. 1936. The mammals and life zones of Oregon. North American Fauna No. 55. U. S. Bur. Biol. Surv., Washington, DC. 416 pp.

Bakeless, J. E. 1964. The journals of Lewis and Clark. New American Library, New York, New York. 384 pp.

Baldwin, G. C. 1962. America's buried past. G. P. Putnam's Sons, New York, New York. 191 pp.

Bancroft-Hunt, N. 1992. North American Indians. Courage Books, Philadelphia, Pennsylvania. 112 pp.

Bandelier, F. and A. F. Bandelier, eds. 1904. The journey of Aluar Nunez Cabeza de Vaca and his companions from Florida to the Pacific. A. S. Barnes and Co., New York, New York. 231 pp.

Barker, A. E. 1960. Vocabulary of the Mountain Stony Indians. Pages 165–180 in M. Barbeau, ed. Indian days on the western prairies. Bull. 163, Anthropol. Series 46, National Museum of Canada, Ottawa. 243 pp.

Barker, M. A. R. 1963. Klamath dictionary. Univ. California Press, Berkeley. 550 pp.

Barrett, S. M., ed. 1970. Geronimo: His own story. E. P. Dutton and Co., Inc., New York, New York. 190 pp.

Barsness, L. 1985. Heads, hides and horns: The complete buffalo book. Texas Christian Univ. Press, Fort Worth. 233 pp.

Bartlett, J. R. 1854. Personal narrative of explorations and incidents in Texas, New Mexico, California, Sonora, and Chihuahua, connected with the United States and Mexico Boundary Commission during the years 1850, '51, and '53. 2 vols. D. Appleton, New York, New York.

Bass, A. 1966. The Arapaho way. Clarkson N. Potter, Inc., New York, New York. 80 pp.

Beaglehole, E. 1936. Hopi hunting and hunting ritual. Yale Univ., New Haven, Connecticut, Publ. Anthropol. 4:1–26.

Beale, E. F. 1858. The report of the superintendent of the Wagon Road from Fort Defiance to the Colorado River.

House Ex. Doc. No. 124, 35th Congr., 1st Sess. Washington, DC. 87 pp.

Bean, L. J. 1972. Mukat's people: The Cahuilla Indians of southern California. Univ. California Press, Berkeley. 201 pp.

Benavides, A. de. 1945. Fray Alonso de Benavides' revised memorial of 1634. F. W. Hodge, G. P. Hammond and A. Rey, eds. Univ. New Mexico Press, Albuquerque. 308 pp.

Benedict, R. 1935. Zuni mythology. 2 vols. Columbia Univ. Contrib. Anthropol. 21. New York, New York. 342 and 345 pp.

Bernabéu, S. 1994. Diario de las expediciones a las Californias' de José Longinos. Ediciones Doce Calles, Madrid, Spain. 315 pp.

Biggers, D. H. 1991. Buffalo guns and barbed wire. Texas Tech Univ. Press, Lubbock. 241 pp.

Bigler, H. W. 1932. Extracts from the journal of Henry W. Bigler. Utah Hist. Quart. 5:35–64, 87–112, 134–160.

Billington, R. A. 1985. Land of savagery, land of promise. W. W. Norton and Co., New York, New York, 364 pp.

Binford, L. R. 1981. Bones, ancient men and modern myths. Academic Press, New York, New York. 320 pp.

Bitner, G. 1943. R. F. Tankersley and family, pioneers of Concho county. W. Texas Hist. Assoc. Yearbook 20:99–108.

Bixby, A. 1880. History of Boulder County. Pages 379–433 in History of Clear Creek and Boulder Valley, Colorado. O. L. Baskin and Co., Chicago, Illinois. 713 pp.

Blair, N. 1982. An historical account of the pronghorn antelope. Wyoming Wildl. 46(9):3–7.

Bleed, P. 1986. The optimal design of hunting weapons: Maintainability or reliability. Am. Antiquity 51(4):737–747.

Boas, F. 1918. Kutenai tales. Smithsonian Inst. Bur. Am. Ethnol. Bull. 59. U.S. Govt. Print. Off., Washington, DC. 387 pp.

Bodine, J. J. 1979. Taos Pueblo. Pages 255–267 in A. Ortiz, ed., Southwest. Handbook of North American Indians. Vol. 9. Smithsonian Inst., Washington, DC. 717 pp.

Boller, H. A. 1972. Among the Indians: Four years on the Upper Missouri, 1858–1862. M. M. Quaife, ed. Univ. Nebraska Press, Lincoln. 385 pp.

Bordes, F. 1968. The old Stone Age. McGraw-Hill Book Co., New York, New York. 255 pp.

Bossu, J. B. (1771). 1962. S. Feiler, trans. and ed., Travels in the interior of North America, 1751–1762. 240 pp. (Reprinted in 1962 by Univ. Oklahoma Press, Norman.)

Botkin, B. A., ed. 1975. A treasury of western folklore. Crown Publishers, Inc., New York, New York. 613 pp.

Bourke, J. G. 1891. On the border with Crook. Charles Scribner's Sons, New York, New York. 491 pp.

———. Unpublished. John Gregory Bourke diaries. Denver Public Library, 1480. Denver, Colorado. (Microfilm)

Bowers, A. E. 1965. Hidatsa social and ceremonial organization. Smithsonian Inst. Bur. Am. Ethnol. Bull. 194. U.S. Govt. Print. Off., Washington, DC. 528 pp.

Brander, M. 1971. Hunting and shooting from the earliest times to the present day. Weidenfeld and Nicolson, London, England. 255 pp.

Brant, C. S., ed. 1969. Jim Whitewolf: The life of a Kiowa Apache Indian. Dover Publications, Inc., New York, New York. 156 pp.

Briggs, W. 1976. Without noise of arms. Northland Press, Flagstaff, Arizona. 212 pp.

Brody, J. J. 1977. Mimbres painted pottery. Univ. New Mexico Press, Albuquerque. 253 pp.

Bromley, P. T. 1977. Aspects of the behavioural ecology and sociobiology of the pronghorn (*Antilocapra americana*). Ph.D. thesis, Univ. Calgary, Calgary, Alberta. 370 pp.

Brook, R. A. 1980. Inferences regarding aboriginal hunting behavior in the Saline Valley, Inyo County, California. J. California and Great Basin Anthropol. 2(1):60–79.

Brown, D. A. 1971a. The Fetterman massacre. Univ. Nebraska Press, Lincoln. 259 pp.

———. 1971b. Bury my heart at Wounded Knee. Holt, Rinehart and Winston, New York, New York. 487 pp.

———. 1977. Hear that lonesome whistle blow. Holt, Rinehart and Winston, New York, New York. 311 pp.

———. 1994. The American West. Scribner, New York, New York. 461 pp.

Brown, J. E. 1976. The roots of renewal. Pages 25–34 *in* Walter Holden Capps, ed., Seeing with a native eye: Essays on Native American religion. Harper and Row, New York, New York. 132 pp.

———. 1992. Animals of the soul. Element Inc., Rockport, Massachusetts. 145 pp.

Brown, M. H. and W. R. Felton. 1956. Before barbed wire. Bramhall House, New York. 226 pp.

Browne, B. 1939. Hunting the pronghorn. Pages 336–343 *in* North American big game, a book of the Boone and Crockett Club, compiled by the Comm. on Records of N. Am. Big Game. Charles Scribner's Sons, New York, New York. 533 pp.

Brumley, J. H. 1984. The Laidlaw site: An aboriginal antelope trap from southeastern Alberta. Pages 96–127 *in* D. Burley, ed., Archaeology Surv. in Alberta 1983. Occasional Pap. 23. Archaeol. Surv. of Alberta, Edmonton. 256 pp.

———. 1986. A radiocarbon date from Laidlaw site, DIOU–7. Pages 205–206 *in* J. W. Ives, ed., Archaeology in Alberta 1985. Occasional Pap. 29. Archaeol. Surv. of Alberta, Edmonton. 287 pp.

Bryant, E. 1936. What I saw in California: Being the journal of a tour by the emigrant route and South Pass of the Rocky Mountains, across the continent of North America, the Great Desert Basin, and through California in the years 1846, 1847. The Time Arts Press, Santa Ana, California. 481 pp.

Bryant, H. C. 1929. Outdoor heritage. Powell Publ. Co., Los Angeles, California. 465 pp.

Buckley, E. C. 1911. The Aguaga expedition into Texas and Louisiana, 1719–1722. Southwestern Hist. Quart. 15(1):1–65.

Buechner, H. K.. 1950. Life history, ecology, and range use of the pronghorn antelope in Trans-Pecos, Texas. Ph.D. thesis, Ohio St. Univ., Columbus. 376 pp.

Burton, R. F. 1862. The City of the Saints and across the Rocky Mountains to California. Harper and Brothers, Publishers, New York, New York. 574 pp.

———. 1966. The look of the West. Univ. Nebraska Press, Lincoln. 333 pp.

Butler, W. B. 1975. The atlatl: The physics of function and performance. Plains Anthropol. 20(68):105–110.

Byers, D. S., ed. 1967. Environment and subsistence. Vol. 1. The prehistory of the Tehuacan Valley. Univ. Texas Press, Austin. 331 pp.

Byers, J. A. 1997. American pronghorn: Social adaptations and the ghosts of predators past. Univ. Chicago Press, Chicago, Illinois. 300 pp.

Cabeza de Vaca, A. N. [1542] 1983. C. Covey, trans. and ed., Adventures in the unknown interior of America. Univ. New Mexico Press, Albuquerque. 160 pp.

Cadieux, C. L. 1986. Pronghorn, North America's unique antelope. Stackpole Books, Harrisburg, Pennsylvania. 254 pp.

Cahalane, V., ed. 1967. The imperial collection of Audubon animals, from the Quadrupeds of North America. Original text by John James Audubon and the Rev. John Bachman. Hammond Inc., Maplewood, New Jersey. 307 pp.

Cancino, J. and F. Reygadas. 1999. Historical notations regarding pronghorn (*Antilocapra americana*) in Mexico. Pronghorn Antelope Workshop (1998) Proc. 18:81–83.

Carlson, P. H. 1998. The plains Indians. Texas A & M Univ. Press, College Station. 254 pp.

Carrington, J. B. 1929. Across the plains with Bridger as guide. Scribner's Mag. 85:66–71.

Carrington, M. 1868. Ab-Sa-Ra-Ka, home of the Crows: Being the experience of an officer's wife on the plains. . . . J. B. Lippincott and Co., Philadelphia, Pennsylvania. 284 pp.

Carter, R. G. 1935. On the border with MacKenzie; Or winning west Texas from the Comanches. Eynon Print Co., Washington, DC. 418 pp.

Castañeda, C. E. 1936. The mission era: The finding of Texas, 1519–1693. Vol. 1. Von Boekmann-Jones, Co., Austin, Texas. 444 pp.

Catlin, G. 1973. Letters and notes on the manners, customs, and conditions of the North American Indians: Written during eight years' travel (1832–1839) amongst the wildest tribes of Indians in North America. 2 vols. Dover Publications, Inc., New York, New York. 572 pp.

Caton, J. D. 1877. The antelope and deer of America. Hurd and Houghton, New York, New York. 426 pp. (Reprinted in 1974 by Arno Press, New York, New York.)

Chamberlain, A. F. 1901. Significations of certain Algonquian animal-names. American Anthropol. (New Series) 3:669–683.

Chittenden, H. M. 1935. The American fur trade of the far West. 2 vols. The Press of the Pioneers, Inc., New York, New York.

Clark, T. D., ed. 1967. Gold rush diaries. Univ. Kentucky Press, Lexington. 206 pp.

Clark, W. P. 1884. The Indian sign language. L. R. Hamersly and Co., Philadelphia, Pennsylvania. 443 pp.

Clyman, J. 1984. Journal of a mountain man. L. M. Hasselstrom, ed. Mountain Press Publ. Co., Missoula, Montana. 295 pp.

Cody, E. E. 1970. Indian talk: Hand signs of the American Indians. New English Library, London, England. 144 pp.

Colbert, E. H. and R. G. Chaffee. 1939. A study of *Tetrameryx* and associated fossils from Pago Spring Cave, Sonita, Arizona. Am. Mus. Novit. 1,034:1–21.

Collinson, F. 1963. Life in the saddle. Univ. Oklahoma Press, Norman. 243 pp.

Connell, E. S. 1984. Son of the Morning Star. North Point Press, San Francisco, California. 411 pp.

Cook, J. H. 1923. Fifty years on the old frontier. Yale Univ. Press, New Haven, Connecticut. 310 pp.

Cope, L. 1919. Calendars of the Indians north of Mexico. Univ. California Publications Am. Archaeol. and Ethnol. 16(4):119–176.

Corbusier, W. H. 1873. Yavapai or Apache-Mojave vocabulary. Smithsonian Inst. Anthropol. Archives, Ms. 2249a. Washington, DC. 124 pp.

———. 1886. Apaches-Yumas and Apache-Mojaves. Part 2 . Am. Antiquarian and Oriental J. 8(6):325–329.

———. 1921. A revised Yavapai or Apachi-Mojave vocabulary. Smithsonian Inst. Anthropol. Archives, Ms. 2249b. Washington, DC. 19 pp.

———. 1922. Additions made in 1922 to his Yavapai vocabulary, made in 1873. Smithsonian Inst. Anthropol. Archives, Ms. 2249c. Washington, DC. 23 pp.

———. 1923. Walapai Indian words, phrases and sentences, and the story of how Wolf's son became a star. Smithsonian Inst. Anthropol. Archives, Ms. 2259. Washington, DC. 43 pp.

Cosgrove, H. S. and C. B. Cosgrove. 1932. The Swarts ruin, a typical Mimbres site in southwestern New Mexico. Pap. Peabody Mus. Am. Archaeol. and Ethnol. 15(1):1–178.

Coues, E. 1893. History of the expedition under the command of Lewis and Clark, to the sources of the Missouri River, then across the Rocky Mountains and down the Columbia River to the Pacific Ocean, performed during the years 1804–5–6, by order of the government of the U.S. 4 vols. Francis P. Harper, New York, New York.

———, ed. 1897. New light on the early history of the greater Northwest: The manuscript journals of Alexander Henry and of David Thompson, 1799–1814. 3 vols. F. P. Harper, New York, New York.

———, ed. 1898. The journal of Jacob Fowler narrating an adventure from Arkansas through the Indian Territory, Oklahoma, Kansas, Colorado, and New Mexico, to the sources of Rio Grande del Norte, 1821–22. Francis P. Harper, New York, New York. 183 pp.

Covey, C., ed. 1984. Cabeza de Vaca's adventures in the unknown interior of America. Univ. New Mexico Press, Albuquerque. 160 pp.

Cremony, J. C. 1868. Life among the Apaches (1850–1868). A. Roman and Co., San Francisco, California. 322 pp.

Cressman, L. S. 1977. Prehistory of the far West: Homes of vanished peoples. Univ. Utah Press, Salt Lake City. 248 pp.

Cressman, L. S., H. Williams and A. D. Krieger. 1940. Early man in Oregon; archaeological studies in the northern Great Basin. Studies in Anthropol. 3. Univ. Oregon Monogr., Eugene. 78 pp.

Cressman, L. S., F. C. Baker, H. P. Hansen and R. F. Heizer. 1942. Archaeological researches in the northern Great Basin. Publ. 538. Carnegie Inst. Washington, DC. 158 pp.

Cronyn, G. W., Jr. 1918. The path of the rainbow, an anthology of songs and chants from the Indians of North America. Boni and Liveright, New York, New York. 347 pp.

Culbertson, T. A. 1952. Journal of an expedition to the Mauvaises Terres and the Upper Missouri in 1850. J. F. McDermott, ed., Smithsonian Inst. Bur. Am. Ethnol. Bull. 147. U.S. Govt. Print. Off., Washington, DC. 164 pp.

Culin, S. 1975. Games of the North American Indians. Dover Publications, Inc., New York, New York. 846 pp.

Curtis, E. S. 1907–1930. The American Indian. 20 vols. F. W. Hodge, ed. Univ. Press, Cambridge, Massachusetts.

Cushing, F. H. 1883. Zuni fetishes. Bur. Am. Ethnol. 1880–1881, Ann. Rept. 2:3–45 to Secretary Smithsonian Inst. U.S. Govt. Print. Off., Washington, DC.

Custer, E. B. 1885. Boots and saddles. Harper and Brothers, New York, New York. 312 pp.

Custer, G. A. 1952. My life on the plains. M. M. Quaife, ed. The Lakeside Press, R. R. Donnelley and Sons, Chicago, Illinois. 626 pp.

D'Azevedo, W. L., ed. 1986. Great Basin. Handbook of North American Indians. Vol. 11. Smithsonian Inst. Press, Washington, DC. 852 pp.

Dale, H. C., ed. 1918. The Ashley-Smith explorations and the discovery of a central route to the Pacific, 1822–1829. The Arthur H. Clark Co., Cleveland, Ohio. 352 pp.

Daly, P. 1969. Approaches to faunal analysis in archaeology. Am. Antiquity 4(2):146–153.

Dane, G. E. 1935. The founding of the presidio and mission of Our Father Sant Francis. California Hist. Soc. Quart. XIV(2):99–110.

Daniel, F. W. 1969. Running Antelope—misnamed Onepapa. Paper Money 8(1) [Whole No. 29]:4–9.

Dansgaard, W., S. J. Johnsen, H. B. Clausen, D. Dahl-Jensen, N. S. Gunderstrup, C. U. Hammer, C. S. Hvidberg, J. P. Steffensen, A. E. Svienbjornsdottir, J. Jouzel and G. Bond. 1993. Evidence for general instability of past climate from a 250-year ice-core record. Nature 364 (6,249):218–220.

Darrah, W. C., ed. 1949. Journal of John F. Steward. Utah Hist. Quart. XVI–XVII:181–251.

Dartt, M. 1879 (M. W. Thompson). On the plains and among the peaks; or how Mrs. Maxwell made her Natural History Collections. Claxton, Remsen and Haffelfinger, Philadelphia, Pennsylvania. 237 pp.

Darwin, C. 1906. The voyage of the Beagle. Everyman's Library, London, England. 496 pp.

Dary, D. A. 1989. The buffalo book—The full saga of the American animal. Ohio Univ. Press, Dayton. 384 pp.

Davies, H. P. 1871. Ten days on the plains. Crocker and Co., New York, New York. 68 pp.

Davis, J. T. 1961. Trade routes and economic exchange among the Indians of California. Rept. 54. Univ. California Archaeol. Surv, Berkeley. 71 pp.

Davis, L. 1986. A thousand winters ago. Montana Outdoors 17(2):15–19.

Davis, T. R. 1868. A summer on the plains. Harper's New Monthly Mag: 36(213):292–307.

de Trobriand, P. R. 1951. Military life in Dakota. Translated and edited from the French original by L. M. Kane. Univ. Nebraska Press, Lincoln. 422 pp.

Deaver, K. and G. S. Greene. 1978. Faunal utilization at 45AD2: A prehistoric archaeological site in the channeled scablands of eastern Washington. TEBIWA 14:1–21.

Delano, A. 1854. Life on the plains and among the diggings; being scenes and adventures of an overland journey to California: With particular incidents of the route, mistakes and sufferings of the emigrants, the Indian tribes, the present and the future of the great West. Miller, Orton and Mulligan, Buffalo, New York, 393 pp.

Denig, E. T. 1930. Indian tribes of the Upper Missouri. J. N. B. Hewitt, ed., Bur. Am. Ethnol. 1928–1929, Ann. Rept. 46:375–628 to Secretary Smithsonian Inst. U.S. Govt. Print. Off., Washington, DC.

———. 1961. Five Indian tribes of the Upper Missouri: Sioux, Arikaras, Assiniboines, Crees, Crows. J. C. Ewers, ed. Univ. Oklahoma Press, Norman. 260 pp.

Denny, C. E. 1938. The law marches west, 1874–1905. W. B. Cameron, ed. Dent, Toronto, Ontario. 319 pp.

Densmore, F. 1918. Teton Sioux music. Smithsonian Inst. Bur. Am. Anthropol. Bull. 61. Washington, DC. 561 pp.

———. 1957. Music of Acoma, Isleta, Cochiti and Zuni Pueblos. Bur. Am. Ethnol. Bull. 165. Smithsonian Inst., Washington, DC. 117 pp.

DeVoto, B. 1947. Across the wide Missouri. Houghton Mifflin Co., Boston, Massachusetts. 454 pp.

Dewdney, S. 1964. Writing on stone along the Milk River. Beaver (Winter) 295:22–29.

Dibble, C. E. and A. J. O. Anderson. 1963. Florentine codex: General history of the things of New Spain. Book 11, Earthly things. The School of Am. Res., Univ. Utah, Salt Lake City, and Mus. New Mexico, Santa Fe. In 13 parts.

Dickson, A. J. 1929. Covered wagon day. The Arthur H. Clark Co., Cleveland, Ohio. 287 pp.

Didear, H. K. 1969. A history of Karnes County and Old Helena. San Felipe Press, Austin, Texas. 187 pp.

Dillehay, T. D. 2000. The settlement of the Americas. Basic Books, New York, New York. 371 pp.

Di Peso, C. C. 1979. Prehistory: Southern periphery. Pages 152–161 *in* A. Oritz, ed., Southwest. Handbook of North American Indians. Vol. 9. Smithsonian Inst., Washington, DC. 717 pp.

Dockstader, F. J. 1954, The kachina and the white man: A study of the influences of white culture on the Hopi kachina cult. Bull. 35. Cranbrook Instit. Science, Bloomfield Hills, Michigan. 185 pp.

———. 1985. The kachina and the white man. Univ. New Mexico Press, Albuquerque. 202 pp.

Dodge, R. I. 1877. The plains of the great West. G. P. Putnam's Sons, New York, New York. 503 pp.

———. 1885. Our wild Indians: Thirty-three years' personal experience among the red men of the great West. A. D. Worthington and Co., Hartford, Connecticut. 653 pp.

Dollar, C. D. 1982. The journal of Charles LeRaye: Authentic or not? South Dakota Hist. Coll. 41:67–191.

Donnelly, J. P., ed. 1967. Wilderness kingdom; Indian life in the Rocky Mountains, 1840–1847: The journal and paintings of Nicolas Point, S. J. Holt, Rinehart and Winston, New York. New York. 274 pp.

Dorsey, G. A. and H. R. Voth. 1901. The Oraibi soyal ceremony. Field Columbian Mus. Publ. 55, Anthropol. Series 3(1):1–358.

Doughty, J. 1833. Prong-horned antelope (*Antilope americana*). Pages 129–150 *in* G. Stewart, ed., The cabinet of natural history and American rural sports. Vol. 3. John , Philadelphia, Pennsylvania. (Imprint Soc., Barre, Massachusetts 1973.)

Driver, H. E. 1972. Indians of North America. Univ. Chicago Press, Chicago, Illinois. 649 pp.

Driver, H. E. and W. C. Massey. 1957. Comparative studies of North American Indians. Trans. Am. Philos. Soc. (New Series) 47(2):1–456.

Driver, J. C. 1985. Zooarchaeology of six prehistoric sites in the Sierra Blanca region, New Mexico. Tech. Rept. 17. Univ. Michigan Archaeol. 103 pp.

DuBray, A. W. 1890. Still-hunting the antelope. Pages 313–332 *in* G. O. Shields, ed., The big game of North America. Rand, McNally and Co., New York, New York. 581 pp.

Duffus, R. L. 1934. The Santa Fe trail. Tudor Publ. Co., New York, New York. 283 pp.

Ebeling, W. 1986. Handbook of Indian food and fibers of arid America. Univ. California Press, Berkeley. 971 pp.

Egan, M. H. 1917. Pioneering the West, 1846–1878. W. M. Egan, ed. Howard R. Egan Estate, Richmond, Utah. 303 pp.

Einarsen, A. S. 1948. The pronghorn antelope and its management. The Stackpole Co., Harrisburg, Pennsylvania. 238 pp.

Ekholm, G. F. 1962. U-shaped "ornaments" identified as finger-loops from atlatls. Am. Antiquity 28(2):181–185.

Elliot, D. G. 1904. The land and sea mammals of Middle America and the West Indies. Zool. Series, Vol. IV, Part I. Field Columbian Museum, Chicago, Illinois. 439 pp.

Ellis, F. H. 1979. Isleta Pueblo. Pages 351–365 *in* A. Ortiz, ed., Southwest. Handbook of North American Indians. Vol. 9. Smithsonian Inst. Press, Washington, DC. 717 pp.

Emmitt, R. 1954. The last war trail: The Utes and the settlement of Colorado. Univ. Oklahoma Press, Norman. 339 pp.

Emory, W. H. 1857. Report on the United States and Mexico boundary survey. House Ex. Doc. 135. 34th Congr., 1st Sess. 2 vols. Cornelius Wendell, Washington, DC. 988 pp.

Euler, R. C. 1972. The Paiute people. Indian Tribal Series, Phoenix, Arizona. 105 pp.

Ewers, J. C. 1939. Plains Indian painting: A description of an aboriginal American art. Stanford Univ. Press, Stanford, California. 84 pp.

———. 1965. Artists of the old West. Doubleday and Co., Garden City, New York. 240 pp.

———. 1975. Intertribal warfare as the precursor of Indian-White warfare on the northern plains. Western Hist. Quart. (Oct):397–410.

———. 1980. The horse in Blackfoot Indian culture. Smithsonian Inst. Press, Washington, DC. 389 pp.

Exley, J. P. 2001. Frontier blood: The saga of the Parker family. Texas A&M Univ. Press, College Station. 332pp.

Feiler, S., ed. 1962 . Jean-Bernard Bossu's travels in the interior of North America 1751–1762. Univ. Oklahoma Press, Norman. 243 pp.

Feltskog, E. N., ed. 1969. Parkman: The Oregon Trail. Univ. Wisconsin Press, Madison. 833 pp.

Fernandez-Armesto, F., ed. 1991. The *Times* atlas of world exploration. Harper-Collins Publishers, New York, New York. 186 pp.

Fewkes, J. W. 1897a. Tusayan katcinas. Bur. Am. Ethnol. Ann. Rept. 15:245–313 to Secretary Smithsonian Inst. U.S. Govt. Print. Off., Washington, DC.

———. 1897b. Tusayan snake ceremonies. Bur. Am. Ethnol. Ann. Rept 16:267–311 to Secretary Smithsonian Inst. U.S. Govt. Print. Off., Washington, DC.

Fichter, E. 1987. Pronghorn groups: On social organization. TEBIWA (J. Idaho Mus. Nat. Hist.) 23:11–22.

Fisher, J. 1967. Zoos of the world. Natural History Press, Garden City, New York. 253 pp.

Flannery, K. V. 1966. The postglacial "readaptation" as viewed from Mesoamerica. Am. Antiquity 31(6):800–805.

———. 1967. Vertebrate fauna and hunting patterns. Pages 132–177 *in* D. S. Byers, ed., The prehistory of the Tahuacan Valley. Vol. 1. Environment and subsistence. Univ. Texas Press, Austin. 331 pp.

Flannery, R. 1953. The Gros Ventres of Montana: Part I, Social Life. Catholic Univ. of Am. Press, Washington, DC. 234 pp.

Fleharty, E. D. 1995. Wild animals and settlers on the Great Plains. Univ. Oklahoma Press, Norman. 316 pp.

Fleming, P. R. and J. Luskey. 1986. The North American Indians in early photographs. Harper and Row Publishers, New York, New York. 256 pp.

Fletcher, A. C. and F. la Flesche. 1972. The Omaha tribe. 2 vols. Univ. Nebraska Press, Lincoln. 660 pp.

Fletcher, B. J. 1966. Up the trail in '79. Univ. Oklahoma Press, Norman. 118 pp.

Forde, C. D. 1931. Ethnography of the Yuma Indians. Univ. California Public. in American Archaeol. and Ethnol. 28:83–278.

Forster, J. R., ed. 1771. Travels through that part of North America formerly called Louisiana. Vol. I. Printed for T. Davies in Russel-Street, Covent-Garden, London, England. 407 pp.

Forsythe, G. A. 1900. The story of the soldier. D. Appleton and Co., New York, New York. 389 pp.

Foster, J. 1978. Working for wildlife. Univ. Toronto Press, Toronto, Ontario. 283 pp.

Fowler, C. S. 1989. Willard Z. Park's ethnographic notes on the Northern Paiute of western Nevada, 1933–1940. Univ. Utah Anthropol. Pap. 114. Univ. Utah Press, Salt Lake City. 160 pp.

Franklin, J. 1823. Narrative of a journey to the shores of the Polar Sea. John Murray, London, England. 768 pp.

Fremont, J. C. 1843. A report on an exploration of the country lying between the Missouri River and the Rocky Mountains, on the line of the Kansas and Great Platte Rivers. U.S. Senate Doc. No. 243. 27th Congr. 3rd Sess. Washington, DC.

Frison, G. C. 1965. Spring Creek Cave, Wyoming. Am. Antiquity 31(1):81–94.

———. 1971. Shoshonean antelope procurement in the Upper Green River Basin, Wyoming. Plains Anthropol. 16(54):258–284.

———. 1974. The Casper site, a Hell Gap bison kill on the high plains. Academic Press, New York, New York. 266 pp.

———. 1978. Prehistoric hunters of the high plains. 2nd ed. Academic Press, New York, New York. 457 pp.

———, ed. 1991. Pleistocene hunters of the high plains. 2nd ed. Academic Press, New York, New York. 532 pp.

Frost, L. A. 1979. With Custer in '74. Brigham Young Univ. Press, Provo, Utah. 140 pp.

———. 1984. The Custer album, a pictorial biography of General George A. Custer. Bonanza Books, New York, New York. 192 pp.

Galvan, J., ed. 1972. A description of the kingdom of New Spain, by Sr. Don Pedro Alonso O'Crouley. John Howell Books, San Francisco, California. 148 pp.

Garrard, L. H. 1850. Wah-To-Yah, and the Taos Trail; or prairie travel and scalp dances, with a look at Los Rancheros from muleback and the Rocky Mountain campfire. H. W. Derby & Co., Cincinnati, Ohio. 349 pp.

Garretson, M. S. 1938. The American bison. New York Zool. Soc., New York. 254 pp.

Garth, T. R. 1950. Atsugewi ethnography. Anthropol. Rec. 14(2):1–128.

Gayangos, D. P. de. 1866. Cartas y relaciones de Hernán Cortés. Anthro. Lib. emperor Carlos V. Imprenta Central de los Ferra-Carriles, Paris, France. 575 pp.

Gebhard, D. W. and H. A. Cahn. 1950. The petroglyphys of Dinwoody, Wyoming. Am. Antiquity 3:219–228.

Ghent, W. J. 1936. The early far West: A narrative outline, 1540–1850. Tudor Publ. Co., New York, New York. 411 pp.

Gifford, E. W. 1931. The Kamia of Imperial Valley. Smithsonian Inst. Bur. Am. Ethnol. Bull. 97. U.S. Govt. Print. Off., Washington, DC. 94 pp.

———. 1932. The southeastern Yavapai. Univ. California Publications Am. Archaeol. and Ethnol. 29:177–251.

———. 1936. Northeastern and western Yavapai. Univ. California Publications Am. Archaeol. and Ethnol. 34:247–354.

———. 1940. Culture element distributions: XII Apache-Pueblo. Anthropol. Rec. 4(1):1–207.

Gifford, E. W. and W. E. Schenck. 1926–28. Archaeology of the southern San Joaquin Valley, California. Univ. California Publications Am. Archaeol. and Ethnol. 23:1–122.

Giorda, J. 1879. Dictionary of the Kalispel or Flathead Indian language. Compiled by the Missionaries of the Society of Jesus. Part II, English-Kalispel. St. Ignatius Print., St. Ignatius, Montana. 456 pp.

Goddard, P. E. 1975. Indians of the Southwest. Cooper Square Publishers, Inc., New York, New York. 205 pp.

Godfrey, E. 1991. Custer's last battle. Century 43(2):358–394.

Godman, J. D. 1826. American natural history. H. C. Carey and L. Lea, Philadelphia, Pennsylvania. 264 pp.

Goetzmann, W. H. 1966. Exploration and empire. Alfred A. Knopf, New York, New York. 674 pp.

Goetzmann, W. H. and G. Williams. 1992. The atlas of North American exploration. Prentice Hall General Reference, New York, New York. 224 pp.

Goldschmidt, W. 1951. Nomlaki ethnography. Univ. California Publications Am. Archaeol. and Ethnol. 42(2): 303–443.

Goossen, I. W. 1967. Navajo made easier. Northland Press, Flagstaff, Arizona. 271 pp.

Grafton, J. 1992. The American West in the nineteenth century. Dover Public., Inc., New York, New York. 199 pp.

Graham, J. D. 1852. Report of the Secretary of War, communicating in compliance with a resolution of the Senate, the report of Lieutenant Colonel Graham on the subject of the boundary line between the United States and Mexico. Memo to 32nd Congress, Washington, DC. 250 pp.

Graham, R. W. and E. L. Lundelius, Jr. 1994. Faunmap: A database documenting Quaternary distributions of mammal species in the United States. Illinois St. Mus., Springfield. Scientific Papers 25(1):1–287.

Grant, C. 1967. Rock art of the American Indian. Thomas Y. Crowell Co., New York, New York. 178 pp.

———. 1978. Eastern Coastal Chumash. Pages 509–519 *in* R. F. Heizer, ed., California. Handbook of North American Indians. Vol 8. Smithsonian Inst., Washington, DC. 800 pp.

———. 1979. The spear-thrower from 15,000 years ago to the present. Pacific Coast Archaeol. Soc. Quart. 15(1):1–17.

Gray. A. B. 1856. Survey of a route for the Southern Pacific railroad on the 32nd parallel. Wrightson and Co., Cincinnati, Ohio. 119 pp.

Greeley, H. 1964. An overland journey from New York to San Francisco in the summer of 1859. C. T. Duncan, ed. Alfred A. Knopf, New York, New York. 375 pp.

Gregg, J. 1954. Commerce of the prairies. M. L. Moorhead, ed., Univ. Oklahoma Press, Norman. 469 pp.

Griffith, E. 1827. The animal kingdom arranged in conformity with its organization, by the Baron Cuvier, with additional descriptions of all the species hitherto not named, and many not before noticed. Vol. 4. Printed for Geo. Whittaker, London.

Griffith, J. S. 1983. Kachinas and masking. Pages 764–777 *in* A. Ortiz, ed., Southwest. Handbook of North American Indians, Vol. 10. Smithsonian Inst., Washington, DC. 868 pp.

Grinnell, G. B. 1897. Range of the pronghorn antelope in 1897. Forest and Stream 48(1):5–6.

———. 1911. When antelope were plentiful. Forest and Stream, October 14:582–601.

———. 1923. The Cheyenne Indians, their history and ways of life. Vol. 1. Yale Univ. Press, New Haven, Connecticut. 358 pp.

———. 1925. American game protection. Pages 201–257 *in* G. B. Grinnell and C. Sheldon, eds., Hunting and conservation. Yale Univ. Press, New Haven, Connecticut. 548 pp.

———. 1956. The fighting Cheyennes. Univ. Oklahoma Press, Norman. 450 pp.

———. 1961. Pawnee hero stories and folk tales. Univ. Nebraska Press, Lincoln. 430 pp.

———. 1962. Blackfoot lodge tales: The story of a prairie people. Univ. Nebraska Press, Lincoln. 327 pp.

———. 1972. The Cheyenne Indians. 2 vols. Univ. Nebraska Press, Lincoln. 806 pp.

Guernsey, S. J. 1931. Explorations in northeastern Arizona. Pap. Peabody Mus. Am. Archaeol. and Ethnol. 12(1):1–123.

Hafen, L. R. 1931. Broken Hand. The Old West Publ. Co., Denver, Colorado. 316 pp.

———. 1966. The mountain men and the fur trade of the far West. 10 vols. The Arthur A. Clark Co., Glendale, California.

Hafen, L. R. and A. W. Hafen, eds. 1955. To the Rocky Mountains and Oregon, 1839–1842. The Arthur H. Clark Co., Glendale, California. 315 pp.

———, eds. 1957. Central route to the Pacific. The Arthur H. Clark Co., Glendale, California. 346 pp.

———, eds. 1959. The diaries of William Henry Jackson. The Arthur H. Clark Co., Glendale, California. 345 pp.

———, eds. 1960. Fremont's fourth expedition. The Arthur H. Clark Co., Glendale, California. 319 pp.

———, eds. 1961a. Reports from Colorado: The Wildman letters, 1859–1865. The Arthur H. Clark Co., Glendale, California. 331 pp.

———, eds. 1961b. Powder River campaigns and Sawyers expedition of 1865. The Arthur H. Clark Co., Glendale, California. 386 pp.

———, eds. 1961c. The far West and Rockies: General analytical index to the fifteen volume series and supplement to the journals of Forty-niners, Salt Lake City to Los Angeles. The Arthur H. Clark Co., Glendale, California. 360 pp.

Haines, A. L. 1976. The plains Indians. Thomas Y. Crowell Co., New York, New York. 213 pp.

Haines, F. 1938a. Where did the plains Indians get their horses? Am. Anthropol. 40(1):112–117.

———. 1938b. The northward spread of horses among the plains Indians. Am. Anthropol. 40(3):429–437.

———. 1970. The buffalo. Thomas Y. Crowell Co., New York, New York. 242 pp.

Hakluyt, R. 1589. Principal navigations, voiages, traffiques and discoveries of the English nation, made by sea and ouer land, to the most remote and farthest distant quarters of the earth, at any time within the compasse of these 1500 yeeres: Divided into three several parts, according to the positions of the regions whereunto they were directed. Pages 499–522 in D. B. Quinn, ed., The Hakluyt handbook. Vol. 2. The Hakluyt Soc., London, England, 1974. 707 pp.

Haley, J. E. 1929. Grass fires of the southern plains. West Texas Hist. Assoc. Yearbook 5:24–46.

———. 1949. Charles Goodnight, cowman and plainsman. Univ. Oklahoma Press, Norman. 485 pp.

Haley, J. L. 1997. Apaches: A history and cultural portrait. Univ. Oklahoma Press, Norman. 453 pp.

Hall, M. C. 1990. The Oxbow archaeological incident: Investigations at twenty-three locations between Owens Valley, eastern California, and Walker Basin, southwestern Nevada. Submitted to Oxbow Geothermal Co. Copies available from Archaeological Res. Serv., Virginia City, Nevada. Vol. 1, 695 pp. Vol. 2, pp. 696–740.

Hall, E. R. and K. R. Kelson. 1959. The mammals of North America. Vol. 2. Ronald Press Co., New York, New York. 79 pp.

Hallock, C. 1879. The sportsman's gazetteer and general guide. 5th ed. Forest and Stream Publ. Co., Orange Judd County, New York. 921 pp.

Halls, L. K. 1978. White-tailed deer. Pages 42–65 in J. L. Schmidt and D. L. Gilbert, eds., Big game of North America. Stackpole Books, Harrisburg, Pennsylvania. 494 pp

Hamilton, T. M. 1982. Native American bows. Spec. Publ. 5. Missouri Archaeol. Soc., Columbia, Missouri. 163 pp.

Hand, G. O. 1862. George O. Hand's diary. Typescript of the Ariz. Hist. Soc., Tucson.

Hanson, J. R. 1986. Adjustment and adaptation on the northern plains: The case of equestrianism among the Hidatsa. Plains Anthro. 31(11):93–107.

Harper, K. T. 1986. Historical environments. Pages 51–63 in W. L. D'Azevedo, ed., Great Basin. Vol. 11. Handbook of North American Indians. Smithsonian Inst. Press, Washington, DC. 852 pp.

Harrington, J. P. 1911. The phonetic system of the Ute language. Univ. Colorado Studies VIII(3):199–222.

———. 1916. The ethnogeography of the Tewa Indians. Bur. Am. Ethnol Ann. Rept. 29:29–618 to Secretary Smithsonian Inst. U.S. Govt. Print. Off., Washington, DC.

———. 1928. Vocabulary of the Kiowa language. Smithsonian Inst. Bur. American Ethnol. Bull. 84. U. S. Govt. Print. Off., Washington, DC. 255 pp.

Harris, W. C. 1888. The sportsman's guide to the hunting and shooting grounds of the United States and Canada. The Angler's Publ. Co., C. T. Dillingham, New York, New York. 207 pp.

Harrod, M. L. 2000. The animals come dancing. Univ. Arizona Press, Tucson. 171 pp.

Hayden, F. V. 1868. Brief notes on the Pawnee, Winnebago, and Omaha languages. Proc. Am. Philosoph. Soc. 10:389–421.

Hayes, A. C., J. N. Young and A. H. Warren. 1981. Excavation of Mound 7, Gran Quivira National Monument, New Mexico. Publications Archaeol. 16. U.S. Natl. Park Serv., Washington, DC. 214 pp.

H. B. 1911. Old time numbers of antelope. Forest and Stream LXXVI(5):177.

Healy, J. J. 1982. Men of the mountains and plains. Pages 112–121 in L. Silliman, ed., We seized our rifles. Mountain Press Publishing Co., Missoula, Montana. 224 pp.

Heizer, R. F. 1938. An inquiry into the status of the Santa Barbara spear-thrower. Am. Antiquity 2:137–141.

———. 1955. California Indian linguistic records, the mission Indian vocabularies of H. W. Anthropol. Rec. 15(2):85–202.

Heizer, R. F. and G. W. Hewes. 1940. Animal ceremonialism in central California in the light of archaeology. Am. Anthropol. 42(4), Part 1:587–603.

Heizer, R. F. and I. W. Johnson. 1952. A prehistoric sling from Lovelock Cave, Nevada. Am. Antiquity 18(2):139–147.

Henderson, J. and J. P. Harrington. 1914. Ethnozoology of the Tewa Indians. Smithsonian Inst. Bur. Am. Ethnol. Bull. 56. U.S. Govt. Print. Off., Washington, DC. 76 pp.

Hernández, F. 1651. A new natural history of the plants and minerals of Mexico. Originally compiled by Francisco Hernández, then edited into [a single] volume by Nardo Antonio Reccho. B. Deversini and Z. Masotti Publishers and printed by V. Masacardi, Rome, Italy. 950+ pp.

Herrick, C. L. 1892. Mammals of Minnesota. Bull. 7. Geological and Natural History Survey of Minnesota, Minneapolis. 300 pp.

Hewitt, J. N. B., ed. 1970. Journal of Rudolph Friederich Kurz: An account of his experiences among fur traders and American Indians on the Mississippi and upper Missouri rivers during the years 1846 to 1852. Univ. Nebraska Press, Lincoln. 382 pp.

Hibben, F. C. 1975. Kiva art of the Anasazi at Pottery Mound. KC Publications, Las Vegas, Nevada. 145 pp.

Hilger, M. I. 1952. Arapaho child life and its cultural background. Smithsonian Inst. Bur. Am. Ethnol. Bull. 148. U.S. Govt. Print. Off., Washington, DC. 240 pp.

Hill, R. B. 1979. Hanta Yo. Doubleday and Co., Inc., Garden City, New York. 834 pp.

Hill, W. W. 1938. The agricultural and hunting methods of the Navaho Indians. Yale Univ., New Haven, Connecticut, Publ. Anthropol. 18:1–193.

Hind, H. Y. 1859. North-west territory: Report on the Assiniboine and Saskatchewan exploring expedition. J. Lovell, Toronto, Ontario. 201 pp.

Hirschfelder, A. and P. Molin. 1992. The encyclopedia of Native American religions. Facts on File, New York. 367 pp.

Hittel, J. S. 1863. The resources of California. A. Roman and Co., San Francisco, California. 464 pp.

Hittel, T. H. 1898. History of California. Vol. I. N. J. Stone and Co., San Francisco, California. 799 pp.

Hodge, F. W., ed. 1907. Handbook of American Indians north of Mexico. Vol. 1. Smithsonian Inst. Bur. Am. Ethnol. Bull. 30. U.S. Govt. Print. Off., Washington, DC. 981 pp.

———. ed. 1910. Handbook of American Indians north of Mexico. Vol. 2. Bur. Am. Ethnol. Bull. 30. Smithsonian Inst., Washington, DC. 1,225 pp.

———. ed. 1984. The narrative of Alvar Nuñez Cabeça de Vaca. Pages 3–126 *in* F. W. Hodge and T. H. Lewis, eds., Spanish explorers in the southern United States 1528–1543. Texas St. Hist. Assoc., Austin. 411 pp.

Hoebel, E. A. 1960. The Cheyennes: Indians of the Great Plains. Holt, Rinehart and Winston, New York, New York. 103 pp.

Hoekman, S. 1953. The history of Fort Sully. Pages 222–277 *in* South Dakota historical collections and report. South Dakota Hist. Soc., Pierre. 567 pp.

Hogarth, P. 1972. Artists on horseback: The old West in illustrated journalism 1857–1900. Watson-Guptill Publications, New York, New York. 288 pp.

Hoig, S. 1979. The battle of the Washita. Univ. Nebraska Press, Lincoln. 294 pp.

Holder, P. 1970. The hoe and the horse on the plains. Univ. Nebraska Press, Lincoln. 176 pp.

Holmes, W. H. 1884. Illustrated catalogue of a portion of the collections made by the Bureau of Ethnology during the field season of 1881. Bur. Am. Ethnol. Ann. Rept. 3:427–594.

Hoopes, A. W. 1975. The road to the Little Bighorn—and beyond. Vantage Press, New York, New York. 336 pp.

Hopkins, S. W. 1883. Life among the Paiutes. G. P. Putnam's Sons, New York, New York. 268 pp.

Hornaday, W. T. 1889. The extermination of the American bison, with a sketch of its discovery and life. Pages 373–548 *in* Ann. Rept., Smithsonian Inst., 1887. U.S. Govt. Print. Off., Washington, DC.

———. 1904. The American natural history; a foundation of useful knowledge of the higher animals of North America. Charles Scribner's Sons, New York, New York. 449 pp.

———. 1914. Wild life conservation in theory and practice. Yale Univ. Press, New Haven, Connecticut. 247 pp.

Howard, J. H. 1965. The Ponco tribe. Smithsonian Inst. Bur. Am. Ethnol. Bull. 195. U.S. Govt. Print. Off., Washington, DC. 191 pp.

Hughes, R. B. 1957. Pioneer years in the Black Hills. A. W. Spring, ed., Arthur H. Co., Glendale, California. 366 pp.

Hull, M. E. 1938. Soldiering on the high plains: The diary of Lewis -Byram Hull, 1864–1866. Kansas Hist. Quart. 7:45, 50–51.

Hummfreville, J. L. 1897. Twenty years among our savage Indians. The Hartford Publ. Co., Hartford, Connecticut. 674 pp.

Huning, F. 1973. Trader on the Santa Fe trail. With notes by L. F. Brown. Univ. Albuquerque, Albuquerque, New Mexico. 153 pp.

Hunt, C. B. 1974. Natural regions of the United States and Canada. W. H. Freeman and Co., San Francisco, California. 725 pp.

Huntington, D. W. 1904. Our big game. Charles Scribner's Sons, New York, New York. 347 pp.

Hurt, W. R., Jr. 1953. Report of the investigation of the Swan Creek site, 39WW7, Walworth County, South Dakota. Archaeol. Studies Circ. 7. South Dakota Archaeol.Commiss., Pierre. 98 pp.

Hutto, J. R. 1932. Big Spring and vicinity. W. Texas Hist. Assoc. Yearbook 8:75–97.

Hyde, G. E. 1959. Indians of the high plains: From the prehistoric period to the coming of Europeans. Univ. Oklahoma Press, Norman. 228 pp.

Hyer, J. K., comp. 1968. Dictionary of the Sioux language. The Carl Purington Rollins Print. Off. of Yale Univ. Press, New Haven, Connecticut. 31 pp.

Inman, H. 1897. The old Santa Fe trail. The MacMillan Co., New York, New York. 493 pp.

Irving, J. T. 1835. Indian sketches, taken during an expedition to the Pawnee Tribes, 1833. 2 vols. Cary, Lea and Blanchard, Philadelphia, Pennsylvania.

Irving, W. 1850. Adventures of Captain Bonneville. George Routledge and Co., London, England. 271 pp.

Ives, J. C. 1861. Report upon the Colorado River of the West. U. S. Gov. Print. Off., Washington, DC. 131 pp.

Jablow, J. 1951. The Cheyenne in plains Indian trade relations, 1795–1840. Am. Ethnog. Soc. Memoir 19. J. J. Augustin, New York, New York. 100 pp.

Jackson, W. 1982. The woman from Sitting Bull's. Pages 180–186 *in* L. Silliman, ed., We seized our rifles. Mountain Press Publ. Co., Missoula, Montana. 224 pp.

Jacobsen, R. B. and J. L. Eighmy. 1980. A mathematical theory of horse adoption on the North American plains. Plains Ethnol. 25(90):333–341.

James, E. 1823. Account of an expedition from Pittsburgh to the Rocky Mountains, performed in the years 1819 and '20; by order of the Hon., J. C. Calhoun, Sec'y of War: Under the command of Major Stephen H. Long. 2 vols. C. Carey and Lea, Philadelphia.

James, S. R. 1983. Surprise Valley settlement and subsistence: A critical review of the faunal evidence. J. California and Great Basin Anthropol. 5(1 & 2):156–175.

Jennings, J. D. 1957. Danger Cave. Pages 1–328 *in* Robert Anderson, ed. Anthropological Papers, vol. 27. University of Utah Press, Salt Lake City.

———. 1986. Prehistory: Introduction. Pages 113–119 *in* W. L. D'Azevedo, ed., Great Basin. Handbook of North American Indians. Vol 11. Smithsonian Inst. Press, Washington DC. 852 pp.

Jennings, J. D. and G. D. Edwards. 1948. Plainsmen of the past: A review of the prehistory of the plains. U.S. Natl. Park Serv., Region 2, Omaha, Nebraska. 70 pp.

Jensen, R. E., R. E. Paul and J. Carter. 1991. Eyewitness at Wounded Knee. Univ. Nebraska Press, Lincoln. 210 pp.

Johnson, O. W. 1969. Flathead and Kootenay. Arthur H. Clark Co., Glendale, California. 392 pp.

Johnston, W. H., Jr. 1890. Signaling for antelope on the Staked Plains. Outing 26(1):2–8.

Josephy, A. M. 1981. The Indian heritage of America. Bantam Books, Inc., New York, New York. 397 pp.

Judson, K. 1910. Myths and legends of the Pacific Northwest. A. C. McClurg and Co., Chicago, Illinois. 145 pp.

Kane, P. 1859. Wanderings of an artist among the Indians of North America (1846–48). Longman, Brown, Green, Longmans and Roberts, London, England. 455 pp.

Karol, J. S. and S. L. Rozman, eds. 1971. Everyday Lakota: An English-Sioux dictionary for beginners. Nebraska Curriculum Development Center, Univ. Nebraska, Lincoln. 122 pp.

Kay, C. E. 1994. Aboriginal overkill—the role of Native Americans in structuring western ecosystems. Human Nat. 5:359–398.

Kellar, J. H. 1955. The atlatl in North America. Indiana Hist. Soc., Prehist. Res. Series 3(3):281–352.

Kelly, I. T. 1932. Ethnography of the Surprise Valley Paiute. Univ. California Publications Am. Archaeol. and Ethnol. 31:67–209.

———. 1964. Southern Paiute ethnography. Univ. Utah Anthropol. Pap. 69. Univ. Utah Press, Salt Lake City. 192 pp.

Kelly, R. L. and L. C. Todd. 1988. Coming into the country: Early Paleoindian hunting and mobility. Am. Antiquity 53(2):231–244.

Kennerly, C. B. R. 1956. Report on the zoology of the [Whipple] expedition. Pages 5–17 *in* Reports of explorations. Vol. 4. House Ex. Doc. No. 91, 33rd Congr., 2nd Session. A. O. P. Nicholson, printer, Washington, DC.

Keyser, J. D. 1977. Writing on stone: Rock art on the northwest plains. Can. J. Archaeol. 1:15–80.

Kidder, A. V., H. S. Cosgrove and C. B. Cosgrove. 1949. The Pendleton ruin, Hidalgo County, New Mexico. Contrib. Am. Anthropol. and Hist. 50:109–152.

Kindig, J. M. 1987. An evaluation of an ethnohistoric account of a plains Indian communal hunt in the Boulder Valley, 1862. Southwest Lore 53(4):17–27.

Kitchen, D. W. and B. W. O'Gara. 1982. Pronghorn, *Antilocapra americana*. Pages 960–972 *in* J. A. Chapman and G. A. Feldhammer, eds., Wild mammals of North America: Biology, management, and economics. Johns Hopkins Univ. Press, Baltimore, Maryland. 1,147 pp.

Kniffen, F., G. MacGregor, R. McKennan, S. Mekeal and M. Mook.1935. Walapai ethnography. Memoirs Am. Anthropol. Assoc. 42. 293 pp.

Koch, R. P. 1977. Dress clothing of the plains Indians. Univ. Oklahoma Press, Norman. 219 pp.

Koster, J. 1980. The forty-day scout. Am. Heritage 31(4):98–107.

Krause, F. 1905. Sling contrivances for projectile weapons. Smithsonian Inst. Ann. Rept. 1905:619–638.

Krause, H. and G. D. Olson. 1974. Prelude to glory, a newspaper accounting of Custer's 1874 expedition to the Black Hills. Brevet Press, Sioux Falls, South Dakota. 279 pp.

Krech, S. III, ed. 1981. Indians, animals and the fur trade. Univ. Georgia Press, Athens. 207 pp.

———. 1999. The ecological Indian: Myth and history. W. W. Norton and Co., New York, New York. 318 pp.

Kroeber, A. L. 1906–07. Indian myths of south central California. Univ. California Publications Am. Archaeol. and Ethnol. 4(4):167–250.

———. 1907. The Yokuts language of south central California. Univ. California Publications Am. Archaeol. and Ethnol. 2(5):165–193.

———. 1917. Zuni kin and clan. Pages 39–205 *in* Anthropological papers. Am. Mus. Nat. Hist. 28. New York, New York. 387 pp.

———. 1929. The Valley Nisenan. Univ. California Publications Am. Archaeol. and Ethnol. 24:253–290.

———. 1932. The Patwin and their neighbors. Univ. California Publications Am. Archaeol. and Ethnol. 29(4):253–423.

———. 1948. Anthropology: Race, language, culture, psychology, prehistory. Harcourt, Brace, New York, New York. 209 pp.

———. 1976. Handbook of the Indians of California. Dover Publications, Inc., New York, New York. 1,013 pp.

———, ed. 1935. Walapai ethnography. Memoirs of the American Anthropol. Assoc., No. 42. Menasha, Wisconsin. 293 pp.

Küchler, A. W. 1964. Potential natural vegetation of the conterminous United States. Spec. Publ. 36. Am. Geogr. Soc., New York, New York. 116 pp.

Kurtén, B. and E. Anderson. 1980. Pleistocene mammals of North America. Columbia Univ. Press, New York, New York. 442 pp.

La Flesche, F. 1932. A dictionary of the Osage language. Smithsonian Inst. Bur. American Ethnol. Bull. 109. U. S. Govt. Print. Off., Washington, DC. 406 pp.

Laird, C. 1976. The Chemehuevis. Malki Mus. Press, Banning, California. 349 pp.

Lake-Thom, B. 1997. Spirits of the north. Penguin Books, New York, New York. 210 pp.

Landes, R. 1968. The Mystic Lake Sioux: Sociology of the Mdewakantonwan Santee. Univ. Wisconsin Press, Madison. 224 pp.

Lang, L. A. 1926. Ranching with Roosevelt. J. B. Lippencott Co., Philadelphia, Pennsylvania. 367 pp.

Lang, R. W. and A. H. Harris. 1984. The faunal remains from Arroyo Hondo Pueblo, New Mexico. Arroyo Hondo Archaeol. Series 5. School of Am. Res. Press, Santa Fe, New Mexico. 316 pp.

Lange, C. H. and C. L. Riley, eds. 1966. Southwestern journals of Adolph F. Bandelier: 1880–1882. Univ. New Mexico Press, Albuquerque. 479 pp.

Lawton, S. P. 1962. Petroglyphs and pictographs in Oklahoma: An introduction. Plains Anthropol. 7(17):189–193.

Laycock, G. 1990. The hunters and the hunted. Outdoor Life Books, Meredith Press, New York, New York. 280 pp.

Leopold, A. S. 1959. Wildlife of Mexico, the game birds and mammals. Univ. California Press, Berkeley. 568 pp.

———. 1959b. Pronghorn antelope. Pages 95–97 *in* Nevada Legislative Counsel Bureau. Survey.

LeRaye, C. 1926. The journal of Charles LeRaye. South Dakota Hist. Coll. 4:150–180.

Levy, R. 1978. Costanoan. Pages 485–495 *in* R. F. Heizer, ed., California. Handbook of North American Indians. Vol. 8. Smithsonian Inst., Washington, DC. 800 pp.

Lewis, O. 1942. The effects of white contact upon Blackfoot culture, with special reference to the role of the fur trade. Monogr. of the Am. Ethnol. Soc., 6. New York, New York. 73 pp.

Lewis-Williams, D. 2001. Paintings of the spirit. Natl. Geogr. 199(2):118–125.

Ligon, J. S. 1927. Wildlife of New Mexico. St. Game Commiss., New Mexico Dept. Game and Fish, Santa Fe. 212 pp.

Linné, S. 1948. El Valle y la Ciudad de Mexico en 1550. New Series, Publ. 9. Ethnol. Mus. Sweden, Stockholm. 220 pp. + 11 map panels.

Linton, R. 1940. Acculturation and process of culture change. Pages 463–501 *in* R. Linton, ed., Acculturation in seven American Indian tribes. D. Appleton-Century Co., Inc., New York, New York. 526 pp.

Little, J. A. 1946. Biography of Lorenzo Dow Young. Utah Hist. Quart. XIV:25–132.

Loeffelbein, B. 1994. Londoner Fred Harvey built a western empire on bountiful meals served by pretty girls. Wild West 6(6):32, 34, 36.

Loisel, G. 1912. Histoire des menageries de l'antique a nos jours. 3 vols. Octave Doin et Fils, Paris, France.

Loud, Llewellyn L. and M. R. Harrington. 1929. Lovelock Cave, vol. 25, no. 1. University of California Press: Berkeley. 252 pp.

Lowie, R. H. 1924. Notes on Shoshonean ethnography. Anthropol. Pap. Am. Mus. Nat. Hist. Vol. 20, Part 3:185–324.

———. 1960. Crow word lists. Univ. California Press, Berkeley. 411 pp.

———. 1982. Indians of the Plains. Univ. Nebraska Press, Lincoln. 220 pp.

Lubinski, P. M. 1997. Pronghorn intensification in the Wyoming Basin: A study of mortality patterns and prehistoric hunting strategies. Ph.D. thesis, Univ. Wisconsin, Madison. 395 pp.

———. 1999. The communal pronghorn hunt: A review of the ethnographic and archaeological evidence. J. California and Great Basin Anthropol. 21(2):158–181.

Lubinski, P. M. and V. Herren. 2000. An introduction to pronghorn biology, ethnography and archaeology. J. V. Pastor and P. M. Lubinski, eds., Pronghorn past and present: Archaeology, ethnography, and biology. Plains Anthropologist Memoir 32, 45(174):3–11.

Lumholtz, C. 1902. Unknown Mexico. 2 vols. Charles Scribner's Sons, New York, New York. 1,013 pp.

MacKenzie, C. 1889. The Missouri Indians: A narrative of four trading expeditions to the Missouri, 1804–1805–1806. Pages 315–393 *in* L. F. R. Masson, ed., Les Bourgeois de la Campagne du Nord-Ouest. Vol. 1. Impr. générale A. Coté et. cie., Quebec, Quebec.

Mails, T. E. 1972. The mystic warriors of the plains. Mallard Press, New York, New York. 619 pp.

———. 1974. The people called Apache. Prentice-Hall, Inc., Englewood Cliffs, New Jersey. 447 pp.

Mallery, G. 1893. Picture writing of the American Indians. Bur. Ethnol. Ann. Rept. to Secretary Smithsonian Inst., U.S. Govt. Print. Off., Washington, DC. 807 pp.

Maloney, A. B., ed. 1945. Fur brigade to the Bonaventura: John Work's California expedition for the Hudson's Bay Company. California Hist. Soc., San Francisco. 112 pp.

Malouf, C. 1974. The Gosiute Indians. Pages 25–172 *in* D. A. Horr, ed., Shoshone Indians. Garland Publishing Inc., New York, New York. 320 pp.

Manly, W. L. 1894. Death Valley in '49. The Pacific Tree and Vine Co., San Jose, California. 498 pp.

Marcy, R. B. 1859. The prairie traveler: A handbook for overland expeditions. Harper and Brothers, New York, New York. 340 pp.

———. 1938. Adventure on Red River. Grant Foreman, ed. Univ. Oklahoma Press, Norman. 248 pp.

Margolin, M. 1978. The Ohlone way, Indian life in the San Francisco-Monterey Bay area. Heyday Books, Berkeley, California. 182 pp.

Marquis, T. B. 1967. Custer on the Little Bighorn. End-Kian Publ. Co., Lodi, California. 64 pp.

———. 1974. Memoirs of a white Crow Indian: Thomas H. Leforge. Univ. Nebraska Press, Lincoln. 377 pp.

———. 1975. Custer, cavalry and Crows. Old Army Press, Fort Collins, Colorado. 183 pp.

Marriott, A. 1963. Saynday's people: The Kiowa Indians and the stories they told. Univ. Nebraska Press, Lincoln. 237 pp.

———. 1968. Kiowa years. Macmillan Publ. Co., New York, New York. 173 pp.

Marryat, F. 1855. Mountains and molehills or recollections of a burnt journal. Longman, Brown, Green and Longmans, London, England. 443 pp.

Martin, C. 1978. Keepers of the game. Univ. California Press, Berkeley. 226 pp.

Martin, P. S. 1967. Prehistoric overkill in Pleistocene extinctions: The search for cause. Proc. 7th Congr. Intl. Assoc. Quater. Res. 6:75–120.

Martin, P. S. and J. B. Rinaldo. 1960. Excavations in the Upper Little Colorado drainage, eastern Arizona. Fieldiana: Anthropol. 51(1):1–127.

Martin, P. S., J. B. Rinaldo and E. Bluhm. 1954. Caves of the Reserve area. Fieldiana: Anthropol. 42. 227 pp.

Mason, J. A. 1910. Myths of the Uintah Utes. J. Am. Folk-Lore 23(89):299–363.

———. 1918. The language of the Salinan Indians. Univ. California Publ. in American Archaeol. and Ethnol. 14(1):1–154.

Mattes, M. J. 1969. The great Platte River road. Nebraska St. Hist. Soc., Lincoln. 583 pp.

Matthews, W. 1874. Hidatsa (Minnetaree) English dictionary. 2:149–168. Cramoisy Press, New York, New York.

Matthiessen, P. 1959. Wildlife in America. Viking Press, New York, New York. 304 pp.

———. 1983. In the spirit of Crazy Horse. Viking Penguin, New York, New York. 645 pp.

Mattison, R. H. 1965. The army post on the northern plains. Oregon Trail Mus. Assoc., Inc., Gering, Nebraska. 27 pp.

Maxwell, J. A., ed. 1978. America's fascinating Indian heritage. Reader's Digest Assoc., Inc., Pleasantville, New York. 416 pp.

McCabe, R. E. 1982. Elk and Indians: Historical values and perspectives. Pages 61–123 in J. W. Thomas and D. E. Toweill, eds., Elk of North America: Ecology and management. Stackpole Books, Harrisburg, Pennsylvania. 698 pp.

———. 2002. Elk and Indians: Then again. In D. E. Toweill and J. W. Thomas, eds., Ecology and Management of North American elk. Smithsonian Inst. Press, Washington, DC. 962 pp.

McCabe, R. E. and T. R. McCabe. 1984. Of slings and arrows: An historical retrospection. Pages 19–72 in L. K. Halls, ed., White-tailed deer: Ecology and management. Stackpole Books, Harrisburg, Pennsylvania. 870 pp.

McClintock, W. 1968. The old north trail. Univ. Nebraska Press, Lincoln. 539 pp.

McCracken, H. 1966. The Frederic Remington book. Doubleday and Co., Garden City, New York. 284 pp.

McDermott, J. F. 1940. Tixier's travels on the Osage prairies. Univ. Oklahoma Press, Norman. 309 pp.

———. 1970. Travelers on the western frontier. Univ. Illinois Press, Urbana. 351 pp.

McDonald, J. N. 1982. North American bison: Their classification and evolution. Univ. California Press, Berkeley. 316 pp.

McDonnell, J. 1889. Some account of the Red River. Pages 267–281 in L. R. Masson, ed., Les Bourgeois de la Campagnie du Nord-Ouest. Vol. I. De L'imprimerie Générale A. Coté et cie, Quebec, Quebec. 413 pp.

McDougall, J. 1898. Pathfinding on plain and prairie (1865–68). W. Briggs, Toronto, Ontario. 277 pp.

McGuire, K. R. 1980. Cave sites, faunal analysis, and big-game hunters of the Great Basin: A caution. Quart. Res. 14:263–268.

McHugh, T. 1972. The time of the buffalo. Alfred A. Knopf, New York, New York. 350 pp.

McMurtry, L. 1999. Crazy Horse. Lipper/Viking, New York, New York. 148 pp.

McNutt, F. A., ed. 1908. Fernanco Cortes—his five letters of relation to the Emperor Charles V. Vol. 1. Arthur H. Clark Co., Cleveland, Ohio. 354 pp.

Mead, J. R. 1986. Hunting and trading on the Great Plains, 1859–1875. Univ. Oklahoma Press, Norman. 276 pp.

Meager, M. M. 1978. Bison. Pages 122–133 in J. L. Schmidt and D. L. Gilbert, eds., Big game of North America. Stackpole Books, Harrisburg, Pennsylvania. 494 pp.

Merriam, C. H. 1979. Indian names for plants and animals among Californian and other western North American Indians. R. F. Heizer, assembler and annotator. Publ. Am. Archaeol., Ethnol., and Hist. 14. Ballerina Press, Socorro, New Mexico. 296 pp.

Meyer, R. W. 1977. The village Indians of the upper Missouri: The Mandans, Hidatsas, and Arikaras. Univ. Nebraska Press, Lincoln. 368 pp.

Michno, G. F. 2000. Indian villages. Wild West. 13(4):48.

Midden, H. F. 1930. Army life on the plains during the Indian wars. M.A. thesis, Univ. Nebraska, Lincoln. 219 pp.

Millais, J. G. 1915. Wapiti. Pages 281–300 in D. Caruthers, P. B. Vander Byl, R. L. Kennion, J. G. Millais, H. F. Wallace and F. G. Barclay, eds., The gun at home and abroad: The big game of Asia and North America. London and Counties Press Assoc., Ltd., London, England. 433 pp.

Miller, D. H. 1985. Custer's fall. Univ. Nebraska Press, Lincoln. 271 pp.

Miller, L. B., S. Hart and D. C. Ward, eds. 1988. The selected papers of Charles Willson Peale and his family. Vol. 2. Charles Willson Peale: The artist in his museum, 1719–1810. Yale Univ. Press, New Haven, Connecticut.

Miller, W. R. 1972. Newe Natekwinappeh: Shoshoni stories and dictionary. Univ. Utah Press, Salt Lake City. 172. pp.

Milner, C. A. II, C. A. O'Connor and M. A. Sandweiss, eds. 1994. The Oxford history of the American West. Oxford Univ. Press, New York, New York. 872 pp.

Minor, M. and N. Minor. 1978. The American Indian craft book. Univ. Nebraska Press, Lincoln. 416 pp.

Mitchell, L. C. 1981. Witnesses to a vanishing America: The nineteenth-century response. Princeton Univ. Press, Princeton, New Jersey. 320 pp.

Mixco, M. J. 1985. Kiliwa dictionary. Univ. Utah Anthropol. Paper No. 109. Salt Lake City. 382 pp.

Möllhausen, B. 1858. Diary of a journey from the Mississippi to the coasts of the Pacific with a United States government expedition. 2 vols. Longman, Brown, Green, Longmans and Roberts, London, England.

Monaghan, J. 1863. The book of the American West. Simon and Schuster, New York, New York. 608 pp.

Monnett, J. H. 1999. Massacre at Cheyenne Hole. Univ. Press of Colorado, Niwot. 143 pp.

Mooney, J. 1898. Calendar history of the Kiowa Indians. Pages 129–445 *in* Seventeenth annual report to the Bureau of American Ethnology to Secretary of Smithsonian Inst., 1895–1896. Part 1. U.S. Govt. Print. Off., Washington, DC. 468 pp.

———. 1979. Calendar history of the Kiowa Indians. Smithsonian Inst. Press, Washington, DC. 342 pp.

Morgan, L. H. 1959. The Indian journals, 1859–62. L. A. White, ed. The Univ. Michigan Press, Ann Arbor. 233 pp.

Morlan, R. E. 1999. Canadian archaeological radiocarbon database. Canadian Mus. Civiliz., Ottawa, Ontario. On disk.

Morris, A. A. 1940. Digging in the Southwest. Doubleday, Doran and Co., Inc., New York, New York. 301 pp.

Morvillo, A. 1895. A dictionary of the Numipu or Nez Perce language. Part I, English-Nez Perce. Saint Ignatius' Mission Print, Saint Ignatius, Montana. 242 pp.

Moulton, G. E., ed. 1986. The journals of the Lewis and Clark expedition. 5 vols. Univ. Nebraska Press, Lincoln.

Munson, E. L. 1897a. Antelope and the great storm. Forest and Stream 48(1):7.

———. 1897b. Range of the antelope. Forest and Stream 48(9):164.

———. 1897c. The antelope in Montana. Forest and Stream 48(12):244.

Murphy, J. M. 1879. Sporting adventures in the far West. Sampson Low, Marston, Searle and Rivington, London, England. 415 pp.

Murphy, V. R. 1891. Across the plains in the Donner party. Century Mag. (July):409–426.

Murphy, W. 1930. The forgotten battalion. Annals of Wyoming 7:383–401. [*in* Brown (1971).]

Murphy, R. F. and Y. Murphy. 1960. Shoshone-Bannock subsistence and society. Univ. California Press, Berkeley and Los Angeles, Anthropol. Rec. 16(7):293–338.

Murphy, T. W. and F. P. Frampton. 1986. Aboriginal antelope traps on BLM lands in the Elko area, northeastern Nevada. 20th Biennial Great Basin Anthropol. Conf.: Las Vegas, Nevada. 16+ pp.

Myers, N. 1989. Is man the fastest animal? Intl. Wildl. 19(5):33.

Nelson, E. W. 1925. Status of the pronghorned antelope, 1922–1924. Bull. 1,346. U.S. Dept. Agric., Washington, DC. 64 pp.

Nevin, D. 1974. The express men. Time-Life Books, New York, New York. 240 pp.

Newberry, J. S. 1857. Report upon the zoology of the route, No. 2, Chapter 1. Pages 70–71 *in* Abbot, H. L., ed., Reports of the exploration and surveys to ascertain the most practicable and economical route for a railroad from the Mississippi River to the Pacific Ocean. U. S. Senate, Ex. Doc. No. 78, Vol. VI. Washington, DC.

Newcomb, W. W., Jr. 1961. The Indians of Texas. Univ. Texas Press, Austin. 404 pp.

Newhouse, S. 1869. The trapper's guide. Oakley, Mason and Co., New York, New York. 216 pp.

Newman, M. T. 1967. Radiocarbon-dated archaeological remains on the northern and central Great Plains. Am. Antiquity 32(4):471–486.

Newman, M. T., A. Woodward, W. J. Kroll and B. H. McLeod. 1957. River basin survey paper 8. Smithsonian Inst. Bur. Am. Ethnol. Bull. 166. U.S. Govt. Print. Off., Washington, DC. 258 pp.

Noonan, J. T., Jr. 1977. The Antelope. Univ. California Press, Berkeley. 198 pp.

Norris, P. W. 1877. Report upon the Yellowstone National Park to the Secretary of the Interior, for the year 1877. U.S. Govt. Print. Off., Washington, DC. 15 pp.

Northern Cheyenne Language and Culture Center. 1976. English-Cheyenne student dictionary. Language Research Department, Lame Deer, Montana. 163 pp.

Nuttall, Z. 1891. The atlatl, or spear-thrower, of the ancient Mexicans. Pap. Peabody Mus. Am. Archaeol. and Ethnol. 1(3):168–198.

O'Bryan, A. 1956. The dîné: Origin myths of the Navaho Indians. Smithsonian Inst. Bur. Am. Ethnol. Bull. 163. U.S. Govt. Print. Off., Washington, DC. 187 pp.

O'Gara, B. W. 2004. Laws and conservation. Chapter 3 *in* B. W. O'Gara and J. D. Yoakum, eds., Pronghorn: ecology and management. Univ. Press Colorado, Boulder.

O'Gara, B. W. and C. Janis. 2004. The fossil record. Chapter 2 *in* B. W. O'Gara and J. D. Yoakum, eds., Pronghorn: ecology and management. Univ. Press Colorado, Boulder.

O'Gara, B. W. and R. G. Dundas. Distribution: Past and present. Pages 67–119 *in* D. E. Toweill and J. W. Thomas, eds., Elk of North America. Smithsonian Inst. Press, Washington, DC. 962 pp.

O'Gara, B. W. and J. D. Yoakum, eds. 2004. Pronghorn: ecology and management. Univ. Press Colorado, Boulder.

Ohlendorf, S. M., trans. 1969. Journey to Mexico during the years 1826 to 1934, by Jean Louis Belandier. 2 vols. Texas St. Hist. Assoc., Austin.

Olmsted, D. L. 1966. Achumawi dictionary. Univ. California Press, Berkeley. 158 pp.

Olmsted, D. L. and O. C. Stewart. 1978. Achumawi. Pages 225–235 *in* R. F. Heizer, ed., California. Handbook of North American Indians. Vol. 8. Smithsonian Inst., Washington, DC. 800 pp.

Olsen, S. J. 1978. The faunal analysis, No. 1. Pages 1–66 *in* Bones from Awatovi, northeastern Arizona. Reports of the Awatovi Expedition, Rept. 11. Peabody Mus. Archaeol. and Ethnol., Cambridge, Massachusetts. 74 pp.

Opler, M. E. 1969. Apache odyssey: A journey between two worlds. Holt, Rinehart and Winston, New York, New York. 301 pp.

———. 2001. Lupan Apache. Pages 941–952 *in* R. J. DeMallie, ed., Plains. Handbook of North American Indians. Vol. 13. Smithsonian Inst. Press, Washington, DC. 1,360 pp.

Ord, G. 1815. Zoology of North America, class Mammalia. Pages 291–361 *in* W. Guthrie, ed., A new geographical, historical and commercial grammar. Vol. 2. 2nd Am. ed. Johnson and Warner, Philadelphia, Pennsylvania. 599 pp. (From an 1894 reproduction by S. N. Rhodes, Heddonfield, New Jersey. 70 pages of Ord's original publication plus a 90-page appendix on the more important scientific and historic questions involved.)

Oregonian, The. 1886. Game abounds in southwest Oregon. Portland, Oregon. (Cited in Einarsen [1948:17].)

Oswalt, W. H. 1966. This land was theirs: A study of the North American Indian. John Wiley and Sons, Inc., New York, New York. 573 pp.

Parfit, M. 2000. Dawn of humans: Hunt for the first Americans. Natl. Geogr. 198(6):40–67.

Parker, A. C. 1954. The Indian how book. Dover Publications, Inc., New York, New York. 335 pp.

Parker, S. 1842. Journal of an exploring tour beyond the Rocky Mountains. 3rd ed. Mack, Andrus, and Woodruff, Ithaca, New York. 408 pp.

Parker, W. B. 1984. Notes taken during the expedition commanded by Capt. R. B. Marcy, through unexplored Texas in the summer and fall of 1854. Texas State Hist. Assoc., Austin, 242 pp.

Parkman, F. 1892. The Oregon trail—Sketches of prairie and Rocky-mountain life. Little, Brown and Co., Boston, Massachusetts. 411 pp.

Parks, D. R., J. Beltran and E. P. Waters. 1979. Introduction to the Arikara language. Mary College, Bismarck, North Dakota. 443 pp.

Parr, R. E. 1989. Archaeological investigations of the Huntoon pronghorn trap complex, Mineral County, Nevada. M.S. thesis, Univ. California, Riverside. 177 pp.

Parsons, E. C. 1936. Taos Pueblo. Geo. Banta Publ. Co., Menasha, Wisconsin. 121 pp.

———. 1939. Pueblo Indian religion. 2 vols. Univ. Chicago Press, Chicago, Illinois. 1,275 pp.

Paterek, J. 1994. Encyclopedia of American Indian costume. W. W. Norton and Co., New York, New York. 516 pp.

Pattie, J. O. 1933. The personal narrative of James Ohio Pattie of Kentucky. T. Flint, ed. John H. Wood, Cincinnati, Ohio. 300 pp.

Peacock, F. W. 1974. English–Eskimo dictionary. Memorial Univ. Newfoundland, Saint John's. 432 pp.

Peckham, S. 1965. Prehistoric weapons in the Southwest. Mus. New Mexico Press, Santa Fe. 28 pp.

Pendleton, L. S. A. and D. H. Thomas. 1983. The Fort Sage drift fence. Anthro. Paper Amer. Mus. Natur. Hist. 58(2):1–38.

Perry, E., C. Z. Quintero, Sr., C. D. Davenport and D. C. Perry, comp. 1972. Western Apache dictionary. White Mtn. Apache Culture Ctr., Fort Apache, Arizona. 135 pp.

Petter, R. 1915. English-Cheyenne dictionary. Privately published, Kettle Falls, Washington. 1,126 pp.

Phillips, P. C., ed. 1940. Life in the Rocky Mountains: A diary of wanderings on the sources of the Missouri, Columbia and Colorado from February, 1830, to November, 1835, by W. A. Ferris, then in the employ of the American Fur Company. Old West Publ. Co., Denver, Colorado. 365 pp.

Phillips, P. C. and J. W. Smurr. 1961. The fur trade. 2 vols. Univ. Oklahoma Press, Norman. 1,414 pp.

Plog, F. 1979. Western Anasazi. Pages 108–130 *in* A. Ortiz, ed., Southwest. Handbook of North American Indians. Vol. 9. Smithsonian Inst., Washington, DC. 717 pp.

Poesch, J. 1961. Titian Ramsey Peale and his journals of the Wilkes Expedition. The American Philosoph. Soc., Philadelphia, Pennsylvania. 214 pp.

Polk, M. R. 1987. Mapping and inventory of seven antelope traps in Elko County, Nevada. Sagebrush Archaeological Consultants, Ogden, Utah. Submitted to U.S. Bur. Land Manage. Copies available from Wells Resour. Area, U.S. Bur. Land Manage., Elko, Nevada. 32+ pp.

Pope, S. T. 1923. A study of bows and arrows. Univ. Publ. Am. Archaeol. and Ethnol. 13(9):329–414.

Potter, D. M., ed. 1945. Trail to California: The overland journal of Vincent Geyer and Wakeman Bryarly. Yale Univ. Press, New Haven, Connecticut. 266 pp.

Press, M. L. 1979. Chemehuevi—a grammar and lexicon. University of California Press, Berkeley. 203 pp.

Priestley, H. I. 1937. A historical, political, and natural description of California by Pedro Fages, soldier of Spain. Univ. California Press, Berkeley. 83 pp.

Progulske, D. R. 1974. Yellow ore, Yellow Hair, yellow pine: A photographic study of a century of forest ecology. Agric. Exp. Sta., South Dakota St. Univ., Brookings. 169 pp.

Rand, S. T. 1888. Dictionary of the language of the Micmac Indians, who reside in Nova Scotia, New Brunswick, Prince Edward Island, Cape Breton and Newfoundland. Nova Scotia Printing Co., Halifax. 286 pp.

Ray, V. F. 1963. Primitive pragmatists, the Modoc Indians of northern California. Univ. Washington Press, Seattle. 237 pp.

Raymond, A. 1982. Two historic aboriginal game-drive enclosures in the eastern Great Basin. J. California and Great Basin Anthropol. 4(2):23–33.

Raynolds, F. W. 1868. Report on the exploration of the Yellowstone River in 1859–60. Senate Exec. Doc. 77, 40th Cong., 2nd Sess. Washington, DC. 174pp

Reagan, A. B. 1922. Hunting and fishing of various tribes of Indians. Trans. Kansas Acad. Sci. 15:443–448.

Reeves, H. M. and R. E. McCabe. 1998. Of moose and man. Pages 1–74 *in* A. W. Franzmann and C. C. Schwartz, compilers and eds., Ecology and management of the North American moose. Smithsonian Inst. Press, Washington, DC. 733 pp.

Reiger, J. F. 1975. American sportsmen and the origins of conservation. Winchester Press, New York, New York. 316 pp.

Reinhardt, R. 1967. Out West in a palace car. The Am. West 4(4):26–33.

Renner, F. G. 1974. Charles M. Russell. Harry N. Abrams, New York, New York. 296 pp.

Richardson, J. 1829. Fauna borealis—Americana; Or zoology of the northern parts of British America. Vol 1. Mammalia. John Murray, London, England. 300 pp.

Riddell, F. A. 1960. Honey Lake Paiute ethnography. Nevada St. Mus. Anthropol. Pap. 4. 87 pp.

Riddell, F. A. and D. F. McGeein. 1969. Atlatl spurs from California. Am. Antiquity 34(4):474–478.

Riggs, S. R. 1890. A Dakota-English dictionary. Contrib. to North American Ethnol., vol. VII. U. S. Govt. Print. Off., Washington, DC. 665 pp.

Rister, C. C. 1929. The significance of the destruction of the buffalo in the Southwest. Southwestern Hist. Quart. 33:34–39.

———. 1938. Southern plainsmen. Univ. Oklahoma Press, Norman. 289 pp.

Robinson, L. W. 1972. An Iowa-Otoe-English dictionary. Kansas St. Univ., Manhattan. 78 pp.

Robrock, D. P. 1992. Missouri 49er: The journal of William W. Hunter. Univ. New Mexico Press, Albuquerque. 299 pp.

Rocky Mountain News. 1871. February 1. Denver, Colorado.

Roe, F. G. 1951. The North American buffalo. Univ. Toronto Press, Toronto, Ontario. 957 pp.

Roe, F. M. A. 1909. Army letters from an officer's wife. D. Appleton and Co., New York, New York. 387 pp.

Roll, T. E. and K. Deaver. 1980. The Bootlegger Trail site, a late prehistoric spring bison kill. Heritage Conserv. and Recr. Serv., Interagency Archaeol. Serv., Denver, Colorado. 174 pp.

Ronda, J. P. 1984. Lewis and Clark among the Indians. Univ. Nebraska Press, Lincoln. 310 pp.

Roosevelt, T. 1885. Hunting trips of a ranchman. G. P. Putnam's Sons, New York, New York. 328 pp.

———. 1888. Ranch life and the hunting trail. The Century Co., New York. 186pp.

———. 1893. The wilderness hunter. G. P. Putnam's Sons, New York, New York. 472 pp.

Roosevelt, Q. and J. W. Burden. 1934. A new species of Antilocaprine, *Tetrameryx omusrosagis*, from a Pleistocene cave deposit in southern Arizona. Am. Mus. Novit. 754:1–4.

Roosevelt, T. R., T. S. Van Dyke, D. G. Elliot and A. J. Stone. 1902. The pronghorn antelope. Pages 98–130 *in* The deer family. Grosset and Dunlap Publ., New York, New York. 334 pp.

Ruby, R. H. and J. A. Brown. 1972. The Cayuse Indians: Imperial tribesmen of old Oregon. Univ. Oklahoma Press, Norman. 364 pp.

Ruddiman, W. F. and H. E. Wright, Jr. 1987. Introduction. Pages 1–12 *in* W. F. Ruddiman and H. E. Wright, Jr., eds., North American and adjacent oceans during the last deglaciation. Geolog. Soc. Am., Boulder, Colorado. 501 pp.

Rudy, J. R. 1953. An archaeological survey of western Utah. Utah Anthropol. Pap. 12. Univ. Utah Press, Salt Lake City. 182 pp.

Russell, C. M. 1929. Good medicine: The illustrated letters of Charles M. Russell. Doubleday and Co., Garden City, New York. 162 pp.

Russell, O. 1965. Journal of a trapper. A. L. Haines, ed.. Univ. Nebraska Press, Lincoln. 225 pp.

Ruxton, G. F. 1861. Adventures in Mexico and the Rocky Mountains. John Murray, London, England. 332 pp.

———. 1887. Life in the far West. William Blackwood and Sons, London, England. 208 pp.

Sage, R. B. 1857. Rocky Mountain life; or, startling scenes and perilous adventures in the far west, during an expedition of three years. Wentworth, Hewes and Co., Boston, Massachusetts. 363 pp.

Sahagún, B. de. 1963. Earthly things. Book 11 *in* C. E. Dibble and R. J. O. Anderson, eds., Florentine codex. Univ. Utah Press, Salt Lake City. 297 pp.

Salisbury, A. and J. Salisbury. 1993. Lewis and Clark: The journey west. Promontory Press, New York, New York. 235 pp.

Sanders, P. H. 2000. Trapper's point. Wyoming Wildl. 64(5):30–35.

Sandoz, M. 1978. The buffalo hunters. Univ. Nebraska Press, Lincoln. 382 pp.

Sanford, M. D. 1959. Mollie: The journal of Mollie Dorsey Sanford in Nebraska and Colorado territories, 1857–1866. Univ. Nebraska Press, Lincoln. 208 pp.

Satterfield, A. 1978. The Lewis and Clark trail. Stackpole Books, Harrisburg, Pennsylvania. 224 pp.

Satterwarte, F. 1889. The western outlook for sportsmen. Harper's New Monthly Mag. 78(468):873–880.

Sawyer, H. and D. McWhirter. 2000. The long trail. Wyoming Wildl. 64(5):36–41.

Saxton, D. and L. Saxton, comp. 1969. Dictionary: Papago and Pima to English, English to Papago and Pima. Univ. Arizona Press, Tucson. 191 pp.

Scarre, C., ed. 1988. Hammond past worlds, the Times atlas of archaeology. Hammond Inc., Maplewood, New Jersey. 319 pp.

Schaefer, J. 1975. American bestiary. Houghton Mifflin Co., Boston, Massachusetts. 287 pp.

Schlissel, L. 1982. Women's diaries of the westward journey. Schocken Books, New York, New York. 271 pp.

Schobinger, J. 1994. The first Americans. William B. Eerdmans Publishing Co., Grand Rapids, Michigan. 195 pp.

Schroedl, A. R. 1977. The Grand Canyon figurine complex. Am. Antiquity 2(2):254–265.

Schultz, J. W. 1957. My life as an Indian. Adapted by R. E. Gard. Duell, Sloan and Pierce, New York, New York. 151 pp.

Seiler, H. and Kokiro Hioki. 1979. Cahuilla dictionary. Makli Museum Press, Banning, California. 291 pp.

Sellers, C. C. 1980. Mr. Peale's museum: Charles Willson Peale and the first popular museum of natural science and art. Norton, New York, New York. 370 pp.

Seton, E. T. 1909. Life-histories of northern animals. Vol. 1. Grass-eaters. Charles Scribner's Sons, New York, New York. 673 pp.

———. 1929. Lives of game animals. Vol. 3, Part 2. Hoofed animals. Doubleday, Doran and Co., Inc., Garden City, New York. 780 pp.

Settle, R. W., ed. 1989. The march of the mounted rifleman. Univ. Nebraska Press, Lincoln. 378 pp.

Sherburne, J. P. 1988. Through Indian country to California. Margaret McDougall Gordon, ed. Stanford Univ. Press, Stanford, California. 285 pp.

Sherratt, A., ed. 1980. Columbia encyclopedia of archeology. Crown Publishers, Inc., New York, New York. 495 pp.

Shields, G. O., ed. 1890. The big game of North America. Rand, McNally and Co., Chicago, Illinois. 581 pp.

Shipley, W. F. 1963. Maidu texts and dictionary. Univ. California Press, Berkeley and Los Angeles. 261 pp.

Simpson, C. D. and T. J. Leftwich. 1978. Historic range change in the Texas pronghorn. Pronghorn Antelope Workshop Proc. 8:121–147.

Sitgreaves, L. 1853. Report of an expedition down the Zuni and Colorado rivers. Robert Armstrong, Washington, DC. 198 pp.

Skinner, M. P. 1922. The pronghorn. J. Mammal. 3(2):82–105.

Smith, A. M. 1974. Ethnography of the northern Utes. Mus. New Mexico, Pap. Anthropol. 17. Univ. New Mexico Press, Santa Fe. 288 pp.

———. 1993. Shoshone tales. Univ. Utah Press, Salt Lake City. 188 pp.

Smith, E. R. 1952. The archaeology of Deadman Cave. Univ. Utah Anthropol. Pap. 10. Univ. Utah Press, Salt Lake City. 41 pp.

Smith, G. H. 1980. The explorations of the La Vérendryes in the northern plains, 1738–43. W. R. Wood, ed. Univ. Nebraska Press, Lincoln. 160 pp.

Smith, V. G. 1997. The champion buffalo hunter. The frontier memoirs of Yellowstone Vic Smith. J. Prodgers, ed. Falcon Publishing. Helena, Montana. 257 pp.

Smith, W. and L. Ewing. 1952. Kiva mural decorations at Awatovi and Kawaika-a. Pap. Peabody Mus. Am. Archaeol. and Ethnol. 37:1–363.

Snow, D. R. 1981. Keepers of the game and the nature of explanation. Pages 61–71 in S. Keech III, ed., Indians, animals and the fur trade. Univ. Georgia Press, Athens. 207 pp.

Snowden, J. H. 1868. Report of J. Hudson Snowden on exploration from the Platte to the headwaters of the Shayenne in 1859. Pages 154–161 in W. F. Reynolds, Report on the exploration of the Yellowstone River. U.S. Govt. Print. Off., Washington, DC.

Spaulding, K. A., ed. 1953. On the Oregon Trail: Robert Stuart's journey of discovery (1812–1813). Univ. Oklahoma Press, Norman. 192 pp.

Speth, J. D. and W. J. Parry. 1980. Late prehistoric bison procurement in southeastern New Mexico: The 1978 season at the Garnsey site (LA18399). Univ. Michigan Anthropol. Tech. Rept. 12. 369 pp.

Spier, L. 1928. Havasupai ethnography. Anthropol. Pap. Am. Mus. Nat. Hist. Vol. 29, Part 3:83–408.

———. 1930. Klamath ethnography. Univ. California Publications Am. Archaeol. and Ethnol. 30:1–338.

Spry, I. M. 1963. The Palliser expedition: The dramatic story of western Canadian exploration 1857–1860. Fifth House Publ., Saskatoon, Saskatchewan. 315 pp.

Standage, H. 1928. The march of the Morman battalion. F. M. Golder, ed. The Century Co., New York, New York. 295 pp.

Standing Bear, L. 1978. Land of the spotted eagle. Univ. Nebraska Press, Lincoln. 276 pp.

Stands in Timber, J. and M. Liberty. 1967. Cheyenne memories. Yale Univ. Press, New Haven, Connecticut. 345 pp.

Stanislawski, M. B. 1979. Hopi-Tewa. Pages 587–602 in A. Ortiz, ed., Southwest. Handbook of North American Indians. Vol. 9. Smithsonian Inst., Washington, DC. 717 pp.

Stansbury, H. 1852. Exploration and survey of the valley of the Great Salt Lake of Utah, including reconnaissance of a new route through the Rocky Mountains. Lippincott, Grambo and Co., Philadelphia, Pennsylvania. 487 pp.

Stein, W. T. 1963. Mammal remains from archaeological sites in the Point of Pines region, Arizona. Am. Antiquity 29(2):213–220.

Stephen, A. M. 1940. Hopi Indians of Arizona—V. The Masterkey 14(5):170–179.

Steward, J. H. 1929. Petroglyphs of California and adjoining states. Univ. California Publications Am. Archaeol. and Ethnol. 24:47–238.

———. 1938. Basin-plateau aboriginal sociopolitical groups. Smithsonian Inst. Bur. Am. Ethnol. Bull. 120. U.S. Govt. Print. Off., Washington, DC. 346 pp.

———. 1941. Culture element distributions 13: Nevada Shoshoni. Univ. California-Berkeley Anthropol. Rec. 4(2):209–259.

———. 1943. Culture element distributions 23: Northern and Gosiute Shoshoni. Univ. California Berkeley Anthropol. Rec. 8(3):263–392.

———. 1974a. Aboriginal and historic groups in Ute Indians of Utah: An analysis. Pages 25–103 in D. A. Horr, ed., Ute Indians I. Garland Publishing, Inc., New York, New York. 159 pp.

———. 1974b. Native components of the White River Ute Indians. Pages 105–159 in D. A. Horr, ed., Ute Indians I. Garland Publishing, Inc., New York, New York. 159 pp.

Stewart, E. I. 1955. Custer's luck. Univ. Oklahoma Press, Norman. 522 pp.

Stewart, O. C. 1941. Cultural element distributions 14: Northern Paiute. Univ. California Berkeley Anthropol. Rec. 4(3):361–446.

———. 1942. Culture element distributions 18: Ute-Southern Paiute. Univ. California Berkeley Anthropol. Rec. 6(4):231–360.

Stiles, H. R. 1906. Joutel's journal of La Salle's last voyage, 1684–7. Joseph McDonough, Albany, New York. 259 pp.

Stratton, J. L. 1981. Pioneer women. Simon and Schuster, New York, New York. 320 pp.

Strong, P. T. 1979. Santa Ana Pueblo. Pages 398–406 *in* A. Ortiz, ed., Southwest. Handbook of North American Indians. Vol. 9. Smithsonian Inst., Washington, DC. 717 pp.

Strong, W. D. and W. E. Schenck. 1925. Petroglyphs near The Dalles of the Columbia River. Am. Anthropol. 27(1):76–90.

Strong, W. E. 1876. A trip to the Yellowstone National Park in July, August, and September, 1875. Privately printed, Washington, DC. 143 pp.

Stuart, G. E., ed. 1983. Peoples and places of the past. Natl. Geogr. Soc., Washington, DC. 424 pp.

Sunder, J. E. 1965. The fur trade on the upper Missouri. Univ. Oklahoma Press, Norman. 295 pp.

Swagerty, W. R. 2001. History of the United States plains until 1850. Pages 256–279 *in* R. J. DeMallie, ed., Plains. Handbook of North American Indians. Vol 13. Smithsonian Inst., Washington, DC. 1,320 pp.

Swanton, J. R. 1940. Linguistic material from the tribes of southern Texas and northeastern Mexico. Smithsonian Inst. Bur. American Ethnol. Bull. 127. U. S. Govt. Print. Off., Washington, DC. 145 pp.

———. 1942. Source material on the history and ethnology of the Caddo Indians. Smithsonian Inst. Bur. Am. Ethnol. Bull. 132. U.S. Govt. Print. Off., Washington, DC. 332 pp.

Swetland, M. J. 1977. A vocabulary of the Omaha language. Nebraska Indian Press, Winnebago. 203 pp.

Tanner, H. H. 1995. The settling of North America. Macmillan Co., New York, New York. 208 pp.

Taylor, C. 1975. The warriors of the plains. Hamlyn Publ. Group, Ltd., London, England. 144 pp.

———. 2001. Native American weapons. Univ. Oklahoma Press, Norman 128 pp.

Tedlock, D. 1972. Finding the center: Narrative poetry of the Zuni Indians, from performances in Zuni. Translated from Andrew Peynetsa and Walter Sanchez. Dial Press, New York, New York. 298 pp.

———. 1979. Zuni religion and world view. Pages 499–508 *in* A. Ortiz, ed., Southwest. Handbook of North American Indians. Vol. 9. Smithsonian Inst., Washington, DC. 717 pp.

Terrell, J. U. 1975. The plains Apache. Thomas Y. Crowell Co., New York, New York. 244 pp.

Thomas, D. H. 1983. The archaeology of Monitor Valley. I. Epistemology. Anthropol. Pap. Am. Mus. Nat. Hist. 58(1):1–194.

Thomas, D. H. and E. H. McKee. 1974. An aboriginal rock alignment in the Toiyabe Range, central Nevada. Am. Mus. Novit. 1534. 17 pp.

Thomas, D. T. and K. Ronnefeldt, eds. 1976. People of the first man. E. P. Dutton and Co., Inc., New York, New York. 256 pp.

Thomas, H. 1993. Conquest. Montezuma, Cortez, and the fall of Old Mexico. Simon and Schuster, New York, New York. 812 pp.

Thompson, D. 1916. David Thompson's narrative of his explorations in western America, 1784–1812. J. B. Tyrell, ed. The Champlain Soc., Toronto, Ontario. 582 pp.

Thwaites, R. G. 1904–1907. Early western travels, 1748–1846. A series of annotated reprints of some of the best and rarest contemporary volumes of travel, descriptive of the aborigines and social and economic conditions in the middle and far West, during the period of early American settlement. 32 vols. The Arthur H. Clark Co., Cleveland, Ohio.

———, ed. 1969. Original journals of the Lewis and Clark expedition, 1804–1806. 8 vols. Arno Press, New York, New York.

Tolmie, W. F. and G. M. Dawson. 1884. Comparative vocabularies of the Indian tribes of British Columbia. Dawson Bros., Montreal, Quebec. 131 pp.

Torquemada, J. de. 1723. Primera parte de los veinte I vne libros rituales 1 monarchia indiana, con el origen y guerras de los Indios Occidentales de sus poblaciones, descubrimiento, conquista, conuersion, y otras cosas marauillosas de la mesma tierra distribugdos en tres tomas Compuesto por f. Juan de Torquemada. Nicolas Rodriguez Franco, Madrid, Spain. 3 vols.

Townsend, R. F. 2000. The Aztecs. Thames and Hudson, Ltd., London, England. 232 pp.

Trefethen, J. B. 1961. Crusade for wildlife. The Stackpole Co., Harrisburg, Pennsylvania. 377 pp.

Trenholm, V. C. 1986. The Arapahoes, our people. Univ. Oklahoma Press, Norman. 367 pp.

Trenholm, V. C. and M. Carley. 1964. The Shoshonis: Sentinels of the Rockies. Univ. Oklahoma Press, Norman. 380 pp.

Trimm, W. P. 1983. Two years in Kansas. Am. Heritage 34(2):65–80.

Tuohy, D. R. 1986. Portable art objects. Pages 227–238 *in* W. L. D'Azevedo, ed., Great Basin. Handbook of North American Indians. Vol. 11. Smithsonian Inst., Washington, DC. 852 pp.

Turney-High, H. H. 1937. The Flathead Indians of Montana. Memoirs No. 48. Am. Anthropol. Assoc., Menasha, Wisconsin. 161 pp.

Tyler, R., C. Clark, L Ayres, W. H. Cadbury, H. J. Viola and B. Reilly, Jr. 1987. American frontier life: Early western painting and prints. Abbeville Press, New York, New York. 202 pp.

Udall, S. L. 2002. The forgotten founders: Rethinking the history of the West. Island Press, Washington, DC. 237 pp.

Uhlenbeck, C. C. and R. H. Van Gulik. 1930. An English-Blackfoot vocabulary. K. akademie van wetenschappen, Amsterdam. 261 pp.

Ulrich, R. 1995. Indian artifacts, remains turn up at Grants Pass. *The Oregonian*. Thurs., April 13. A1, A19.

Umber, H. and C. Bihrle. 1989. The early days. North Dakota Outdoors LI(7): 2–8.

Umfreville, E. 1790. The present state of Hudson's Bay. Printed for C. Stalker, London, England. 230 pp.

Underhill, R. 1991. Life in the Pueblos. Ancient City Press, Santa Fe, New Mexico. 154 pp.

Underhill, R. M. 1948. Ceremonial patterns in the greater Southwest. Am. Ethnol. Soc., Monogr. 12. New York, New York. 62 pp.

Unrau, W. E., ed. 1979. Tending the talking wire: A buck soldier's view of Indian country, 1863–1866. Univ. Utah Press, Salt Lake City. 397 pp.

U.S. House of Representatives. 1852. Report of the Commissioner of Patents for the year 1851. Part 2. Agriculture. Ex. Doc. 102. Robert Armstrong, Printer, Washington, DC. 676 pp.

U.S. House of Representatives. 1858. Reports of explorations and surveys to ascertain the most practicable and economical route for a railroad from the Mississippi River to the Pacific Ocean, 1853–6. Vol. IX, Ex. Doc. 78, 33rd Congr., 2nd Sess. A. O. P. Nicholson, printer, Washington, DC.

U.S. Navy. 1959. Dictionary of American naval fighting ships. Vol. 1. Naval Hist. Div., Washington, DC. 349 pp.

Utley, R. M. 1984. The Indian frontier of the American West, 1846–1890. Univ. New Mexico Press, Albuquerque. 325 pp.

———. 1997. A life wild and perilous. Henry Holt and Co., New York, New York. 392 pp.

Van Wormer, J. 1968. The world of the pronghorn. J. B. Lippincott Co., New York, New York. 191 pp.

———. 1969. The world of the pronghorn. J. B. Lippincott and Co., Philadelphia, Pennsylvania. 191 pp.

Vaux, W. S. W., ed. 1854. The world encompassed by Sir Francis Drake . . . carefully collected out of the notes of Master Francis Fletcher, preacher in this employment and divers others his followers in the same. Hakluyt Soc. 16. London, England. 295 pp.

Vestal, S. 1957. Sitting Bull, champion of the Sioux. Univ. Oklahoma Press, Norman. 349 pp.

Voegelin, E. W. 1938. Tubatulabal ethnography. Anthropol. Rec. 2(1):1–84.

———. 1942. Culture element distribution, 20: Northeast California. Univ. California Anthropol. Rec. 7(2):46–252.

Voth, H. R. 1903. The Oraiba summer snake ceremony. Field Columbian Mus. Publ. 83. Anthropol. Series 3(4):261–358.

Wagner, F. H. 1978. Livestock grazing and the livestock industry. Pages 121–145 in H. P. Brokaw, ed., Wildlife and America. Council Environ Qual. U.S. Govt. Print. Off., Washington, DC. 532 pp.

Wagner, W. F., ed. 1904. Adventures of Zenas Leonard, fur trader and trapper 1831–1836. The Burrows Bros. Co., Cleveland, Ohio. 317 pp.

Waldman, C. 1985. Atlas of the North American Indian. Facts on File Publ., New York, New York. 276 pp.

Walker, D. E. 1978. Indians of Idaho. Univ. Idaho Press, Moscow. 207 pp.

Walker, J. R. 1980. Lakota beliefs and ritual. Univ. Nebraska Press, Lincoln. 329 pp.

Wallace, E. 1978. The journal of Ranald S. Mackenzie's messenger to the Kwahadi Comanches. Red River Valley Hist. Review 3:227–246.

Wallace, E. and E. A. Hoebel. 1952. The Comanches: Lords of the south plains. Univ. Oklahoma Press, Norman. 398 pp.

Wallmo, O. C. 1978. Mule and black-tailed deer. Pages 31–41 in J. L. Schmidt and D. L. Gilbert, eds., Big game of North America. Stackpole Books, Harrisburg, Pennsylvania. 494 pp.

Ward, G. B. and R. E. McCabe. 1988. Trail blazers in conservation: The Boone and Crockett Club's first century. Pages 47–121 in Records of North American big game. Boone and Crockett Club, Dumfries, Virginia. 498 pp.

Warren, E. R. 1942. The mammals of Colorado. Univ. Oklahoma Press, Norman. 330 pp.

Warren, G. K. 1856. Explorations in the Dacota country in the year 1855. U. S. Sen. Exec. Doc. 76. A. O. P. Nicholson, Washington, DC. 79+ pp.

Waters, F. 1963. Book of the Hopi. Viking Press, New York, New York. 345 pp.

Watkins, E. A. 1938. A dictionary of the Cree languages. R. Faries, ed., Church of England in Canada, Toronto, Ontario. 530 pp.

Wear, D. W. 1886. Report of the superintendent of the Yellowstone National Park. Pages 837–845 in Report of the Secretary of the Interior being part of the message and documents communicated to the two Houses of Congress at the beginning of the 2nd Sess., 45th Congr., Vol. I. U. S. Govt. Print. Off., Washington, DC.

Weaver, D. 1991. Prehistoric Missouri: Crossroads of America's ancient cultures. Missouri Resour. Rev. 8(1):16–19.

Webb, W. E. 1872. Buffalo land. E. Hannaford and Co., Cincinnati, Ohio. 503 pp.

Webb, W. P. 1931. The great plains. Grosset and Dunlap, New York, New York. 525 pp.

Weber, D. J. 1968. The Taos trappers, the fur trade in the far Southwest, 1540–1846. Univ. Oklahoma Press, Norman. 263 pp.

Webster, G. S. 1978. Dry Creek rockshelter, cultural chronology in the western Snake River region of Idaho, ca. 4150 B.P.–1300 B.P. TEBIWA 15:1–35.

———. 1980. Recent data bearing on the question of the origins of the bow and arrow in the Great Basin. Am. Antiquity 45(1):63–66.

Wedel, W. R. 1961. Prehistoric man on the Great Plains. Univ. Oklahoma Press, Norman. 355 pp.

Wedel, W. R. and G. C. Frison. 2001. Environment and subsistence. Pages 45–60 in R. J. DeMallie, ed., Plains. Handbook of North American Indians. Vol. 13. Smithsonian Inst. Press, Washington, DC. 1,360 pp.

Weems, J. E. 1976. Death song. Doubleday and Co., Inc., Garden City, New York. 311 pp.

Weitzner, B. 1979. Notes on the Hidatsa Indians based on data recorded by the late Gilbert L. Wilson. Anthropol. Pap. Am. Mus. Nat. Hist. Vol. 56, Part 2:181–322.

Welch, J. 1994. Killing Custer: The battle of the Little Bighorn. W. W. Norton and Co., New York, New York. 320 pp.

Weltfish, G. 1977. The lost universe: Pawnee life and culture. Univ. Nebraska Press, Lincoln. 519 pp.

West, E. 2001. A look back at bison. Wyoming Wildl. 65(1):6–17.

Wheeler, H. W. 1923. Buffalo days. Bobbs-Merrill Co., Indianapolis, Indiana. 361 pp.

Whipple, A. W. 1941. A pathfinder in the Southwest. G. Foreman, ed. Univ. Oklahoma Press, Norman. 298 pp.

White, L. A. 1932. The Pueblo of San Felipe. Memoirs Am. Anthropol. Assoc. 38. 69 pp.

———. 1935. The Pueblo of San Domingo, New Mexico. Memoirs of the American Anthropol. Assoc., No. 43. Menasha, Wisconsin. 210 pp.

———. 1942. The Pueblo of Santa Ana, New Mexico. Memoirs Am. Anthropol. Assoc. 60. 360 pp.

———. 1962. The Pueblo of Sia, New Mexico. Smithsonian Inst. Bur. Am. Ethnol. Bull. 184. U.S. Govt. Print. Off., Washington, DC. 358 pp.

White, T. E. 1952. Observations on the butchering technique of some aboriginal peoples: No. 1. Am. Antiquity 17(4):337–338.

———. 1954. Observations on the butchering technique of some aboriginal peoples, Nos. 3, 4, 5 and 6. Am. Antiquity 19(3):254–256.

Whitworth, R. 1965. Journal of Robert Whitworth. Tucson and the West 7:127–160.

Wied, M. 1843. Travels in the interior of North America. Translated by H. E. Lloyd. Ackermann and Co., London, England. 520 pp.

Wilke, P. J. 1986. Aboriginal game drive complexes at and near Whiskey Flat, Mineral County, Nevada. Paper presented at the 20th Biennial Great Basin Anthropol. Conf., Las Vegas, Nevada. 12 pp.

Will, G. F. and H. J. Spinden. 1906. The Mandans. Peabody Mus. Am. Archaeol. and Ethnol., Harvard Univ. Papers 3(4):78–219.

Williamson, J. P. 1886. An English-Dakota school dictionary. Iapi Oaye Press, Yankton Agency, Dakota Territory. 144 pp.

Winship, G. P. 1896. The Coronado expedition, 1540–1542. Bur. Am. Ethnol. 1892–1893 Ann. Rept. 14, Part 1:329–613.

Wishart, W. 1978. Bighorn sheep. Pages 160–171 *in* J. L. Schmidt and D. L. Gilbert, eds., Big game of North America. Stackpole Books, Harrisburg, Pennsylvania. 494 pp.

Wissler, C. 1910. Material culture of the Blackfoot Indians. Anthropol. Pap. Am. Mus. Nat. Hist., Vol. 5, Part 1. New York, New York. 175 pp.

———. 1966. Indians of the United States. 3rd ed. Handbook Series 1. Am. Mus. Nat. Hist., New York, New York. 172 pp.

Wister, F. K., ed. 1958. Owen Wister out West: His journals and letters. Univ. Chicago Press, Chicago, Illinois. 269 pp.

Wood, R. W. and T. D. Thiessen. 1985. Early fur trade on the northern plains: Canadian traders among the Mandan and Hidatsa, 1738–1818. Univ. Oklahoma Press, Norman. 353 pp.

Woodhouse, S. W. 1853. Mammals. Pages 43–57 *in* Report of an expedition down the Zuni and Colorado rivers, by L. Sitgreaves. Robert Armstrong, Washington, DC. 198 pp.

Wright, L. B., ed. 1965. The Elizabethan's America. Harvard Univ. Press, Cambridge, Massachusetts. 291 pp.

Yoakum, J. D. 1978. Pronghorn. Pages 103–121 *in* J. L. Schmidt and D. L. Gilbert, eds., Big game of North America: Ecology and management. Stackpole Books, Harrisburg, Pennsylvania. 494 pp.

Yohe, R. M., II. 1984. A report on faunal remains from a special purpose site in the western Mojave Desert. Pacific Coast Archaeol. Soc. Quart. 20(4):56–72.

Young, R. W. and W. Morgan. 1980. The Navajo language. Univ. New Mexico Press, Albuquerque. 1,069 pp.

Young, S. P. 1946. The wolf in North American history. Caxton Printers, Ltd., Caldwell, Idaho. 149 pp.

Young, S. P. and H. H. T. Jackson. 1951. The clever coyote. The Stackpole Co., Harrisburg, Pennsylvania. 411 pp.

Page numbers in italics indicate illustrations.

Front endsheet credits: artist, source

1. *Frederic Remington*, from McCracken (1966)
2. *R. A. Müller*, Library of Congress, Washington, DC
3. *Charles M. Russell*, Amon Carter Museum, Fort Worth, Texas
4. *Frederic Remington*, from Roosevelt (1888)
5. *Ernest Thompson Seton*, Philmont Scout Ranch, Cimarron, New Mexico
6. *F. Lee Jaques*, James Ford Bell Museum, Minneapolis, Minnesota
7. *Ernest Thompson Seton*, Philmont Scout Ranah, Cimarron, New Mexico
8. *John D. Caton*, from Caton (1877)
9. *Charles M. Russell*, from Russell (1929)
10. *C. A. Lesueur* (artist), *G. B. Ellis* (engraver), Smithsonian Institution, Washington, DC
11. *Artist Unknown*, from Shields (1890)
12. *Artist Unknown*, Smithsonian Institution, Washington, DC
13. *Frederic Remington*, from Roosevelt (1888)
14. *Making Medicine*, Smithsonian Institution Anthropological Archives, Washington, DC
15. *Artist Unknown*, from Elliot (1904)

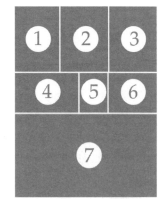

Back endsheet credits: artist, source

16. *Ernest Thompson Seton*, Philmont Scout Ranch, Cimarron, New Mexico
17. *John D. Caton*, from Caton (1877)
18. *G. Mützel*, Library of Congress, Washington, DC
19. *Artist Unknown*, Library of Congress, Washington, DC
20. *Carl Rungius*, from Roosevelt et al. (1902)
21. *C. Hamilton Smith* (artist), *T. Landseer* (engraver), Smithsonian Institution, Washington, DC
22. *Stanley Del*, after Gustav Sohon, Union Pacific Railroad Museum, Omaha, Nebraska
23. *Alfred Jacob Miller*, David Warner Foundation, Tuscalosa, Florida
24. *Carl Rungius*, Glenbow Museum, Calgary, Alberta
25. *Ernest Thompson Seton*, Philmont Scout Ranch, Cimarron, New Mexico
26. *J. Stewart* (artist), *D. Linzars* (engraver), Southernprints, United Kingdom
27. *Heinrich Baldwin Möllhausen*, Library of Congress, Washington, DC
28. *Ernest Thompson Seton*, from Seton (1929)
29. *Heinrich Baldwin Möllhausen* (artist), *R. Metzeroth* (engraver), Library of Congress, Washington, DC